AN EAST WIND BLOWING

MEL KEEGAN

AN EAST WIND BLOWING

THE GAY MEN'S PRESS

First published 1999 by GMP Publishers Ltd
in association with Prowler Press Ltd
3 Broadbent Close, London N6 5GG

World copyright © 1999 Mel Keegan
Mel Keegan has asserted his right to be identified as the
author of this work in accordance with the
Copyright, Designs and Patents Act 1988

A CIP catalogue record for this book is available
from the British Library

ISBN 0 85449 286 0

Distributed in Europe by Central Books,
99 Wallis Rd, London E9 5LN

Distributed in North America by InBook/LPC Group,
1436 West Randolph, Chicago, IL 60607

Distributed in Australia by Bulldog Books,
P O Box 300, Beaconsfield, NSW 2014

Printed and bound in the EU by WSOY, Juva, Finland

1

He lay so still, so silent in the heather and so well camouflaged by the green and blue pattern of his tunic that the yellow brimstone butterfly came unconcernedly within a hand's span of his face. Unblinking, he watched the fragile wings as it settled on his outstretched forearm to sun itself, and then his eyes moved on beyond it to the throwing knife that lay with its honed blade in his upturned palm.

The spring day was mild, one of the first warm days of the season. The sun was pleasant on his back and the whole world was so quiet, he might have been the last human being alive as he lay on the crest of the low, heather-clad hillock and scented the breeze. Not far away was a straying flock of black-faced sheep; he heard their voices, and the wind rustling in the young bracken, the hum of bees working among the yellow gorse flowers, and the larks high overhead. It would have been easy to set his head down and doze but he was waiting, working, not lounging here.

Bellow the hillock was an old, well-worn track leading between the burrows of several colonies of hares, and today Ronan was hunting. Hares were creatures with short memories. He had hunted here only days before, and already they were using the same track again, their signs were everywhere. As he flexed his fingers that blade moved in his palm, catching the sun, and the brimstone butterfly spread its wings. A dog fox had been here before him. He could smell it, and it might have cheated him today: hares were not entirely stupid.

Almost imperceptibly he stretched and decided to wait a little longer before abandoning this hunting ground in favour of another where the fox had not drawn blood recently. Six foxes lived on this part of the moor, he knew them all by sight and they knew him, for humans and foxes shared the same territory, the same game. Sometimes he would cheat them instead, but it did not much matter. Spring had come early this year and the hunting season would be rich.

The old folk were prophesying a good year and a late winter, but to Ronan of Whitestonecliff even summer seemed years away, and winter was too distant to be anxious about. Every day was almost long enough to lose track of in itself, and he was too busy to spare a thought for other seasons, other years.

To his hands fell a variety of duties, some he cherished, some he scorned, but he had no authority to choose his own work. As the eldest son still living in his father's house, it was his duty to most of the hunting, but this at least was no imposition. He would have chosen to leave the settlement under the whitestone cliff face and immerse himself in the the solitude of the moor. Only there did he feel free, unfettered, where no man gave him orders he was honour-bound to obey, no one watched over his shoulder as he worked, told him he was lazy or inept, or reminded him of who, of what he was.

He should have been a warrior, the son of a warrior. He had always said so, for he could feel the heart of a warrior inside his chest. But the gods had made their own plans for him, before he was born. The father they gave him was an artisan — a good one, but no matter how he tried, Ronan could not discover any enthusiasm for the trade. Every bone in his body was that of a warrior, but not only his father's wishes barred him from the way of the sword. Tradition also denied him. The implacable gods of tradition seemed determined to strangle him before he reached his seventeenth summer. He was born to a peasant household that owned no land and had never owned any. His place was working the land for others, and if not that labour, then serving them in some useful trade. He was a freeman — his family were not landed but neither were they bonded, and he could carry a warspear in the ranks of the soldiers who marched to battle for the chief in Derventio.

But that was not being a *warrior*, as Ronan had often argued to his father. A peasant freeman could either farm or fight. A fighter made to farm would lose his wits in the sheer tedium of the work, and a farmer made to fight would just as swiftly lose his life through his own ineptitude. One or the other trade was possible, not both. So Ronan would tell his father, and then duck as the man aimed a cuff at his ear.

He was on the point of stirring, abandoning the heather slope, when his narrowed eyes caught the tiny movement, the twitch of long ears beyond the fronds of the small spring bracken at the edge of the trail. The ears twitched again, and Ronan's sensitive fingers closed about the blade. He came fully awake, his attention focusing on the creature whose quivering nose had just appeared from the bracken fronds. He commanded the accuracy of long practice and the hare died so quickly, so soundlessly, its fellows blinked bewilderedly at it. As they came out of the bracken Ronan got to his feet and brushed down his tunic and leather breeches.

The moor was wide and green, stretching away to the mountains fifty miles in the west, darkened by intermittent woodland, crossed by many streams, and it was his. Ronan did not own it, nor would he ever, but he felt that he held dominion here. for he used the moor, served it and was served by it. If it did not belong to him, then no one held dominion over it.

He was broad-shouldered and lean with youth, not a boy any longer and yet not properly a man, though he was as strong as many a grown man. The sun and wind had tanned him deeply, bringing light streaks among the chestnut-brown mass of his hair. His jaw was clean-shaven, his face smooth, his features handsome, with warmth and candour that would render him boyish for many years to come. He was not permitted to be a warrior, but his hands were hard, leathery, and the fingers that retrieved the throwing knife were callused by hard work.

The hare was a large buck, fattened after the winter, his third catch of the day, and his last. He took it back to the tall, solitary pine where he had hung the others out of reach of the marauding foxes, and there he gutted it, cleaned the knife and slid the blade back into the sheath that rode at his right side,

Mid-afternoon was warm, the sky pale but clear until it was sullied in the northeast by a pall of massing cloud. Ronan set his back against the rough bark of the pine, rubbing his shoulders there as he watched the clouds. They were coming up on a strong wind, and it would rain this evening. Even to Ronan, the moor was a desolate place in the rain, and he bit his lip, not relishing the thought of being tied to Whitestonecliff and home for the whole day. He would run errands, endure the childish bickering of his younger brothers and sisters, while his father worked up the road on the chieftain's land, plying his trade. On the outskirts of the old Roman town of Derventio, the houses had begun to tumble down with age, and there was work aplenty for a good stonemason.

The wind swung about and all at once had the cold, cutting edge of a knife. Ronan pushed away from the tree, gathered the hares and thonged them together. He slung them over his left shoulder and then he was moving, picking his way through the thorny gorse bushes toward home. On his left hand was the old road Caesar had driven across the moor, a slightly elevated ribbon of white stone, unrepaired in longer than anyone could recall. It cut across the open moorland from Derventio on the banks of the river, to Catreath in the northeast, another garrison town built by Rome.

Rome — city and empire alike — was a hazy concept to Ronan. It was a city he might reach by ship, a long way from the moors of Brigantia, his home. A city where the Caesars sat in grand palaces, so the ballad singer said. Once, Romans had lived in Albion, fighting, building forts and roads, even cities, but they were gone now, and Ronan could not be exactly sure who they were, why they had come, why they had gone away again, unless it was to build roads and forts elsewhere. He had heard great stories of the old days, the hand-me-downs bequeathed by one generation upon the next: how the tribes of Albion fought and died, how Holy Mona, the last fortress of the Druidai, fell, how the Warrior Queen was whipped and outcast, and how she turned like a she-wolf at bay and for a time devoured the conquerors in a lake of blood until she too fell. But at the last many Britons themselves became almost Roman on the southeast coast, and all the blood that had been split was for nothing.

Ronan kicked at the white stone of the old road with a leather-booted foot. It stretched away into the southeast like a long, bleached rib, eventually entering Derventio, but he would follow it for only a mile and leave it again as it passed by Whitestonecliff, within sight of the village. The brace of hares swung at his back and he gazed up, eyes slitted to follow an eagle, hunting, as was he. Now, *that* was freedom, he told himself, not for the first time. The freedom of the wind, and the mountains that had always remained free even when the invaders came.

His ears were so accustomed to the quiet that he heard the sounds of iron-shod hooves ringing on the road while the horses were still far off and, turning, he shaded his eyes to watch them approach at a trot. These were good horses, finely bred and leggy — horses Ronan recognised, for they belonged to the stables of the old chief who sat at Derventio.

Gruffydd was grey as a badger now, but his body was still thick with muscle. Much of the time he employed Ronan, and often employed his father too, and out of respect for that the youth stood aside to give Gruffydd the road. Five horses trotted up, one on a leading rein. Accompanying their master were the grooms, Cullen and Rua, and at Gruffydd's left hand was his eldest son, Bryn.

Drawing level with Ronan, Gruffydd reined in and tossed back the folds of his blue-striped cloak. He was a bluff man, silver-bearded, shrewd, with eyes like an old raven and skin like leather. It was difficult to see any shared blood between him and Bryn, for the two were as dissimilar as strangers. A sword slapped at the old man's left thigh, for though he had not fought for years he still considered himself a warrior. Ronan glanced ruefully at the weapon. Brys also was armed, and well he should be, since he had been taught by the swordmasters and would be chief in Derventio himself one day, perhaps one day soon. Gruffydd was not young.

Bryn was Ronan's age, but taller, broader, a dark youth, smouldering, with blue eyes and features as handsome as Ronan's, though in a quite different way. He wore his beauty like a young horse, it sat well on him, and he was arrogant. His tunic was black and yellow, his cloak was green, and among his fingers heavy rings caught the sun as he reined back beside his father.

The chief's face creased pleasantly as he smiled at the youth on the roadside. Ronan was pleased to return the expression. A smile lit his face, though he did not know it, transforming earnestness into lush beauty that was engaging.

"Just the boy I wanted," Gruffydd said cheerfully. "I'd have come looking for you if you'd not been here. Set your eyes to what I've brought, boy, and tell me what you see."

On the leading rein Rua held in his left fist was a little roan stallion, sturdy, barrel-chested, well made and groomed till he shone. Ronan's green eyes passed shrewdly over the speckled red-grey coat, and he put down the hares to take the little horse's bridle, run his hands over muscled shoulders and forelegs. "More breeding stock, my lord?"

"Eventually." Gruffydd watched the boy from Whitestonecliff look over the roan. Shrewd, was Ronan, and clever, especially when it came to nags. "I'll race him once or twice first. And you'd be interested, I'd wager."

The understatement made Ronan laugh. "Aye, my lord, I would, if you're in need of a rider, or someone to train him."

"We're looking for both." Bryn gazed off across the moor as if he had pressing interests elsewhere. His left hand closed about the jewelled pommel of his sword. "You're the best there is with nags, Ronan, so you'll come to Derventio and run him for us."

"Of course you will," Gruffydd agreed, "but for today, I think it is we who must take lodgings in Whitestonecliff. It's too late to press on for home, and there's bad weather coming up."

As he spoke, Ronan gathered up the hares and glanced into the dull northeast. Clouds boiled there and the wind had lately grown very sharp. The village kept a guest house, and the chief's party would enjoy the best food Whitestonecliff could provide. It would still be rough fare for Gruffydd and his son. The settlement was small, hardly wealthy, no better or worse than the other outlying villages that clung to Gruffydd's moorside domain.

The horses moved off and Ronan swung the hares back over his shoulder as he fell into step by the chief. His eyes searched ahead for the shallow stream. It trickled across the old Roman road, no more than ankle deep, and ran down by the village, on the south side of the embankment. Gryffydd looked down at him, appraising the boy's face and liking what he saw. "And you, lad. What will you have for your troubles on our behalf? Some gold coins? A pony of your own? A warspear or a battleaxe?"

It was tempting to claim the pony, but for Ronan it would have been a useless luxury. There were always other people's horses to ride, and a pony was beyond his needs. He shrugged, his smile lopsided and resigned as he looked up at the chief. "I'd like the axe, my lord, but I should take the money for my family's sake."

Gruffydd chuckled. "Duty to family is one of a man's greatest strengths, lad. If my little horse wins, Ronan, an axe for you as well. He runs like the wind but he has a mind of his own. I can tame him with the whip and the spur, but I'd break his spirit, and I like spirit in a horse as in a man. Work your own kind of magic on him, boy. What is it you do?"

Again, Ronan shrugged. "Understand them, my lord. They're no different from men. You can drive them with spurs or speak gently. When they crave your gentle words, they try to please you. like people."

The insight was uncommon from one so young, and from a poor household. Gruffydd frowned thoughtfully, clearly mulling over the words as he, his son and the stable hands turned off the unkempt old road and followed the shallow stream through the woodland. Before them, Ronan jumped nimbly from dry place to dry place, knowing every rock, every sheep trail. He could just see the telltale curtain of woodsmoke from the hearths of home.

The village drew its name from the great chalk cliff that stood guard over it like a rampart, where the moor gave way to the woods bordering Gruffydd's rich farmland. In places the rain and snow had washed the turf away from the underlying chalk, and artists many centuries ago had cut into one face of the undulating hills the enormous likeness of a horse. Today, Gruffydd's people kept the image cut out, for it could be seen for miles and marked his territory.

The overcast came up fast out of the northeast, iron grey and brewing into a mass that threatened serious rain. As they entered the woodland it began with great droplets that fell in a thickening curtain while they followed the winding trail along the forested slope. The air was rich, earthy in the rain, and Ronan liked it, though Gruffydd swore lividly.

More centuries ago than anyone knew, men had burned back the woodland and now the village stood in an open area, a cluster of wooden houses with roofs thatched in woven heather. The smoke of cookfires had begun to hug the ground, driven down by the rain, and the sky was heavy, the earth a thickening quagmire.

Ronan raised his hand in greeting to the chieftain. Ewan stood waiting for his guests, a brown wool cloak wrapped about his sheepskins. He was some distant kinsman of Gruffydd's, and quiet pleasantries were exchanged between the two as Ronan took his leave.

Geese honked at him at the door of his own house, and he threw a stick at them. In spring they could be vicious. He swung the brace of hares off his shoulders and pushed on the heavy timber door. It creaked inward on dry, protesting pivots and he ducked in under the thatch, pushed through a patchwork of door skins that shut out the draught.

The house was companionably dim and he was momentarily blind. It had one room; two hearths were alight and the smell of baking bread wafted from the one in the corner. The younger children had their feet in the big fireplace that was sunk in a depression in the middle of the floor. Brass lamps flickered, augmenting the firelight, but the house was still dim, warm and inviting. The air was smoky and the wind rustled constantly in the thatch.

Across the hearth, Ronan's two younger sisters gave him a look of reproach as he shut the door. The youngest piped, "You're late!"

Ignoring the child, he held up his hares. His mother and the eldest girl were ladling water into the black iron cauldron, while his brothers occupied their hands in the lamplight, cutting hide into thonging. "I met my lord Gruffydd and Bryn on the road and had to walk back with them, or I'd have run and been here in half the time." He handed the hares to his mother. "I'm not *that* late."

"But you're soaked," she observed. "Put your tunic by the fire to dry before you get your death of cold."

She was the last human being who cared enough for him to say such things, and Ronan did as he was told with a smile. He shrugged out of the tunic, spread it on the hearth stones and crouched there to warm himself as he listened to the wind singing about the house and the voices of the children. Boyd and Brian were busy with their hide, but little Caelia and the youngest girl, Fiona, were unoccupied and chattering endlessly. Ronan rubbed his eyes, watching his mother and the eldest daughter, Camilla, skinning the hares.

His sister was lovely, red-haired, with a quick temper if she was angered. She was promised in marriage to one of Ewan's four

11

sons, and would wed in a month. When she was gone it would be easier to provide for the remaining brood. Boyd and Brian were nine and eleven years, and gave Ronan a kind of respect he did not get from the girls. They saw how he was muscled, how hard he had become, how skilled a hunter he was. When they looked at him they saw a man, and they wondered how the years would change them.

Bearing six children had not troubled his mother greatly. Ronan smiled as she caught his eye over the fire, She wore her dark hair in three long braids. Silver streaks had begun at her temples and wove into the black tresses in lovely patterns. She wore plain grey wool, as did Camilla, but the two were anything but plain, Ronan thought. He sat with his chin on his arm and closed his eyes, growing drowsy as he warmed.

If he chose to wed he could have a house of his own, but even now Ronan knew his heart too well for that. He was restless, yearning for freedom, wary of being burdened by a wife and a brood of his own. He longed only to be free, to do as he pleased, to leave when and if he chose, and to love where he pleased. His father chided him about his restlessness, which he called idleness, but oddly his mother understood. She never troubled Ronan, and he was grateful.

The woman dropped the quartered hares into the cauldron as the water began to seethe, and watched her first born drowsing by the fire. Ronan was called wayward because he went against tradition, refusing the peasant loyalties that had shackled poor men for as long as anyone could remember. But he was also clever, and he was like no other boy she knew. In his own way, he was beautiful, putting many a girl to shame, blessed with skin like pale gold, and green eyes. Yet it was the beauty from within that won him other's hearts in a moment. A mother had soon recognised that power in him.

He was little like his father in either looks or temperament, but both were stubborn. Ronan was no artisan, nor could he be made into one, of that his mother was certain. For now he would hunt for the family, work horses for the chief, and where he was going, even Ronan did not know, freeman though he was. He would never be allowed to carry a sword among the sons of chiefs and chieftains — being low-born cost him that. He was just young muscle that was needed on the land, to work it and defend it, often with his bare hands, like the rest of the freemen labourers. And perhaps to die one night, when an east wind brought invaders from the sea.

The Angles had come often, and they would come again soon. When the seas calmed in spring and the wind swung around in the invaders' favour, men waited, watched for signal fires and kept their weapons sharp. Next time the Angles came, Ronan was of an age to fight, and his mother's face betrayed the dread that squeezed her heart.

* * *

In the guest house that occupied a place of some prestige beside the long, low chieftain's hall, fires and lamps had been lit for Gruffydd and his son. Rain pattered again but the heather thatch was newly repaired after winter and the house was dry.

Servants brought in platters of mutton, pork and cheese, and pitchers of ale stood on the table, some still steaming, while the pokers were thrust back into the fire to heat again. It was not a feast by the standards of Derventio, but Gruffydd was satisfied. He broke the dark bread into pieces and studied the swirl of frothy liquid in his cup as if it were a scrying glass. At the other end of the table, Bryn carved deeply into a pork haunch, and Ewan fingered a strand of his unbraided hair as Gruffydd sampled the ale.

"Fires were seen the coast two weeks ago," he mused as he soaked a piece of bread in the ale and chewed mechanically.

"Fires?" Ewan reached for the pitcher to refill his own cup. "There was a fight?"

The chief passed a leathery palm across his breast. His fingers locked about his heavy amulet, the warrant of his rank. "Aye, a victory, but not a rout. The Angles went away to lick their wounds and choose other prey. They did not panic, nor run like curs beaten for their impudence. Other prey, Ewan."

"Us." Ewan crumbled bread between his fingers. "We've been lucky, my lord. Two summers have gone by peacefully. Our luck may stretch a little further."

But Gruffydd shook his head. His teeth worked diligently on a piece of pork rind. "Our luck is at breaking point, Ewan. You cannot win against these Angles, for there is no end to them, they never stop coming. I have said this to my brother chiefs — that we should take the battle to them, across the water, stop them on the shores of Gallia before they reach us, before they even unfurl a sail. But it would take a talent I do not possess to make the tribes of our coast fight together, *with* one another instead of against each other, for a change. The Angles are coming, Ewan, sure as an east wind is blowing to fetch them here. We'll give them a fight they'll tell stories about for two score years, eh, boy?" He was looking along the table then, where Bryn was draining a third cup of mulled ale. "And you shall be blooded, my son. For that at least, this season is timely."

Imperceptibly, Bryn's wide mouth compressed. Warmongering was of no interest to him. He was not keen to be blooded, but nor did he fear it. He was hard, with the resilience of youth, and complacent. He was strong, and he knew it; he had been taught well, by the finest swordmasters in the north, and he knew that, too. His wide shoulders lifted in an expressive shrug that made him feel the cold tackiness of his damp tunic and he said to his father, "The horse concerns me more. That, and Aemelia."

The old man blinked in surprise. "Your wedding day is set too far in the future for your liking?"

"Not far enough," Bryn corrected gloomily.

"She is well bred and her dowry will be a fine price." Gruffydd was clearly attempting to be practical, but to Bryn's ears he sounded merely mercenary.

"She has all the winsome qualities," Bryn said tartly, "of a buzzard, which would be all well and good, were I also a buzzard!" He paused, drank the third cup of Ewan's potent ale to the bottom and slammed down the cup. His head had already begun to swim. "But I am not a buzzard, and in any case, I'd as soon not wed with anyone, least of all not the last spoiled daughter of a Christian house! They never know when enough is enough. It's simple enough, so they tell me, to *wed* one, but when you try to unmake the marriage because you have had enough, you learn what they're made of."

Gruffydd would have liked to rebuke his son or at least contradict him, but he could hardly argue the truth. Instead, he merely made disapproving noises and turned his attention back to his meal. "Then choose another woman. One your mother will approve of, mind! Save your handsome lads for your own time, we'll have none of that at home. I've seen the lads you chase in the fields, and your tavern wenches, and I'll have none of them marrying into my house. If you'll not take Marcus Duratius's daughter, who will you take?"

Bryn replied with a sullen, stony silence, and Gruffydd sighed, looking along at Ewan.

The chieftain was almost of Gruffydd's age, and amused. His dark eyes laughed, nested in deep creases, while he concealed his humour behind his cup. "No matter," Gruffydd said at last. "You'll keep a while longer, rascal. And with the Angles coming we'll not be short of diversion to keep us all busy. How many men can you spare, Ewan, to fight? A hundred will come with their own weapons from Catreath, but the rest say they'll hold their ground in case their own homes need defending. . . which may likely be the case. We'll pull a hundred from our neighbours, if we're lucky. Catreath is full of mercenaries, as usual, looking for a fight — and wanting pay."

"How many men?" Ewan rubbed his face. His broad, hard fingers traced the creases about his brow, smoothed his mustache. "Twenty or thirty, my lord, not many more. We're a small village. Aye, and kill thirty of our young men, and we'll feel it for a generation."

The words were telling, since they were all too true. Each year, with the warming winds of spring, the invaders came. Each year, greater numbers came ashore from more ships, and with the close of the fighting season another Angle tribe had settled on British land, ousting the Britons or locking slave iron about their necks. Their fences spread north and west from the coast, pushing inland, and Gruffydd had long known that his rich farmland was a prize that enjoyed an uneasy, insecure peace. He kept his warband armed and well mounted, and maintained lookouts along the coast, using the old, crumbling Roman signal towers. The fires were lit when sails showed on the horizon, and every year those fires burned.

Only weeks before the barbarians had attacked to the south, at Eboracum, but the chief there held the strongest warband in the north country, and though the Angle ships were said to have sailed right up the River Ambri and into the smaller Usan River, almost to the walls of Eboracum itself, the invaders were turned back. But it had not been a decisive victory, as Gruffydd had said. The ships turned south, down the coast, when they should have been forced back out to sea. In the south they would find safe ports, friendly camps in which to heal, grow strong, and arm to attack again.

Some of the chiefs wanted to mass a warband, send out a call to arms to any man who had the heart to fight, and make war in Gallia, Germania, across the Narrow Sea. The chief at Eboracum, Gareth Ironhand, had counselled war for years. His city had run to seed since the Romans left, but it was still a trophy worthy of conquest. The Angles came nearer every season, and skirmishing in Gareth's river country was commonplace, even in winter.

No one doubted that war was coming, but some disregarded it. Gruffydd watched Bryn soaking an old, wrinkled, last season's apple in a cup of hot wine, and wondered if it was the lot of every father to despair over his sons. Bryn was unconcerned. He was too wealthy, too handsome and too idle for his own good; drinking and bedding were already the death of his reputation — unless he actually desired the reputation of a shameless rake. While weapons amused him he plied the sword and the axe with the easy grace of the master, and then he cast them aside as if they were mere toys.

He was good, to him the skills were natural, as they should be to the born warrior, but to Bryn it was just a game. To him, the Angle threat mattered less than the fall of the dice, the odds on a horse — and *much* less than tumbling a peasant's lusty young son in the hay.

Still, Gruffydd smiled ruefully and let Bryn go his way. He had a level head and would come into line soon enough when the fighting began. And he was right about Amelia Duratius. Her father had been trying to get that girl wed for years, repeatedly raising the price of her dowry with the hopes of luring a man to his doom with that, since his daughter had become a woman with all the charm of a cantankerous old she-badger.

Sensing his father's scrutiny, Bryn looked up, brow arched in question. In one so young, the innocently saturnine expression sat uneasily on his features. It was an attractive quality which women of all ages, and many men, found irresistible. Gruffydd smiled faintly and turned back to Ewan.

"Our thanks for your hospitality tonight, but we shall move on in the morning. My little stallion is safely out of the rain? Then we'll bid you good night, Ewan. Your men will have heard news of the battle. Tell them to listen now for the call to arms. No one can say when it will come, but it cannot be long."

"Aye, my lord." The chieftain scraped back his chair and swung a damp cloak about his shoulders. "We'll listen. We've a few of our own young men to blood in this. It's timely, as you say." He settled the cloak about his knotted sheepskins. "If you've all you need, I'll be away to my own hearthside."

"Everything but a hot bath," Bryn said when Ewan had banged shut the door. "These peasant rat holes are wretched."

"But dry enough to suffice." Gruffydd stretched, listening to his joints creak in protest of the rain. "If we'd pressed on we'd still have been on the road! A little gratitude would go a long way, Bryn."

"Gratitude for what?" Bryn remained unimpressed. "It's their duty to extend their hospitality, and an honour, if they know what's good for them! For my money, I'd have stayed in Catreath."

"I know you would," Gruffydd said drily. "I saw him. The lad with the brown eyes and the yellow hair." Bryn grinned impishly.

16

"You're enough to make a father despair!" But Gruffydd chuckled.

"Or be proud," Bryn added, with a flex of his supple body as he examined the sleeping skins and turned up his nose.

2

The rain was gone before dawn, leaving the village under the chalk cliff sodden and muddy. The sky had cleared and the wind fell. Woodsmoke drifted as the hearths were rekindled, and Ronan wrinkled his nose as he pulled on his grey sheepskins and went out to taste the morning. He smelt the woods, and beyond them the moor, but today was not his own. Today, his brothers must hunt for the family, since Ronan himself would be in Derventio by evening.

Whitestonecliff shook itself awake as he watched. Hounds and children alike scurried about, water and firewood were carried, eggs gathered from the unlikely nests of chickens that wandered where they would. The chieftain's guests appeared late as Ewan's servants ran with breakfast, and while Bryn was still yawning his father ambled to the stable to check on the welfare of his horse.

A boy ran to find Ronan and summoned him to Gruffydd's service. The little stallion stood knee deep in straw with Ewan's own horses. Ronan stroked his bony face and the animal rubbed his head against the grey sheepskin, making Gruffydd laugh quietly.

"He likes you."

"He'll come to know me," Ronan said. "Won't you, boy?" He looked up at the old chief with a smile. "I'll ride him today, if you like."

"I've no saddle for him," Gruffydd cautioned.

"It makes no difference." Ronan locked his fingers into the bridle straps, rubbing the smooth leather between thumb and forefinger. "I'd like to ride him, my lord. How soon will he race?"

The old man patted the smooth, speckled rump. "In a month, back at Catreath, all being well. You'll have heard of the fight that's coming in like a storm on the east wind. Aye, well, that could lay waste to every man's plan, and who'll care which nag wins a race when the Angles are beating on your door?" He twitched bushy brows at Ronan. "Will you carry a spear for me?"

"If Ewan orders it," Ronan said evenly, but the chief heard the reluctance in his voice and grunted. Ronan took a breath and chose his words with care. "I would sooner swing a sword or an axe with the *real* warriors, my lord." He looked up at Gruffydd, whose seamed brown face was frowning at him over the horse's withers. He had half expected to see anger or derision there, but Gruffydd was taking him seriously and Ronan's pulse quickened. "The farmers in the spearmen's ranks march out just to be cut down, my lord. They die bravely and with honour, but how shall I envy them? I've no wish to die! I'd march with them if you commanded it, but. . ."

"But you're too young to throw your life away on Angle spears, you'd be wasted in such service, and you're wise enough to know it." Gruffydd's eyes narrowed, buried in deep creases. "You hold yourself in high regard for a peasant's brat, young Ronan."

Ronan felt the swift heat flush his face and looked away, more resentful than contrite, and was about to mumble an apology. Gruffydd cut him off with an impatient gesture.

"You're a prideful young tyke, but that's often no bad thing. Do you think you're good with a sword? An axe? How good?"

Pulse quickening again, Ronan lifted his head, very much aware that he was being judged. "I can ride as well as any man, and better than most," he began, hearing the eagerness in his own voice, thinking how boyish it sounded and castigating himself for his own youth. "And I'm strong. I've the eyes, the ears of a hunter. I've fed my family for years, not with a bow or a javelin, but with these." He palmed the throwing knives that even then were sheathed on his belt, at his right side. "I could learn to use the sword and the axe, my lord — and quickly, if I was well taught."

"Young rascal," Gruffydd chided, but he was not angry. The rebuke was gentle, even thoughtful, and Ronan waited, hardly daring to breathe. Had he been impudent? Was ambition so much a sin? Surely he had shown the kind of initiative and spirit that were commended in men, qualities Gruffydd liked in horses and warriors alike.

Before the old man could properly answer, footsteps, splashing in the thin mud, announcing Bryn's arrival, and Gruffydd said quietly to Ronan, before his son was in earshot, "Let me think on it. See to the nag, do me that service, and then we shall decide. You'll not have handled a sword before. It may be harder than you think, boy."

With that he stamped out of Ewan's stable, and Ronan blinked after him as the old chief hailed Bryn and took a cup of ale. Ronan had spoken almost defiantly, fully expecting to be rebuked, perhaps even punished, and he could have shrugged off a cuffed ear more easily than he could grasp the answer he had received.

He schooled his face as Gruffydd and Bryn turned toward

him to look over the horse. Ronan grasped the little stallion's bridle and backed him out of the stable, all the while speaking softly to him, petting him, so that he grew accustomed to the sound of a stranger's voice, the touch of his hands. He would ride this pony to Derventio, and of a sudden it was imperative that he should do well before Gruffydd, that the chief should approve of a boy from Whitestonecliff.

Warrior. The thought clamoured in Ronan's mind as he turned the horse about, showed him off. *Warrior!*

The road to the old Roman town ran through a vale of many rivers and streams. To the north, one rushing stream bypassed the settlement of Elmgrove, and the River Rhiw flowed west through Gruffydd's rich, coveted pastureland to join the Dervent itself, four miles north of the town. Ronan had often made the ride, and always enjoyed it. A little more than twenty Roman miles through lush country that wore the new, almost virgin green of the season.

He took his leave of his family with a few words of advice to his brothers, Boyd and Brian, about the duties that fell to them in his absence. He cuffed them affectionately and wished them well, for they were good boys, loyal to their home and good to their mother. She had a kiss for Ronan's cheek before he left, and a thick slab of bread and cheese, for his breakfast.

The little horse blinked soft, dark eyes at him, and Ronan shared the last of his food with him before he passed the trailing leather reins up over the twitching, sensitive ears. The lovely head came up and tossed, and Ronan grinned. He rubbed the animal's bony nose and said quietly to him, "The chief has bought you. Now, that means he owns you. . . no, it means he *thinks* he owns you. That's right, isn't it?" He pulled gently at the roan's ears, and the horse blew through his nostrils. "But if you could get loose, run free — he'd see how much he owned you then!" As if he understood, the horse snorted, and Ronan chuckled. "But we must work for him, you and I. You must run, and I. . . one day soon, Gruffydd will very likely expect me to go out and die in his service with a smile. Given the choice, little horse, I think I'd sooner run!" He patted the sleek, muscular neck and took the reins in his left hand. "Trust me, I'll not hurt you."

As he swung up the horse stood like a statue, but as Ronan's weight settled and steadied on his back he came up on his hind legs, squealing in annoyance. Ronan clung tight with his knees and spoke words of gentle chastisement as he came down again. "You must make me look good," he told the animal, patting his neck when he was able. "You must run for me, and then perhaps Gruffydd will put a sword into my hands, instead of a spear, let me march to war with the warriors, and give me a chance to march home again." The stallion danced from foot to foot, bucking slightly, but Ronan was well seated and in no danger of being dislodged. In a few moments he steadied and snatched impatiently at the bit as Ronan took a firmer hold on the reins.

He came about, responding more readily, and at the stable door Gruffydd nodded, and nudged Bryn with one elbow. Bryn chuckled as they waited for Cullen and Rua to finish saddling the other horses. "What odds, father, that little red demon will have him off before we're two miles down the road?"

"Throw off young Ronan?" Gruffydd echoed. "Long odds on that, Bryn. My money's on the lad. He's a better hand with nags than either of us. That animal showed you just yesterday who was master! Is your rump still bruised?"

Bryn gave his father a disdainful look. "Ronan should be a good hand with a horse. It's a peasant skill, after all. I could bring you a dozen slaves as gifted."

"It's a skill I'd pay good gold to discover in myself, save that it can't be bought," Gruffydd retorted. "But like your mother, Bryn, I imagine you're too high and fine for such things."

"When I keep a hound," Bryn observed with a ghost of a smile as he looked down a long, aquiline nose at Ronan, "I don't expect to have to rush about barking myself."

The old man gave Bryn a hard look. "Working horses is also a warrior skill. Ronan might have the makings of a warrior, if I took him off the land and put him in the warband. What think you of that?" He paused, watching as Ronan coaxed the horse to stand still, learn good manners. "All that lad needs is a patron."

Bryn did not comment. Turning away, he took his own horse from Cullen, and Ronan watched as he swung up into the saddle. Supple, fluid, filled with cat-like grace, was Bryn. Long-limbed, tall and darkly beautiful, and much too aware of it for his own good. Ronan only sighed as Bryn mounted, and Rua led up the other animals. Like as not, Bryn considered the whole question beneath him. A chief's son had better things to occupy his time than wondering and worrying about a peasant's dubious honour. The Angles were probably heavy on Bryn's mind, Ronan realised, for this was the season of Bryn's blooding, too.

The thought was sobering, and Ronan still wore a frown as they trotted out of Whitestonecliff, headed south for Derventio. All about him were woods and pastures, so rich and fecund, they must be like booty to the invaders who came in on the east wind from the sea. Gruffydd had every reason to wear that anxious face; and Bryn? What Bryn was thinking or feeling was kept too well hidden for Ronan to guess, but if he was not concerned with the night of his warrior blooding, then by gods, he should be. Many high born warriors, chiefs, chieftains and their sons, died on the field of battle, too.

Before they saw the town Ronan could smell it, the intriguing, not too unpleasant odour of a large number of people and their industries. Derventio was a ramshackle chaos of crumbling Roman buildings and the wood-and-wicker houses that gradually replaced them as they tumbled down or were razed by fire or fighting. It spread along the river's lush banks, and they rode down an avenue that skirted the southern perimeter until they were within sight and hearing of the water.

The swollen Dervent was still running fast and deep after the thaw, but it was a lovely river. The trees about it displayed a patchwork of spring greenery and white blossom, and beneath them grazed a dozen black-faced sheep, a flock of goats, and big, white geese.

The walls of the legionary fortress itself still stood but were obscured by the freemen's houses clustering about them. Look-outs dozed along those walls, and the enclosure that had once been used to defend the Empire's presence in these hills was used to pen animals and drunks now. The Roman structures were slowly being taken apart by time and wind and weather, or by stonemasons who used them as an easy quarry to supply other sites.

The chief lived in an enduring Roman house. Half the roof had been thatched, after a storm stripped away the old tiles, and Gruffydd had added to it with a long timber section that sat oddly on the original building. He was proud of the house; it had once belonged, so people of his father's generation said, to a Roman officer, the legate of a legion, but no one was really sure. The legions had left the wild, hard north country so long ago.

The walls imprisoning the garden and courtyard were still sound. The gate squeaked on unoiled pivots, and the little stallion's iron shoes rang on the cobbles as he danced to a halt. Ronan slid gratefully to the ground. The horse was tired after the ride, and since morning his manners had been quite good.

Ronan took his reins over his arm as Gruffydd and Bryn slid out of the saddle. "I'll take him to the stables, my lord," he offered, "and rub him down."

"Aye, good lad," Gruffydd agreed. "Have him fed, as well. Then come to the kitchen and eat yourself. You've a fine knack with horses, Ronan. I'll tell you now, that little red demon threw three riders to the ground yesterday." He cast a mocking glance at Bryn.

"He just needed a kind word," Ronan said easily. "You're a fine judge of horses, my lord. This one will serve you well." He smiled up at the chief, and at Bryn, but Bryn's thunderous expression made him recoil. "Am I at fault?"

Gruffydd tousled Ronan's hair with rough affection. "In no way, boy. Bryn is smarting, since the nag threw him, and he hoped to see you flat on your backside in the road too! We had a wager on it, and he lost a coin. Now, go and see to the nag."

They called him a demon, but for Ronan he was docile. He clattered on ahead of Cullen's and Rua's tired ponies, and into the stable that backed onto the cobbled courtyard, a long, double-storeyed building, with a hayloft above the stalls where once a legate's horses were accommodated. Ronan knew it well. Since he had been old enough to work, he had spent much of his time here, riding horses, grooming them, watching as they were gelded and, later, helping in the forge where the farriers made and mended horse-shoes and stirrup irons.

And often he had watched the warband train. The swordmaster was a crusty old veteran to whom rank meant less than nothing. He barked at officers and men alike, and not even Bryn was exempt the rough edge of his tongue. Beyond the stable, running down to the river's edge and along it, was an open paddock, most of which was visible from the hayloft. Ronan had often sat in the loft, watching noblemen's sons his own age and younger swinging first wooden swords and then iron ones at each other in practice. It did not look difficult to him, no matter what the swordmaster said about it exceeding a peasant's capacity.

And just once, he had picked up a real sword, had held it, felt its weight and balance. How sweetly it fit his palm, as if a crafts-man had moulded it for the purpose. And then his ears had been boxed for the impudence, for 'fooling about' with Bryn's weapons. His face had prickled with the heat of shame and he had rushed away.

That day was almost two years ago, and Ronan still felt the sting as he forked a pile of fresh hay into the little stallion's stall and picked up brushes and combs to groom away the dust and mud of the road. He would run like the wind, and he would win. He would earn a battleaxe for his rider, at the very least.

"Will you do that, Red?" Ronan whispered to him as the horse thrust his nose into the hay and began to eat. "Will you win for me, and win a fortune for the chief, so that Gruffydd owes me a favour or three?" The horse did not seem to hear.

An hour later, sore and weary after a long day, he bathed at the deep stone trough in water so cold it stole his breath away, and jogged through the servants' long yard to the kitchen. In command of the hearths was a matron, stout and fierce, with fists like hams and a deep, mannish voice. When he was younger Ronan had been terrified of her, but now he teased her, made her laugh, and when he was in Derventio she fed him is if he were for the slaughter. He enjoyed the cosseting, but more than that he loved to listen to the woman's stories.

She knew every ancient tale of the warlike Brigante people. She knew of the Iceni, and of Boudicca, whose name was still whispered, whose shade was still glimpsed through the mists when Samhaine was foggy, hushed and haunted. Sometimes at night, when the chief's household was abed and the servants and slaves counted their duty done, Ronan sat by the smoldering hearth with the bonded people to listen to the woman, whose name was Sian, as she spun the ancient tales again.

The kitchen was warm and steamy. Ronan smelt the pig that had been turning over the fire since morning, and he was hungry. At the open door he paused in a patch of evening sun, smiled at the woman, and at the lad who helped her. They were dawdling through odd chores at the table, mother and son, both wind tanned and dark as the Brigante, but there the similarities between them ended. Where the woman was tall as a man and strong as a warrior, the boy was frail. Dafydd was well enough, but he would never run or fight, never swing a sword, nor ride a horse. A wooden crutch leaned on the table where he sat, shelling peas into a basket. Ronan smiled, and his belly warmed.

"Can you spare a cup of ale for a weary traveller?" he asked from the door. The two hounds lazing by the hearth lifted their heads, but they knew him and only flung themselves at Roan to be petted as he came inside.

"Ronan of Whitestonecliff! Come and sit you down, don't stand there at the door like a stranger!" Sian always scolded him, but she was laughing. "If you've come from home this morning you'll be hungering, and it'll not be like Gruffydd to have sense enough to feed a growing lad."

"I could eat a nag," Ronan confessed as he pulled a chair up to the table beside Dafydd, who was young and dark, and very beautiful. He was Sian's last born, a full year younger than Ronan, almost to the month. It was autumn since Ronan had visited here last, and that time had done much for Dafydd. He was a young man now, which made his beauty all the more disturbing, made Ronan painfully aware of him. He looked up almost shyly, as if he knew what Ronan was thinking. Long, inky eyelashes fluttered and his cheeks pinked a little. "I've come to work the chief's new horse," Ronan said as a platter of bread and pork was set down before him, making conversation to distract himself from the boy at his side.

Sian snorted rudely. "Gruffydd and his horses. He'd spend his last *solida* on a pony." She pulled back her big shoulders, tossed back braids that were like thick coils of black and silver, and smoothed the scuffed leather apron she wore over breeches and long skirted tunic.

"What's wrong with horses?" Ronan asked through a mouthful of meat.

"Nothing, pet," she said, setting a cup of ale beside his plate, "so long as there's profit in it for *you*. If you're doing well out of it, old Gruff can't be losing, but he'll gamble his fortune on a nag's nose one day, aye, and lose the lot."

The idea made Ronan chuckle. "Not while I'm riding it, I hope!"

"You?" Sian shook her head as she sat down again, opposite her son. "No, the old gods smile when they see you coming, young rascal. They'll do no such thing to you, mark my words well. The waters will be stormy where those old gods send you, but for Ronan there'll be something special."

"Special?" he echoed between bites, feeding scraps to the dogs at his feet. "All I want is a place in the warband, Sian. They're saying a fight's fast coming, and I don't care to march to my death with the farmers. What will the old gods say about that? It's a lot to ask."

"And if you don't ask, pet, how will you ever get anything?" Sian drank a cup of ale and looked sidelong at her shy, silent son. "Look at him. My Dafydd. Hasn't he grown since you saw him last?"

And Dafydd blushed, ducked his head, while Ronan felt a sudden race of warmth. Oh yes, Dafydd had grown in every way. He was almost a man now, and save for the crutch that was never far from him, he would have been looking forward to his own warrior blooding in the same battle as haunted Ronan, and likely Bryn too. Ronan cast a glance over his shoulder in the direction of the wing of the house where Gruffydd held court, and wondered just what was going on behind Bryn's handsome face. Perhaps a turmoil of doubt, such as often seized Ronan? Flocks of butterflies in his belly, that took him uawares and almost sickened him? Ronan sighed. He and Bryn might sit and eat tonight beneath the same roof, but they were a world apart, separated by fate at the hour of their birth, and Ronan would probably never know what Bryn thought or felt. Even to ask would earn him a whipping.

* * *

The debris of the meal had been cleared but the guests stayed on, to Gruffydd's annoyance. Marcus Duratius was a merchant, a dealer in anything and everything, from jet jewellery to saddles and swords, from nails and twine to ships and sails. His company was always amusing, often profitable, but the company of his daughter was *not*. And she almost always accompanied him these days.

Why should she not, when the arrangement had been made, wrists clasped and wine drunk on the agreement? Aemelia Duratius was Bryn's betrothed, she would be his wife one day in summer, and she would come to live in this house. Gruffydd sighed heavily. It took a lot to make Bryn run — Gruffydd had never seen him back off from anything he could answer with the edge of a sword. But Bryn was fleeing now, like a coward.

"Make my excuses for me," he hissed into his father's ear. "Tell Marcus, politely if you can, rudely if not, what he can do with his dowry and his daughter. Say I've gone to Germania to try the whores there. Say I've taken ill and may expire. Say I'm dying already!"

"And what," Gruffydd chuckles, "shall I say when they expect an invitation to the funeral?"

But Bryn was already gone, escaping into the back of the house. Gruffydd sighed again as he dispatched a bondsman for wine. So it was down to him to settle the business of a broken marriage contract, was it? He would tackle that subject with Marcus later, in private, over the best barley spirits he possessed. No need to humiliate the girl by shredding the contract before her very eyes.

Marcus Duratius was of Roman extraction. One of his grandsires was an important officer, generations before, when the legions abandoned Brigantia to her uncertain, stormy future, and Duratius liked to claim that some Gallic forefather had been with the Roman invasion fleet. Gruffydd was not entirely sure if that was any cause for pride.

The merchant and his disagreeable daughter reclined on leather couches, enjoying the evening sun that slanted in through the windows opening onto the courtyard. The room was light and pleasant since Gruffydd's wife had replastered the walls to erase the dark, cheerless old religious murals. Some martyred saint still suffered behind the fresh plaster, but Gruffydd was pleased to be rid of the pious, angry image. His Christian visitors might have called it sacrilege to plaster over saints; they were well known for their piety. Aemelia wore a little silver cross at her throat, and Marcus's earrings were in the design of fishes, which had something to do with their religion, though Gruffydd was not sure what.

The girl lacked nothing in beauty, he thought as he graced her with a polite smile. She was comely, but her expression was sour enough to curdle a churn of milk at a glance. Gruffydd fixed his smile in place and seated himself, wondering if Aemelia was angry about anything in particular, or everything in general. He tried to imagine Bryn married to her, and choked back a chuckle. Surely, it was a marriage wrought be demons, even if Bryn's taste had been for lovely women. . . and Gruffydd well knew, Bryn's taste lay elsewhere.

"Marcus, how goes the trade?" he prompted as the bondsman hurried back with the wine and the silence left by Bryn's sudden exit became taut.

He was a small man, olive skinned, due to that Roman blood. Black hair was cropped very short about a well-shaped skull, and Marcus kept himself clean shaven. He wore the conservative colours his ancestors would have approved of, a white woolen tunic, grey breeches, costly leather boots made in Germania. He took a cup from the servant without otherwise acknowledging the old man's existence, while Aemilia lounged indolently and gave her father and Gruffydd alike a sullen look.

"The trade goes badly," Marcus said at last. "Worse every season, which is to be expected. The lands across the Narrow Sea are a shambles."

And that was where Duratius's family had done half their business, for generations. A knife slid into a wedge of cheese, carved off a finger-thick slice, and Gruffydd sat back against the leather. Duratius's thoughts were plain on his face, and Gruffydd gave him a bleak look. The Angles were coming, it would be this season, it must be. Every man knew it. "It is as I told you before," Gruffydd growled. "We must go and fight them in *their* land, not wait for them to come here. We would suffer less, not having our own country burned and overrun. If we are to make war, I'd sooner do it in Gallia or Germania, and keep the Angles and the Saxons out of this island altogether."

"As would I," Duratius agreed, "but it is a war neither you nor I could organise. I was in Karitia a week ago. There has been fighting in the Great Forest, in the east, and we know we can expect trouble here when the tribesmen sail west, looking for refuge."

"Refuge, my eye," Gruffydd scoffed. "They've never come here begging for our help, pleading for succour, with tales of brigands and barbarians in their forests, looting and raping through their villages. If they fled to us with those tales and beseeched for our aid, they would get it! But they come with fire and sword, Camulus damn them, ready to burn us out, if they can. They'd as soon overrun us, and lock the slave iron around our necks!" He took a long draught from his cup. "You call that seeking refuge? By gods, Marcus, we have a different name for it. We call it invasion!" Duratius could not argue, and Gruffydd studied his guest with a deep frown. "So, what do they say in Karitia? How long, before they come at us again?"

The other man studied his knees for a moment. "A day, a week, a month. Who can be sure? Perhaps we shall escape the assault this season. Perhaps they will strike at Gareth Ironhand again."

Perhaps, Gruffydd allowed bitterly, yet what respite would that buy? A little more time to prepare, and to race his new horse. But it was a bad way to buy peace — with the blood of allies. Gareth Ironhand had already fought once this year, and if Gruffydd had heard correctly, he had been injured. The Angles had tried his defenses and been turned back, their losses also were heavy. How foolish would their captains be, to test Eboracum again so soon?

With a wordless grumble, Gruffydd buried his nose in his cup and glared at Aemilia. One trial at a time!

*　*　*

The shadows were long across the paddocks by the river, and the little roan stallion ran for the joy of it, kicking his heels. For the moment Ronan was happy to lie in the grass, watching him, and had dozed for a time while the midges dances over the water. Coots and mallards were on the river, some with ducklings paddling behind them, but he had eyes only for the horse. Until he saw Bryn ap Gruffydd.

Tall, unmistakable in his black tunic, tight black breeches and boots, Bryn swung out of the house with a mug in one hand, a bundle of bread and meat in the other, and for some moments was unaware that he was watched. But as he came closer he saw Ronan there in the grass, and checked in surprise.

The youth from Whitestonecliff came slowly, reluctantly, to

his feet, brushed down his breeches and ducked his head as if he expected a rebuke. Bryn said nothing, but finished the food and drink, deliberately appraising Ronan as if he were a slave on the auction block. Ronan waited, reminding himself that Bryn was a chief's son and heir, and yet his hackles still rose, his cheeks began to prickle with heat. With an effort, he curbed his tongue and held his silence until Bryn spoke.

"You there," Bryn said abruptly, "what are you doing?"

"Nothing," Ronan told him honestly. "Just sitting here, watching the horse."

"You've no duties?" Bryn had a quiet, pleasant voice, despite the sting of his words. The river breeze tossed his dark hair, lifted his fringe from his brow, and the sun picked up the intense blue of his eyes.

"Only to your father's horse." Ronan's eyes narrowed as he looked across the meadow at the grazing stallion. "And he looks content enough to me."

"Cullen and Rua could likely use you in the stable," Bryn suggested darkly.

Ronan took a deep breath. He was being goaded — he knew that. He just did not know why, and the not knowing irked him. It was almost as if Bryn was trying to provoke him into lashing out, with fists or words. Such an outburst would earn Ronan a whipping, and even as he deliberately curbed his temper and his tongue, he wondered why Bryn would want to see him whipped. What had he ever done to anger Bryn ap Gruffydd?

He shook his head, stubborn, but patient and polite. "Cullen and Rua are both sleeping off the ale they poured into themselves when I was still working. They told me your betrothed is visiting. I thought you'd be keen to spend your time with her, not me."

Bryn looked sidelong at him, and the vivid eyes travelled slowly, deliberately from Ronan's hair to his feet and back, making him almost squirm. It was a look of naked sensuality. Not the first such look Ronan had seen or felt, but surely the most studied. Then Bryn's face broke into a grin of boyish mischief. "How little you know of my lady Aemilia Duratius!"

"But I thought she was beautiful," Ronan said awkwardly, still feeling the weight of Bryn's eyes.

"Certainly, she's no concern of yours," the chief's son said tartly. "And she is betrothed to me no longer, no matter what you've heard, so neither will she be any concern of mine after this, thank all the gods!" He drew himself up to his full height. He was a fraction taller than Ronan, but Ronan was a little better muscled, since he had worked long and hard while Bryn enjoyed a gentler life. Bryn set his left hand deliberately on the hilt of his sword and cocked his head at Ronan. "So you've an ambition to be a warrior, have you?"

The idea seemed to vastly amuse him, but Ronan heard no aggression in his voice, and took no offence. Bryn had every right to trade on his rank, as and when he saw fit. He would be chief here in his own right when his father was gone, and with the constant threat of the Angles, that day could come at any time. Perhaps tomorrow. Vaguely, Ronan wondered if he should count it some kind of honour that Bryn took any interest in him, especially if it were the sensual interest he had seen moments before.

A perverse kind of ambition governed Ronan. If Gruffydd did meet his death soon, then Ronan's livelihood could easily depend on the prideful young heir to Derventio. A little respect for rank shown today might go a long way. "I would like to be a warrior," he said carefully. It could hardly hurt to speak the truth.

Unexpectedly, Bryn smiled, a crooked, handsome, winsome expression. "This," he said almost to himself, "I shall watch with interest. You don't think like a peasant's brat, do you?" One hand reached out. Its fingers cupped Ronan's chin, stopping his breath, but the caress was withdrawn just as abruptly and Bryn strode away.

No, Ronan thought as he watched the long limbed youth. *No, I don't think like a peasant's brat, and I'm not going to die like one, either! Not if I can help it.*

As sunset blazed along the western horizon and the day's work finished, lights were doused and hearths banked, he prowled Gruffydd's property. Thumbs hooked into his belt, three of the dogs at his heels, he made and unmade a hundred plans for his future and the roan stallion's, and when Sian's strident voice called the bonded people to the kitchen to eat, he sat between Dafydd and Cullen and ate better than his kin ate at Whitestonecliff.

As usual, he slept in the stable loft, listening to the horses and the night wind that sang under the eaves. And he remembered Sian's strange, fey words: *The old gods smile when they see you coming. For Ronan there'll be something special.* Something special? He wondered on the brink of sleep. How could it be?

Most people still swore by the old gods as well as by those of Rome, but the Christians denied the existence of any god at all except their own mysterious, benevolent one, of whom they were so afraid. Did their beliefs mock the hearts and minds of other men? Sian was almost the last true daughter of the Deer people, and proud of it. With her left hand she would make banishing signs, symbols to ward off ill fortune, and call the names of Camulus and Andrasta.

The old gods, Ronan thought as he slid down into the web of dreams. No Druid teacher or lawgiver had been seen in Gruffydd's lands in years. Could the old gods still be here, and care enough to hear a boy's prayers?

3

Steel was ringing in the paddock where the warriors trained, interrupting the stillness of the morning while the sun was still low. Ponies' hooves thudded on the turf and bowstrings sang as the archers worked. Bryn was with them, under his father's strict supervision, and for a time Ronan had watched from the fence before he grew bored and busied himself with the horse.

Bryn was also bored, but the exercises were a necessary evil. His boast was that he was a warrior, with a privileged place in the warband. He must at least maintain his dexterity with the tools of his trade, but the novelty had worn off a very long time before. Gruffydd worked his men relentlessly, and Bryn would rather have been in the tavern, where dice rattled through the night and the boys were lissome, lovely, and friendly.

From the warriors' paddock he could see the lad from Whitestonecliff, working with the latest addition to Derventio's stable. Ronan passed into and out of view beyond the sycamores that separated the twin paddocks. The meadows cushioned the chief's house from the noise and bustle of the town, and Derventio could have been miles away. Ronan was working the little horse with a sure hand and a firm ambition, and Bryn was certain the audacious young jockey had the best of the arrangement.

He was not alone. The crippled boy sat on a fallen log, watching him work the horse. Bryn had been aware of Dafydd since winter, and often lamented the gods' incomprehensible schemes. They crippled the beautiful boy and consigned him to the kitchen, while Aemilia Duratius was born to loll about in priceless gems, draping her plump carcass on a couch and doing nothing much but turn a sour eye on any man unfortunate enough to approach her. Bryn had never understood any of it.

Three days had mended most of the horse's bad habits, and in Ronan's hands he seemed a lamb. That same morning, however, Cullen swore he had been bitten, and had the wound to prove it. "Aye, and how did you provoke him?" Ronan had demanded, before he ducked nimbly under the groom's fist. Cullen would have liked to cuff his ear or black his eye, and gave him a blistering oath. He shouted after Ronan that the horse called Red was a Samhaine demon that loathed everyone but its own handler, and there was something 'not right' about Ronan of Whitestonecliff, if the demon loved him.

It might have been true. Bryn suspected as much when even Gruffydd complained about being nipped, but Red was gentle and well mannered when he was left alone, or in hands he preferred. The chief merely grumbled about making a new couch out of the animal if he failed to win, and left him to Ronan.

For himself, Ronan was more than satisfied. He was sure enough of the stallion to take him out of Derventio and amble miles down the riverbank without even a saddle on him, and without fear that he would throw his rider and bolt, as Cullen had warned. If the horse was lost on the moor, Ronan would certainly be flogged, and it would fall to Cullen's hand to administer the punishment. He was a churlish, blaspheming drunkard, a swineherd's son, with enough brains to keep a pigsty clean, but not enough to give himself a headache while he was doing it. Ronan was scornful of anything he said or did. Rua made more sense, at least when he was sober, but that was not so often. Sian often sent their food to the stable, to keep them out of her kitchen and her way.

Red cantered to a halt and Ronan slid off, passed the reins over his neck and brought him back to the log where Dafydd sat. The breeze tossed Dafydd's long, unbraided hair, which was dark and glossy as the wing of a raven; his skin was like milk after the long cold of winter, and his teeth gleamed white in the sun as he smiled. Ronan let go the reins and sat down on the log beside him as the horse put his nose into the grass.

"He'll run the legs off anything in Catreath, will that one," Dafydd observed. Ronan only nodded, for he was right. "If my lord Gruffydd doesn't make a couch of him first," Dafydd added.

"He's no fool," Ronan said easily. "Cullen may have the wound to show that he was bitten, but Gruffydd knows he provoked the horse. My lord bought him to run, not to be sociable, and he'll do that well enough. Look at those legs!"

But Dafydd was much too preoccupied looking at Ronan's legs to spare the horse much attention. "After this race," he mused softly, watching the way the wind teased Ronan's bright hair, will you be staying here?"

The question surprised Ronan, but he could only shrug.

"Who can say? It defends on Gruffydd. If he gives me a place in the warband, I'll be here, and glad to be. If not, well, maybe he'll get another horse and I'll ride that and still be here." He paused, looking sidelong at the boy. "Why, Dafydd?"

The boy's mouth quirked, an expression of annoyance that was still beautiful on so lovely a face. "It would take a dolt to ask that! I should have had more sense than to mention it."

"Mention what?" Ronan blinked in surprise. "What did I say?"

"Nothing." Dafydd sighed. "Nothing at all. Just like a man."

At that, Ronan chuckled. How good it felt, to be called a man! "Oh. Oh, I see. There's better to choose than me, Dafydd. I'm not much to catch. I'm not looking for a home yet! But if I was, I'd build a house, aye, and invite you to share it."

"You would?" Dafydd was hushed. "Last time you were here, you ignored me."

"I didn't ignore you," Ronan protested. "I was busy! And besides, last time I was here, you were a child, weren't you?"

He had the grace to blush. "No, I wasn't. And you didn't bother to ask. Do a couple of seasons make so much difference?"

"When a boy is becoing a man, they do." Ronan met his eyes and sought a smile. "Oh yes, they do." He cupped one soft cheek in his right hand. "I'll not make promises about a home, because I can't. I've not the heart to settle now, and I won't ask you to waste your life, waiting for me. You're too winsome a flower for that. But, ignore you? What man with eyes to see could ignore you?" And while Dafydd was still speechless with amazement, Ronan took the boy's face between his hands, leaned over and kissed his lips.

It was not an awkward kiss. Ronan was too lovely, too blessed with charm, to be awkward in love. He had not known many lovers, but even one night in the embrace of a man who really knew the arts of love was enough. Dafydd caught his breath as Ronan's arms closed about him and the kiss deepened.

For some moments they were rapt, lost in each other, and then Ronan lifted his head away and Dafydd pressed tightly to him. "I'm right, aren't I?" Ronan whispered.

"I suppose. Damn you," Dafydd sighed. "But still, I would have chosen you first before all others, and it — it irks me."

It irked Ronan more than a little too, for he liked Dafydd, and he felt a certain tug toward home and hearth. It would have been nice to have his own roof, his own bed, and someone warm and welcoming in it. But not yet. Not here, and not yet. Over the boy's head, he watched the horse again, and felt another kind of tug. Ambition was a fearsome taskmaster, and although Dafydd muttered his annoyance Ronan slid away and got to his feet.

Behind him, Dafydd laughed quietly, ruefully. Ronan was more than a little like that horse — coltish, unruly, beautiful. Little wonder they understood each other. "You speak his language," Dafydd called, shaking his head over Ronan, recalling his mother's counsel and recognising its wisdom. "Let him go his way," Sian had said, amused, without being asked for advice. "Let him go free, for it's the wildness and the freedom that draws you to Ronan, and you'd bestroy both in a week if you break his wings." Wise, was Sian of the Deer people.

Raucous singing issued from the stable as they led the horse back to his stall: Rua was drunk again. He sang better drunk than sober, even if he did tend to forget the words, and this morning he was shrilling his way through an old song that told of the great old days when the Brigantes and a few solicitous Caledones held out against Rome at the fortress of Petravic. Ronan gave the horse his pile of sweet hay, fetched his water, and offered Dafydd the prop of his shoulder once more. With the crutch under his other arm, Dafydd was quite agile, though he would never walk properly. His birth had been difficult, his hips were badly damaged. He would never walk without a crutch, and was resigned to it.

The kitchen was deserted. They found themselves bread and venison, onions and ale, and sat by the baking hearth to eat. It would be comfortable, Ronan thought, to work for Gruffydd and live here, especially if he had the station of a warrior to sweeten the arrangement. He was not so restless that he would turn down the invitation, but the wind beckoned, he heard it speak softly to him of other places, lands he could barely even imagine, with names he could not pronounce.

The lust to wander tormented him, even as he looked into Dafydd's dark, liquid eyes and saw such promise there as poets sang of. Ronan sighed, and with a kiss for the boy's brow he took his leave. Time to return to work, before he *was* at fault, and earned himself an honest thrashing.

He was checking and mending harness in the afternoon, sitting on a low stool in the stable yard with an expensive red leather saddle across his knees and a thick, bent needle in his fingers, when Gruffydd appeared with a broken dirk for the smithy. Ronan came politely to his feet, expecting some tiresome errand, but Gruffydd simply frowned at him in silence until Ronan was sure he had done something wrong. He dropped his eyes to the cobble stones by the chief's muddy boots and waited for whatever storm to break.

At last, Gruffydd stirred and Ronan dared look up. The old man's frown had deepened, and he drew the sword from the sheath at his left side. For a breathless moment Ronan's whole spine stiffened as he thought the fine steel blade would come at him, but Gruffydd reversed it, presented it to him, leather-bound hilt first.

He blinked foolishly, looking up into the seamed, wind-tanned face to see eyes sparkling now with some kind of mischief. They were very like Bryn's eyes, and for just a moment Ronan saw them as father and son. "My lord?" he prompted cautiously.

"When you're offered a sword, boy," Gruffydd said wryly, "you can't afford to hesitate. Swords, like crowns, are offered only once."

Impulsively, even rashly, Ronan took it. His fingers closed on the grip's tight leather binding and the polished blade rose, heavy and sweetly balanced. "It's beautiful," he said honestly as he recognised the craftsman's mark, an engraving below the crosspiece.

"And it fits your hand well," Gruffydd observed as he watched the boy turn the weapon this way and that. The blade caught the sun, cast intermittent sheets of light, like a dance of sprites in the dusty air. "What have you used? Swords, javelins, the axe?"

"Knives," Ronan told him as his eyes followed the twist and turn of the sword. "I've hunted wild pigs with the javelins, and I've swung an axe against trees often enough to know the weight of one."

"Trees and pigs don't strike back at you," Gruffydd growled. "You're a hunter, then? And you could learn the warrior's trade quickly, if you were well taught, could you?"

The blade stilled, lowered, and Ronan lifted his chin before the chief's probing look. "That's what I said, my lord, and what I still say." And then, reluctantly, he reversed the sword and handed it back.

Gruffydd took it, accepting Ronan's audacity for the moment. "Then take yourself to the swordmaster when you've done with your duties tomorrow, boy. He'll see what you're made of soon enough. He'll not have to teach you which end of a horse is which, at least! So, how fares my little red stallion?"

"Well enough to win twice what you paid for him, on one race alone, my lord. If the gods allow it, I'll serve you as well."

"Brave words." The old chief smiled. "Let's see how brave you are when Cuddy has finished with you! I shall tell him to expect you — and I shall be watching, remember that."

Little chance of forgetting it, Ronan thought ruefully. He was haunted through the afternoon, silent as he ate with the bonded people in the kitchen, and he told no one what Gruffydd had said to him.

But, good as his word, that evening Gruffydd spoke to Cuddy, the swordmaster, and Cullen heard the news from him — that the peasant's brat from Whitestonecliff was to train with the warband. The story spread like wildfire, and Ronan endured the taunts with all the patience he could muster. Cullen glared at him but knew better than to speak out. Though he was Ronan's senior by sixteen years or more, and his master's trustee, he was bonded to Gruffydd's household, while the youngster was a freeman. Something Cullen would never be.

Sleep eluded Ronan and he was still wide awake, staring into the darkness between the loft's roofing timbers, when the night was old. The door below opened, then closed again quickly. One of the three stable cats mewled from an empty stall and Ronan listened, wondering if Rua had come to. He was drunk down there, somewhere, and should be unconscious till late morning. Almost soundless footfalls approached, and the ladder up to the loft shifted under someone's weight. Ronan shuffled over to look down, and smiled as he extended a hand. Dafydd took it gratefully, hauling himself up the last few feet.

"By the gods, it's dark. I've a hard time on ladders, and I might have broken my neck, falling over that cat!" The boy hoisted himself onto Ronan's rugs and made himself comfortable.

"Does your mother know where you are?" Ronan asked softly as he slipped one arm about Dafydd.

"I don't know! Does yours?"

"I don't know either," Ronan admitted ruefully. "If Sian wants you, she has only to call. Her voice would rouse the dead." Then he gentled. "I'm glad you came. I can't sleep."

"Nor can I! But it's not Gruffydd and his horse keeping me awake. Nor Cuddy the swordmaster You're to go to him in the morning," Dafydd muttered. "Little wonder you can't sleep."

He could not see the boy's face clearly, since the loft was lit only by the spilling glow from the single lamp left burning in the stable below, but a note in Dafydd's voice suggested scorn. He was hugging his knees, peering at Ronan in the gloom. "Speak your mind," Ronan invited, amused.

"You will kick yourself in future, Ronan," Dafydd said boldly, "that you did not handfast with me when you had the chance."

The humour was infectious, and Ronan chuckled as he shuffled closer. His lips touched the boy's throat, felt it bob. "I suppose I will. I'll kick myself black and blue." For a moment he reconsidered the decision he had made, to embrace freedom and give an ear to the wind that beckoned from far-off places. Soft hands fluttered on his skin, his breath caught in his throat and his heart began to race.

It would be so easy to be caught in the gentle snare of belonging. Dafydd was beguiling, warm, so good to touch and hold. But Dafydd did not ask that Ronan gave his heart, and what Dafydd wanted tonight, Ronan could give so easily, and with such delight. He rolled the boy over on the rugs, and his hands wriggled up under the soft wool tunic. Dafydd was bare beneath it, and Ronan chuckled as he found a hard young boycock, and palmed it.

"Ah! What have I here?"

"Something little used before, Dafydd murmured in a rueful voice, "but much used hereafter, I hope." He pulled the tunic off over his head and sprawled back on the rugs. "What are you waiting for?"

What indeed? Ronan wore only his linen, all he wore to sleep on mild nights, and he was naked in moments. In the darkness he felt his way around Dafydd's slender body, kissed him inch by inch, tasted his skin and found it sweet, and at last clamped tightly to him as they humped and rubbed. His fingers clenched into the boy's pliant buttocks, and between them discovered the slickness of body oil.

Surprise stopped him while Dafydd was wriggling and mewling like a kitten. "Did you want *that*?" he asked breathlessly, and his heart hammered, for it had not occurred to him that Dafydd might be hungry for everything at once. "Dafydd, would you have me that way?"

"I have been ready for you that way for a long time." Dafydd reached up to kiss. His tongue thrust deeply into Ronan's mouth before he turned over on his belly and spread his long legs. "But take care, Ronan. You know how my right hip is crippled. . . and I am a virgin." His voice was taut.

Ronan's heart slowed a little. He kissed Dafydd's thin shoulders, stroked his spine with gentle hands. "I shan't hurt you, sweeting. How could you think that of me?"

"I trust you," Dafydd whispered. "Would I be here tonight, like this, if I did not? I want to remember you always as my first. My first man."

So Ronan gently pillowed himself on him, kissed his neck and ears, and slowly, very carefully, entered him. He stopped when Dafydd cried out, recalling his own first time, when the woodcutter had tumbled him in the forest. It had hurt, but the pain eased away and the pleasure began. Gradually Dafydd calmed, and Ronan murmured softly, nonsense words to put him at his ease.

At sixteen years, Ronan was a man in all ways, and he never forgot this while Dafydd lay beneath him. His cock was already quite thick, and many a full-grown man was less well endowed, despite Ronan's youth. He moved only slowly, with great gentleness, and the next cry from Dafydd was a sound of pleasure.

"You're all right now?" Ronan kissed the boy's slender neck. His own body burned as he held himself in check, waiting for Dafydd to be ready for more. His reply was a lush little wriggle, and he smiled. "Indeed, you *are* all right! I shall make love to you now, little one, if you'll allow it. Nothing else will pain you."

"Make love," Dafydd sighed. "Oh yes, make love to me."

It did not take long, for they were too young and too eager, and afterward Ronan held him, kissed him. They spent an hour exploring one another, time they would always treasure, no matter to whom they gave their hearts at last — or where the elder gods of this island chose to send Ronan after that night.

Fortune shifted at the mention of his name. Ronan felt it, and shivered. His pulse quickened, a fast heavy beat that had nothing to do with Dafydd's touch, the hot draught of his breath. Tomorrow would begin the proving of it, and though the boy's weight was warm and welcome on his chest as Dafydd slept at last, Ronan's restless thoughts wandered back to Gruffydd's promises.

The chief would watch him like a hawk, he would forgive nothing, and Cuddy, the old swordmaster, would be determined to prove a point at his new student's expense. If he could. Ronan's mouth compressed with resolve. It was *his* point that would be proved, not Cuddy's, for the swordmaster was wrong. A 'peasant's brat' could become a warrior. The boy from Whitestonecliff could do it — and he *would*.

4

Cuddy was grey as a badger now, much more than double Ronan's age, but he was still nimble, almost as quick as a boy. If the battlefield trick existed, he knew it. Years before, his family had been landed, wealthy, but squabbling clan elders disposed of the wealth before Cuddy or any of his long-dead brothers could claim their inheritance. He had carved out for himself the rank and respect he commanded today, first as a warrior swinging an axe beside Gruffydd when they were two young men together, and later as swordmaster of Derventio's warband.

He trained new warriors in ancient arts, and he himself was hard as ship nails, seasoned as old cask wood. His body was covered in scars, and his right hand, the sword hand, was missing a whole finger to bear testimony to his battles. His voice cracked like a whip, he rarely smiled, and most of the boys respected him. The rest merely feared him. Ronan felt respect for the man's experience and authority, his learning, but Cuddy would be less his teacher than his opponent, and they both knew it.

The old warrior scorned peasants, no matter what Gruffydd said. Peasants belonged to their masters, their place was on the land, tilling and harrowing, and ambition among them was intolerable. Ronan accepted this, and merely nodded to himself. Tolerance was something his new rival would have to learn.

With morning the sky was low, sullen, and the easterly wind was cold. Thunderheads massed behind it, and while Ronan worked the little horse along the river bank the rain began to fall. Vast drops splashed into the water, shattering the wind-rippled surface, and lightning flickered, forks of brilliance dancing along the horizon, before the thunder spoke with a voice some men said was that of a god.

When the thunder rolled and echoed across the northcountry, the roan stallion snorted in fright. Ronan felt him snatch at the bit with a strength that jerked at his wrists, and the iron-shod hooves came up as he began to panic. Mallards bolted low overhead on noisy wings and the horse plunged forward with a mind of his own. Ronan's shoulders suffered the jolt, and it took all the muscle he possessed to hold the horse as Red reared, trying to throw him.

The rain was much harder as he brought the roan into the shelter of an old oak, a little way back from the river bank, and talked soft, coaxing nonsense to him. Gruffydd had not given him a name, but now everyone was calling him Red, for the colour of his coat. A horse that was easily startled by loud noises was of dubious value on the battlefield or in a crowd, such as could be expected at a race. It was a fault, and a bad one, a flaw that must be set to rights. Red was no more than three years old, and as yet untried. He had his faults, and Gruffydd was not blind to them. They were the reason he had employed Ronan.

There was a fascinating, earthy smell in the shelter of the oak, and the light was filtered, green. Ronan slid down from the saddle and stood at the horse's head, fingers locked into the bridle straps, just talking to him. Red stood still, intent on his voice, trusting him enough not to bolt, though his ears lay flat and every nerve was taut.

The storm passed by, miles to the east, leaving the world cool, wet and quiet. The wind was cold on Ronan's damp skin, and when he judged Red to be calm enough to behave, he swung back up onto the broad sheepskin saddle.

The warband had trained and dispersed by noon. The paddock they used was empty when Ronan finished his meal of bread and honey, and Cuddy was waiting for him, sitting on the bench before the hut where the swordsmiths worked and where the weapons were stored. His scarred old hands tore a roast squab to greasy tatters as Ronan watched, and he chewed methodically on the pungent meat.

He wore a heavy brown tunic, leather collared and studded with coin-sized iron pieces that would turn aside an ill-placed sword. For Ronan he had a glare, accusing and condemning at once, and Ronan drew himself up to his full height, squared his shoulders, lifted his chin.

The swordmaster looked him over thoroughly and rudely while he finished the bird and threw the scraps to a big, black hound that lounged at his feet. He wiped his hands on his tunic, pulled a leather gauntlet onto his four-fingered sword hand, and stood. He was not quite as tall as Ronan, but the daunting bulk of his muscle, his arrogance and authority more than made up for his lack of height.

"You're the freeborn, Ronan of Whitestonecliff?"

"Yes, my lord," Ronan responded, for it was the truth, though Cuddy made it sound like the accusation of a sin.

The old man's voice was whip-crack brittle. "Don't 'my lord' me, boy. I've no lands, no rank, and you're well aware of it. But I'll be your master until you come to your senses and go home. You're the boy who knows horses."

"I am." Defiance clipped Ronan's voice, and he met Cuddy's eyes levelly now.

For some time they were silent, each judging the other, appraising an opponent, then Cuddy nodded slowly. "You've pride enough to make a warrior, boy, and enough impudence. Take off your tunic." He waited as Ronan dropped the grey sheepskin and blue tunic to the grass at his feet, then walked around him, evaluating the worth of what he saw as if he were buying a slave at market. "You've the muscle for it," he said as he came to rest at Ronan's left hand. "And your bare back says you've never had a whipping heavy enough to scar. Good luck, is it, or good sense?"

"I have good manners." Ronan endured the old tyrant's scrutiny and the cold wind with a shuttered expression. "It takes bad manners or idleness to earn a whipping. My lord Gruffydd trusts me."

"You'll have to make Cuddy trust you now!" Cuddy grunted as Ronan's profile hardened with determination. "You're well muscled for one of your years. Broad in the shoulders. But it takes more than that to make a warrior." The swordmaster exhaled noisily. "Show me your hands." When Ronan held them out, palms up, they were closely inspected, and Cuddy muttered to himself. "They're not soft, but you've none of the warrior's calluses yet. You'll blister, you know that. When you do, you'll soak your hands in brown vinegar and blind them with linen strips. You'll work hard, you'll do as you're told, you'll speak civilly to me, or I'll see that you *are* whipped, and soundly. If you're as good as you think you are, one day you'll throw an axe further than me, cast a javelin truer, swing a sword harder, and knock me in the dust, because Cuddy the swordmaster is old now, no matter that he knows every trick of this trade, and if you're good. . . you shall be a warrior."

They looked levelly at one another again, appraising, and Ronan felt an odd, unbidden thrill of pity as he perceived the tragedy of old age, something he had not felt before. Pride was Cuddy's greatest weapon now, the greater part of his strength, and yet once he had been an incomparable warrior.

"You still want to try?" he was asking. "To back out now will be no dishonour. It took courage to come even this far, I know."

Ronan folded his arms across his cold chest, studying the grass at his feet as his mind raced over the threats and promises he had just heard, and his mouth tugged into a reluctant but genuine smile as he looked back at the swordmaster. "My head says 'go home,' master. My heart says 'go on.' You have me confused now. Which shall I follow?"

Abruptly, startlingly, Cuddy laughed. He poked Ronan in the chest with the steel tip of one gauntleted finger. "Your heart, boy. Always follow your heart when it comes to warring and whoring and the gods, the head is no good for those things. Now, put your clothes on and come with me."

He led the way into the smith's workshop, a dark place where the forge was forever alight, roaring, attended by three brawny young slaves and a master smith. All worked on Gruffydd's orders, and slaves and master craftsman alike spoke in undertones of the coming fight, the pillaging Angles. When the east wind fetched death in one night, the gods would not even notice which man was free, and which was a slave. High born and slaves would die side by side.

They were making swords, axes, javelin blades, against that night. Cuddy paced to the back of the hut, and from a rack in the corner chose a black iron shortsword. Without a word, he gave it to Ronan.

Ronan took it by the hilt, knowing instinctively how to hold it, balance it. Cuddy grunted, not caring to comment as he turned back into the light and air and left Ronan to follow when he would. The sword was not at all a good weapon — crudely made, rough, the blade poor and blunt, and it lay in Ronan's hand like a dead thing. It was the ordinary, cheap piece of ironmongery that was handed out to cavalrymen at little cost to be used, broken, discarded by the score on the day of battle. Still, Ronan was in no mind to complain, and waited for Cuddy to suggest some lesson. Cuddy just frowned at the hand holding the sword and seemed to be preoccupied, by what thoughts or memories, Ronan could not guess.

"Swordmaster?" he prompted at last.

"How does it feel in your hand?" Cuddy asked shrewdly.

"Dead," Ronan said without hesitation. "Dead as mutton. I'd not give you a bent *denarius* for it, if you were trying to sell it."

The sparkle in the old, raven eyes was at odds with the man's sternness. "I did not ask for your opinion of the sword, rascal, but of your own hand. How does it feel to you? Heavy?"

"A little." Ronan shifted as he held the blade up at shoulder height.

"Oh, a little, is it? And I suppose you could hold it all day?" Cuddy gave a gap-toothed grin. "Aye, well, we'll start with just holding it a little while, and we shall see. Hold your arm out, boy. *Out*, I said, as if you have the enemy there before you. And bring the sword up. Higher! Now, hold it there." He sat down on the bench, and before Ronan's bemused eyes, unstoppered a jar of wine.

"Why?" Ronan wondered aloud, moments later.

"Why are you holding it, rascal?" Cuddy chuckled. "You'll know yourself soon enough."

"But, how long shall I hold it?" Ronan demanded.

"You'll know that, too." Cuddy's chuckle was wicked now.

And in minutes, Ronan knew. It became a battle of wills which he could not win, and knew he could not win. Cuddy sat it out in silence, whittled a stick with a razor-sharp knife, dispatched the wine, shouted and waved to his fellows as they rode by the fence, but no matter where his attention seemed to be, he was intimately aware of the battle being fought out before him. How long would it take the boy to break? And in what spirit would he break, when the time came, when no amount of stubbornness and pride would serve him any longer.

In minutes, the sword in Ronan's outstretched hand seemed to triple its weight, and while Cuddy drank his wine it tripled again. The effort of holding it became enormous, and Ronan's face was white, sweat-sheened with concentration and intense effort. The swordmaster ignored him, watching instead the eagle that hunted over the north slope of the paddock on unmoving wings. But he was listening.

Stubborn as a mule, Ronan held up the sword. The whole world began to revolve about the effort, the iron, his arm, and he lost track of time. He was in pain now, a burning agony of protesting muscles, inflicted by his own will, which would not let him drop the sword, no matter what happened, while Cuddy was watching. He would never have believed that such intolerable torture could be so innocently inflicted, and so suddenly. As the impossibility of ever winning this battle of wills became apparent, he worked harder than ever, holding his breath now in an effort to squeeze a little more, just a little more, from his spent muscles.

It was this that Cuddy was listening for: the ragged, broken breathing. His eyes returned to Ronan as he heard it, and he watched with narrowed eyes as the boy fought on. Oh, it was a battle, still and silent and terrible. The point of the roughly beaten sword trembled now, but Ronan would not let it drop more than a fraction. The effort to hold it brought his neck up in cords and ropes of strain and he could barely breathe, and as his eyes stung with sweat he realised how near to his limit he was. Every moment was a mountain climbed.

How much more he had left to give, he would never know, but all at once Cuddy was there, the sword was swiped out of his hand and the master shook his head with a faint, rueful smile that grudgingly approved. "You're a fool, boy," Cuddy told him roughly. "If I let you go on, you'd cripple yourself, cost yourself a week's healing, wouldn't you?"

As the sword was plucked from his nerveless fingers, Ronan sagged to his knees, his left hand clutching at his limp right arm. He whooped for air and looked up dazedly as Cuddy tossed the sword away and gave him a wry grin. The four-fingered hand tousled Ronan's hair and Cuddy accused, "You're a stubborn tyke."

"You told me to hold it," Ronan said hoarsely between clenched teeth, still hugging his arm.

"Did I tell you to cripple yourself?" Cuddy demanded. "Are you hurt?"

"No," Ronan lied, but it was obviously a lie.

The old swordmaster pulled off the leather gauntlet and gave him a push. "Over you go, flat in the grass with you." And as Ronan thankfully went down, Cuddy knelt beside him and applied his hands and a lifetime's sure knowledge to the bunched muscles and abused sinews. His rubbed and pounded Ronan's arm, chest and back until they were merely throbbing and numb, while Ronan averted his eye, grateful for the treatment, yet filled with resentment that it should be necessary.

"You'll be stiff and sore," Cuddy warned as he worked. "And it's a feeling you'll get used to, boy, if you're to work with me. If you're to fight beside the warriors. When you have swung a sword from dawn till dusk against two score men who only want to knock the head off your shoulders and cut the rest of you to tatters, you'll feel like his. You'll hurt, though there's not a mark on you. But you shall be a *warrior*, because you'll have won. You will be alive at the end of the day, to feel your hurts." He paused, looking down into Ronan's face. "Do you understand me, boy?"

The grass was cool and damp beneath Ronan's hot cheek. He said nothing for a time, intent on Cuddy's words, and when he did speak his voice was reserved. "My name is Ronan. And I understand." He looked up at the old man, eyes narrowed against the glare of the steadily brightening sky. "Do you do that to all your students?"

Cuddy shook his head, concentrating on the knotted shoulder. "Not all. Only the ones I'm not sure of."

"Not sure of?" Ronan echoed. "What's wrong with me?"

"With you? Nothing. You're sound, Ronan, you're true as an arrow, which is what I wanted to know. You're as stubborn as a mule and as honest as a priest. Aye, Gruffydd was right about you. If you were a peasant to the heart, you'd have cracked wide open like rotten wood. I had to know. Have you ever heard a peasant given a whipping? He whines like a mangy cur at the first lash. A warrior will bite his tongue to blood to silence his cries till the scourger has flayed him, and walk away from it on his own feet. It's the heart of the man that's different."

Ronan rubbed his face with his left hand as he began to tingle beneath the pummelling. "But what does that mean?"

It means that rotten wood cannot be carved, and I've no liking for wasting my time in the attempt." Cuddy straightened, complaining of his back, and sat in the grass. "Peasants are a mixed bag.

You've got half-bloods and quarter-bloods, people who don't know who they are, don't know who or what they want to be, and half of them, you can't trust. I've learned that the hard way."

Stretching, Ronan began to get up, and then thought better of it and simply turned over, flat in the grass. He pillowed his head on his left forearm and looked up curiously at Cuddy. "Half-blood, quarter-blood? What do you mean?"

"Half-Romans, soft bellied and whining," Cuddy said scathingly. "The legions have gone, but they left their Roman blood behind them, it's still here, it'll be here for generations yet, and it weakens us. When the legions pulled out they all scurried to Londinium, clinging like parasites, sucking up every last *solida* Rome would leave behind. Then, there's the half-Saxons, half-Angles. The raping bastards have been raiding into our lands since before I was born, and they leave behind a mongrel scourge on us. We've been betrayed in the past by halflings, and they'll betray us again, the way the Roman halflings were our betrayal when we were invaded by the legions.

"I've heard the stories, everyone has." Ronan frowned up at the swordmaster. "But are they true? It's all so long ago."

"D'you not trust the Druidai?" Cuddy demanded. "They still tell the stories of how we were sold to the Romans, for favour and for gold. Men with two bloods in their veins, boy. Where do their loyalties lie? Can you ever be sure of them? And it's not that I blame them! If I were half Angle or half Saxon, and I saw the invaders coming over that hill, and I knew there was no chance to survive if I stood here and fought against them, where do you imagine I would be?"

"Standing on your honour," Ronan hazarded.

"In a puddle of my own blood, dying for loyalty and duty, while men who share my own blood will tomorrow be living in the same houses, tilling the same fields, where I grew up?" Cuddy gave him a curious look. "It's easy to speak of honour, fealty, duty, boy. But when his back is up against the wall and the blade is against his throat, a man will usually choose to live, to survive, and hope to win honour back another day." He sighed heavily. "Oh, I don't blame the halflings. We call them mongrels, these men and women born out of rape, but in the end they have the same needs as you or me or anyone ... which makes them dangerous. Can you ever be sure which way their quest for survival will take them? Rome had traded on our coasts for generations before they destroyed us at the last, and the south was full of halflings. Caesar offered those halfling brats lands and riches, if they fought with him, opened our back door and let Rome slither in like a snake, and they betrayed Albion like that." He snapped his fingers. "And then a few more years passed by, and Rome betrayed *them*, and soon enough even the tame lapdogs like Prasutagas were abused, and it was left to warriors like his wife, Boudicca, to shout the call to arms."

An odd quiver coursed through Ronan's gut. "This is all true? You're sure?"

"Aye, lad, I am." Cuddy nodded, engrossed in his thoughts and blind for a moment as his eyes looked through the veil into another world. "I had the tales, all of them, from a Druid when I was little older than you, and travelling in the west."

"I believe," Ronan whispered, and swallowed hard. His arm felt well enough to move, and he sat, trying his joints one by one. "Will you teach me, then?"

The swordmaster seemed to return to the present with a jolt. "I'll teach you," he said, taking a breath as if it might dispel some fog from his mind. "Tomorrow, when your arm will serve you, you shall begin. The sword, lad. The axe, the javelin, and then from what I hear of you, you'll be teaching us a thing or two about nags!"

Dismissed, Ronan wandered alone, aching and sore but not unhappy. He saw Bryn, up on a skittish white gelding with gaudy red harness, on his way out and dressed in his finest. Gruffydd was nowhere to be seen, so it was a safe wager that Bryn was going courting. A man only dressed in his best when he was determined to impress. He did not even turn his head and see Ronan, and Ronan's teeth worried at his lip in a moment's empty, futile envy, before the ache in his right side sent him to the kitchen in search if Sian and a cure.

No such cup was forthcoming, since Sian was out at market, and instead Dafydd spent an hour pampering Ronan with hot water and liniment. The two shared secretive smiles and a lover's kiss when they had a moment alone, and Ronan whispered a promise, that Dafydd was welcome in his arms, any time.

The aches eased with the hot cloths, but a hangdog face and a hopeful smile won Ronan further petting. In all his life, he had never been coddled enough to grow accustomed to it, much less spoiled by it, and even as he luxuriated in the indulgence today his mind was wandering, one thought consuming him. *The swordmaster will teach me!*

He was awake long after Gruffudd's household retired, still rubbing his arm and remembering. He hoped Dafydd would come to him again, yet knew it was a selfish hope and thanked the gods for the their gift when the boy limped into the stables very late, long after Ronan had given him up.

They lay in the deep piles of hay, stroking one of the stable's white kittens, while outside the wind sang and Ronan's eyes wandered over Dafydd's shadowy form. He was almost lost in the dimness, a sprawl of pale limbs filled with the artless promise of delight, laughing at the kitten, which was chewing his fingers with sharp teeth.

Ronan settle back into his blankets with a rueful smile Dafydd could not see. *The lover, the employment, the cat,* he thought, mocking himself. *All I need now is the house and the hearth!* And it was so tempting, which disturbed him deeply. He put the kitten aside, closed his arms about the boy's lean body, and took a sharp breath as his joints pulled.

"You're still hurting," Dafydd whispered, close by his ear. "Whatever did he do to you? There's not a mark on you!"

"Not even a bruise to show for a battle fought and wounds brought home," Ronan agreed. "You could say I did this to myself." He kissed David's hair. "It was a test, of a kind, and I think I must have passed, because he says he'll teach me. Cuddy's a character! There's not a lot of men like him — which is probably a good thing. I wonder what he intends for me next?"

It was said with rueful humour, but Ronan suspected that even had he known a nightmare was before him, he would have gone on. He felt that his feet were on a trail that diverged neither left nor right, with his retreat cut off and no way left to go but forward. Perhaps he should have felt hounded, hunted, but that night he felt only eagerness, and after Dafydd's loving he slept deeply, dreamlessly.

The boy was gone when he woke, and no one heard him yelp as his muscles began to move. The swordmaster was right — he had stiffened from head to foot while he slept, and it took a half hour's vigorous exercise to limber him so that he moved once more like a youth and not like a creaking old man. Ronan simply mocked himself, and wondered if Bryn, tall, sensual, elegant, beautiful Bryn, had gone through this. And if he had, how much would Bryn allow his face to betray?

He was halfway through his morning's work with the horse before he felt happy with his arm, but he would never have admitted it to Cuddy, any more than Bryn would confess that he had been hurt, for pride or any reason. The swordmaster's shrewd, cynical look said he knew anyway.

The warband had already left the paddock when Ronan arrived, and only the rough iron sword awaited him like his nemesis. He lifted it from the grass as the teacher finished his customary jar of wine, and Cuddy drew his own sword from the sheath at his left side. It whined on the oiled leather as it slid free, with a voice like a live thing. *This* was a sword, Ronan decided covetously. Finely made from the best steel, the blade engraved in whorls and ribbonwork, the hilt tight-bound in emerald green leather, the pommel fixed with a big red stone the size of an egg. It caught the sun as Cuddy lifted it, shining as the black iron weapon never would.

Ronan already knew every cut and thrust, from careful observation of the warriors, but Cuddy showed him again, made him duplicate the moves a hundred times, before he led him to a stout, notched wooden post in the corner of the paddock and stood back. Ronan did not have to be told what to do. He had often watched the others — boys much younger than himself, men old enough to be his father, even his grandfather — and he swung the sword against the wood, duplicating each cut he could remember, again and again.

It was not the same, when the blows were stopped dead by the wood, which absorbed each swing, as if a colossus stood against him with a massive sword. It felt to Ronan like the shocks of swinging an axe against a tree when he was sent logging, and his wrist jerked, ached. He frowned curiously, seeking a way to absorb the shocks into his arm and shoulder, as the wood absorbed them, so as not to injure himself. Cuddy watched mutely with a deep frown, but he nodded as if he might be chalking up a mark to the boy from Whitestonecliff. Many noblemen's sons must learn this lesson the hard way — they, who had never done the job of logging timber in their lives.

He worked until his breath failed, and then Ronan flopped down beside Cuddy on the lush riverbank. Now, the swordmaster questioned him closely about his family, back through several generations, and Ronan answered faithfully, for he knew why. Today, Cuddy was imparting warrior skills that could easily be turned against the people of this very town, if Ronan had the blood to turn traitor and save his own hide on the night of battle. For himself, Ronan was much less quick to judge halflings harshly, but Cuddy's lifetime of bitter experience had made him suspicious. He need not have worried, for Ronan's ancestors were just artisans, farmers, poor working people from the moorland, and at last Cuddy was satisfied.

As Ronan got his breath back, the old man put a heavy, iron-banded shield onto his left arm, watched him adjust its weight and balance several times, and then sat back down on the bench by the armoury. "All right, boy. This is your lesson. The shield is your only protection on your blind side. It must feel as if it is part of your body, not a weight that weighs you down. It is not a burden, it is your good companion. Get used to it. Go out and run. Run, I said!"

Ronan ran like a deer under normal circumstances, but not with the drag of dead weight on his arm, and he understood at once the purpose of the exercise. A warrior might have to carry a shield throughout a whole day, fight with it, ride, live with it. If the shield was made with a lethal steel boss, it could be a weapon in itself, so long as a man was its master, not an abject hopeful clinging desperately to it.

He settled into an easy lope he could keep up for miles. This would not be easily learned, and he saw no reason to exhaust himself to impress Cuddy or Gruffydd. They had both done this themselves in their youth, and they knew the effort.

On the bench before the smithy, Cuddy watched him run, noted the young man's balance, his measured stride, and how he matched his gait to the unfamiliar weight. The swordmaster nodded as he took the cork from a skin of ale and wet his throat. "Give Gruffydd his due," he said to himself, or to the big black hound that lounged at his feet, "he can pick lads as well as horses."

In half an hour Ronan loped back, tired but not spent, and he held the shield with a certain ease and grace. The old man waved him to the ground to rest. "Bright lad," he said, not grudging enough to ignore effort. "You'll do that every day, and swing the sword at that post every day for a while. Those will be your exercises to begin with, and you'll know when you don't need them any more. I'll not tell you when to stop, you'll know when. Your own hide and neck will depend on your honesty with yourself, Ronan. Be idle, shirk, lie to yourself, and you'll die for it. You'll be dead in your first battle, for you'll have no endurance, even though you might know the skills the way a monkey can learn them." He lifted his chin and fixed Ronan with a hard look. "Tomorrow, you'll cross my sword. How are your arms?"

The time for bluff was long past. "Like lead," Ronan admitted. "I'm sorry, Cuddy. I thought I was strong."

"And you are." Cuddy chuckled. "As strong as an ordinary man. But a warrior is no ordinary man. If he was, he'd be pushing a plough, digging a ditch. When you're done with your work, go down to the baths and soak yourself in hot water. It's as good a cure as any I know for what ails you." He dug into a pouch at his belt for a coin. "That'll pay for it. Gruffydd'll not have thought to pay you yet."

Astonished, Ronan took the coin and thanked him for it. Normally he disliked water, but he was tired enough, sore enough, to be grateful for the bath tonight.

The public baths were still in decent repair, still a meeting place for merchants, chieftains, warriors and athletes, as they had been when the legions marched through Derventio on their way from the great fortress at Eboracum to the frontier beyond the wall. Many of the town's large houses had their own baths, but this old Roman garrison had not lacked for amenities.

Scenes of wrestlers and hunters decorated the walls in colourful mosaics, and Ronan was enthralled. He had never been into the public baths, nor bathed in any real bath before, and while Cuddy was right — the hot water worked magic on his tired limbs — he was not at all sure that he liked it. Bathing like this was a very *public* affair.

Tonight only men had come in to bathe, and many of them had paired off into couples. Ronan was sure sex was taking place in the humid, steamy shadows, and his own body was overtly appraised by the idlers who sat on the sides, dangling their feet in the water. Ronan was no stranger to sex between men, but he had never been publicly naked, nor publicly ogled. He kept to one corner of the wide, deep pool, shoulder-deep in the water, and closed his eyes until he heard a voice he recognised.

He turned about toward it, just as Bryn ap Gruffydd slid neck deep in the water, and for a split second Ronan caught a glimpse of smooth, pale skin and heavy genitals, before Bryn said acerbically, "This is the last place I'd have expected to find you." He wet his dark hair and plastered it back from his face. "Are you sure you're in the right place?"

"Cuddy sent me," Ronan said warily. "It's paid for! It's supposed to mend ailing muscles, so they tell me."

"It's good," Bryn said tartly, "for keeping *clean.* You look three shades lighter."

Refusing to take offence, Ronan only shrugged. "Some of us have chieftains for fathers, others were not so favoured by the gods. If those who were honoured parted sooner with their money, those who weren't would probably live a lot better — aye, and cleaner."

For a moment Bryn's eyes widened, flashed daggers at Ronan, and then he laughed, and the sound made a pulse in Ronan's temple hammer. "Perhaps there's a grain of truth in that, but I know men who'd have you whipped as a rascal for saying it. Don't we treat you well enough? I'd say you're enjoying all the creature comforts at our expense. And Dafydd is mooning about after you like a lovesick wench."

Ronan shot a hard look at him and had taken a breath to warn Bryn to leave Dafydd's name out of this conversation when Bryn asked, "How is Cuddy treating you?"

"Fairly." Ronan drew his palms across his chest. His hands were sore but had not yet blistered, as the old teacher had warned. He glanced shrewdly at Bryn's hands, and one brow arched. Bryn was high born, but his hands had the calluses of a man who worked hard. Oh, he had gone through Cuddy's rough, painful school. Warriors were made, not born. But the wood must be good, as Cuddy said, for rotten wood could not be carved. Ronan smiled faintly. "I'll learn," he told Bryn. "I'm not too much of a dullard."

The chieftain's first-born son turned toward him, weight propped on his elbow on the side of the pool. "You call me 'my lord', or have you forgotten?"

"You're not the chief yet," Ronan muttered, furious with himself as he felt the rush of heat in his cheeks.

Bryn chuckled. "But one day I shall be. What will I remember of you, when I am?" His voice almost purred, filled with some naked sensuality that made Ronan's belly churn, made his cheeks brighten again. Bryn moved closer, and beneath the water his hand settled on Ronan's hip. "Well, well. You're a hot-blooded little creature, aren't you?" Bryn asked, as if it amused him. His hand slipped about to palm Ronan's buttock and kneaded it. Against his will, Ronan's cock got up hard as a javelin shaft in the water, and as Bryn looked down, he saw it. "My gods," he chuckled, "hot-blooded indeed! Come here to me. I know what you'd like from me."

The tone of command cut right through the purring voice of the seducer and Ronan dived away through the hot water. "Not tonight, Bryn." *And not any night, not without caring and affection. I'll not be a chief's son's convenience!* He pinned on a brittle, mask-like smile.

"Some other time," Bryn purred unconcernedly as he leaned back in the water and began to pamper himself with lazy indulgence.

From the other end of the bath, Ronan watched him covertly. Bryn was handsome, his body was taut and smooth, with white, perfect skin, and desire licked through Ronan like a flashfire. But he mocked himself for it, warned himself against it. In his heart, he wanted nothing more than to go with Bryn tonight — and Bryn must know it, or he would never have laid hands on Ronan — but what a mistake it would surely be. Bryn would count Ronan of

Whitestonecliff among his conquests and possessions, and Ronan's pride would have none of that.

When his quick, untimely erection had subsided and his limbs were comfortable, he lifted himself out of the water, scrubbed his skin dry, and hurried away from the lewd looks of men who seemed to lounge about here only to watch boys bathe. Many eyes were on him as he left, but when Ronan glanced back from the door for just a moment he saw only Bryn, and the pulse in his throat jumped again.

5

Under the swordmaster's unforgiving eye, Ronan performed the ritualised exercises with an exhausting dedication. The afternoon sun was hot, sweat streamed across his bare back and he shook salt droplets out of his eyes as he attacked the wooden post as if it were his enemy. Relentless, more stubborn than ever as his torso began to tire and ache, he swung the old iron sword until Cuddy actually knocked it out of his hand and pushed him down in the grass to rest.

Panting, Ronan lay with his forearm over his eyes, aware of the cool prickles of clover against his hot skin, the drone of bees working the nearby orchard, a lazy wind in the woods on the opposite riverbank. And he heard that slithering sound as Cuddy drew his own sword. Ronan took his arm from his eyes and peered at the old man. Cuddy had dug the tip of the blade into the earth and was leaning on it, glaring at Ronan as if he had done something terrible. Ronan was about to ask where he was at fault when the swordmaster beckoned ominously with that four-fingered hand.

Tense, alert, Ronan hoisted himself to his feet and picked up his sword. He was balanced like a dancer on the balls of his feet when Cuddy growled, "Cut off my head. Cut off my arms, Ronan of Whitestonecliff. Cut me in two. . .if you can."

The levity was not entirely wasted on Ronan, and he wore a brash grin as he tried all the set forms of cut and swing and thrust he had been taught. Cuddy blocked them all with a flurry of blows that would have been astonishing in a man half his age. The good steel of his broadsword rang like a bell on the black iron thing Ronan held, and at last Ronan was thrown so far off balance that he sprawled in the grass again.

The flat of Cuddy's sword smacked hard across his buttocks, but the blow did not draw so much as a yelp or a curse from Ronan.

His eyes narrowed in the bright, warm afternoon sun as he got back to his feet, bent to snatch up the sword, and began again. No more success rewarded him this time, and again he was flat in the grass with the flat of Cuddy's sword smarting his rump for his efforts.

But now he grinned broadly, even chuckled as he clambered back to his feet, for now he was learning. Cuddy had not said a word, and nor did he offer one as he watched a boy's basic clumsiness being slowly pared away and his discovering for himself how to ply not the sword, but his own wrist, his own body. The weight of the shield dragged at his left side, unbalancing him, and Ronan wanted to discard it, but Cuddy would have none of that. Instead, Ronan learned to use it *for* balance, and to interrupt his opponent's rhythm with it.

In an hour his right palm blistered, and when the blisters bled Cuddy called an end to the session. With a grunt he inspected Ronan's hands, and sent the smith's boy to fetch brown vinegar and strips of stiff linen. It was the quick, common cure for any mishap in the paddock or armoury. Ronan swore, his eyes watered, as he put his right hand into the shallow dish of biting liquid, but after a time the fierce pain eased. Cuddy bound his hand tightly, tied off the frayed ends of the ragged bandage and sent him to fetch out a javelin.

Ronan had the eye of a hunter, and he had learned the huntsman's craft long before. With the javelin, his shot was as true as Cuddy's, and soon the swordmaster nodded his approval of this part of the training, save to confound Ronan with a simple challenge.

"Now, lad," he invited, "throw the javelin with your left hand and let's see how true your aim is." Ronan blinked tiredly at him, and Cuddy's seamed old face split into an amused grin. "An odd thing to ask, is it? Then, think of this: your right arm is cut to the bone, you cannot use it for long and long, while it heals, yet the battle is raging all about you. Your friends, your blood-kin, your lovers, are screaming your name and begging for your help, while your enemies bay at your heels and your warband's camp is overrun. Are you finished, then and there, or do you use your left hand? Perhaps the surgeon has cut off your right arm to save your life. It can happen to any warrior, in any battle. Will you go home, bemoan your luck and do the old woman's work, minding the children?"

Without a word, Ronan shifted the javelin into his left hand, balanced it as best he could and threw it. It fell short and wide of the target, which was a wicker butt with a black boar painted on it. He was fatigued, and leaned both palms on his thighs, not too proud to let Cuddy see his weariness. "Do all warriors learn this?"

The old man shook his head. "Not all. Only the great ones, the ones with sense. I had to learn once myself." He held up his sword hand, displaying the space where a finger had once been. "A Pict took that off with an axe. I didn't use the hand for over a year, but I fought again in three months."

"Did Bryn learn the skill?" Ronan asked impulsively.

"Bryn?" The suggestion made Cuddy guffaw rudely. "Now, there's a jest!"

"But he's a fine warrior," Ronan said with grudging admiration for another's abilities. "I've seen him work. I sometimes watch from the fence there, while the horse rests."

"Aye, Bryn is a fine warrior," Cuddy agreed, "as far as he goes. But he doesn't go far enough. He has the knack with a sword and bow, he's passing fair with the javelin, not clever with the axe, and useless with his left hand. He sees no reason to work, when he's the apple of his father's eye."

"Then I'll work till I have it," Ronan decided, and jogged out to fetch the javelin.

"Rascal," Cuddy said quietly, watching as the boy loped down the paddock like a lithe young animal, "you'll be as good as your word, won't you? You'll learn to spite Bryn!" And he lowered his buttocks onto the bench with a groan. The youth's energy and pace could wear an old teacher to a shadow. Ronan seemed almost tireless, while Cuddy's bones and joints demanded rest. And Ronan would drive himself until he mastered his left hand — nothing would stop him, short of chaining him up, but Cuddy had to chuckle over the reason for his determination.

One-upmanship was not the most laudable motive, but it often worked better than more honourable arguments. So Ronan had engaged in some kind of contest with Bryn, had he? It would serve as a lesson to ap Gruffydd's heir, to be bested by a peasant brat whose only assets were his ambition and his skill. Ronan's heart and mind were well known, by now, to Cuddy, and that stubborn streak. Bryn was very good, no one disputed it. But he was born to rank, and his worst fault was complacency. To the boy from Whitestonecliff, every day was a battle, everything before him was a challenge. His heart was set on victory, and he would push himself to the end. Bryn had the same natural ability, but he had no battle to fight, nothing to drive him. He was born to rank and honour, while Ronan would sacrifice the skin of his hands, his sweat, perhaps even his blood, with a grim smile. Cuddy wished him well.

It was impossible to dislike Ronan. The swordmaster envied him his youth and strength, his lush good looks and even his sunny disposition, but the envy stopped short of bitter jealousy, for Cuddy's life had been long and full, and looking back on his own youth, he pictured himself as very like Ronan. How could he resent a youth in whom he saw so much of himself?

Cuddy plucked off his gauntlets, dropped them by the bench and bawled for a skin of ale. The same apprentice who had fetched the vinegar brought it to him, and Cuddy emptied it as he watched the left-handed javelin throws come nearer and nearer the target. At last Ronan dropped down at the master's feet, flushed and panting, and Cuddy tousled his hair. Ronan looked up with the smile that had been beguiling women and men alike for several years already, and Cuddy crooked a brow at him. Was this at the root of the contest between Ronan and Bryn? Had Bryn decided that he wanted this lad? He was well known in Derventio for his taste in boys. But Ronan would never share the bed of a future chief! The notion made Cuddy chuckle.

"I nearly had it," Ronan panted. "Did you see? I'll have it tomorrow."

"A silver coin for you, if you do," Cuddy growled as he stripped the linen from Ronan's right hand to see the blisters. "Soak this again, in fresh vinegar. You'll cross swords with me till you have my match, and then you'll swing against one of the men, Padraic or Brock, perhaps. And then you'll learn how to handle an axe."

"And after that?" Ronan asled, beginning to drowse in the heat of afternoon as fatigue settled into every muscle and bone.

The swordmaster cuffed his ear. "Then? Then you shall be a warrior, won't you?"

*　*　*

In a week Cuddy was not quick, strong or clever enough to deal his young student the flat of his sword across the backside, and Ronan's hands had healed and hardened under the punishment until they were rarely sore and never blistered. He carried both sword and shield when he ran, and every day he loped out along the river as far as the bridge and back, which took the better part of an hour. Only when he returned without being winded was Cuddy satisfied.

He was harder and leaner than he had ever been in his life, and

Ronan was prideful of his body. He was less like a youth, more like a man every day, and he knew it. At Cuddy's request, the freeman warrior Brock came to exercise with him, and Ronan rose eagerly to the challenge.

It was not at all like crossing swords with Cuddy. Brock was five years Ronan's elder, taller, heavier, and he fought with the sword and axe, one in either hand, while Ronan ducked and wove and cut his way around both weapons until he had their measure. Cuddy stood aside with his black dog, offering scarcely a word, letting Ronan teach himself, for the arts of the warrior could not be learned by talking, only by doing.

The freeman, Brock, was good enough to tax Ronan in every way. Ronan's physical endurance was tested to the limit, and his patience too. Brock found a student's mistakes amusing, and though Ronan made few errors and was much nimbler than Brock, still the man laughed, and the sound stung Ronan.

To the bigger, stronger warrior, Ronan applied that stubborn patience, and in three days Brock, despite his stature, experience and strength, went down in the grass. His error was perhaps the most fundamental. He had attempted to make a fool of Ronan, and was too clever for his own good When he tumbled in the grass at last Cuddy slapped his thigh and laughed. Brock, knowing what was wisest, gave Ronan his hand.

Standing unobtrusively at the corner of the smithy shed, Gruffydd had watched the whole contest, and when Brock sprawled at Ronan's feet, Cuddy turned and gave the chief a wink. Brock was sitting in the grass, the sword plucked neatly from his grasp. Ronan was not fully trained yet, but he had little left to learn.

"He's changed," Gruffydd said quietly as Cuddy joined him. "See how he gives his hand to the man who has just tested his mettle?"

"He has nothing much left to prove," Cuddy agreed. "He has discovered his own worth, Gruffydd. The man inside, the man he felt in his heart, when you and I looked at him and saw only a peasant's brat from Whitestonecliff."

Gruffydd dropped a hand on his old friend's shoulder, squeezed it companionably, and ambled away toward the stable.

But perhaps only Dafydd knew just how much Ronan had changed. To the touch, he was only bone and muscle, and Dafydd whispered this as they sat by the big hearth in the kitchen, one night that was stormy and cold. Ronan was drowsy, comfortable, watching the firelight cast shifting patterns across Dafydd's lovely face. He smiled, knowing how right Dafydd was. The boy from

Whitestonecliff was a boy no longer. Should he mourn the passing of his boyhood? He suspected that he should, but instead Ronan rejoiced in it.

The wind was wild, blowing up a rainstorm, but the kitchen was sound, humid, almost hot. They had the hearth to themselves just then, for the servants and bonded people had been summoned to wait on Gruffydd, and the warmth and privacy invited intimacy. The firelight fetched red lights into Ronan's hair, softened his features, and Dafydd told him all this too, in the song-song, crooning whisper of one who should have been a bard. "You'll be staying here, then," he added. "They've trained you for the warband, they'll want you in Derventio now. And a warrior can't be sleeping in the hayloft! You'll have to have a house, when Gruffydd pays you."

Ronan nodded but said nothing. His eyes were heavy, intent on the embers at the heart of the fire, and Dafydd's words twisted through him like the growing roots of a sapling tree. He took a deep breath, held it, let it out slowly, and only looked away from the fire when Dafydd said suddenly,

"You're a stubborn man, Ronan."

"Cuddy says that." Ronan cocked an ear to the wind. "Cuddy says a lot of things. I'm to have my own sword soon, and an axe, so Gruffydd said."

"And when the Angles come?" Dafydd demanded. "A dead warrior is no use to me, Ronan." He snatched a stout black poker from the rack by the heart and began to stir the fire.

"A dead peasant spear-carrier would be even less use to you." Ronan caught the boy's hands as the poker clattered down. "Pickle the Angles in barrels of brine, Dafydd! They'll come when they come, _if_ they come, and I'll not waste my life fretting about them till they're here." He lifted the boy's soft hand and touched his lips to the slender fingers. "Soon now, Cuddy will be finished with me."

"And you'll ride with the warband, as I said. And you'll have your own house." Dafydd licked his lips, frowning at Ronan with dark, sober eyes. "You don't want me, do you?"

"Don't say that," Ronan admonished. "I don't want to be tied to home and hearth. That's the truth of it. I'm young and — and footloose! Perhaps next season I shall go to Eboracum and seek my fortune there, or go north of the wall, or west to Caerleon, where great things are happening. Have you not heard the name of the young chief, Artos, who was born in Cornwall and taught by the archdruid, the sorcerer. There is a place with Artos's warband for any man who will raise his sword against the Saxons." Ronan leaned over and kissed Dafydd's mouth deeply. "Home and hearth would be manacles to me."

"Or is it that — that *rake*," Dafydd muttered. "It's him you want, isn't it? I knew you would want him, as soon as he cast those hot blue eyes on you. Ah, damn you, Ronan. Go and warm his sheets, then, since you don't want me any longer!"

"What are you talking about?" Ronan caught Dafydd by the upper arms before he could escape. How soft he was, almost but not quite like a girl. But his cheeks were flushed with annoyance and he would not look Ronan in the eye now. "What is this nonsense?" Ronan whispered, and kissed his forehead to coax.

"Bryn," Dafydd whispered. "I know you want him, and I don't blame you for it."

"I don't want Bryn!" Ronan protested.

Dafydd did not seem to hear. "I know he's handsome, and he's. . .he's whole in body, unlike myself. I'll always limp, and it's not pretty to look at, and Bryn is very beautiful."

"I said, I don't want Bryn," Ronan repeated, louder. And yet he heard the ring of a lie in his own words, and was painfully aware of the untruth. In fact he wanted Bryn very much, and had for some time. Was it so obvious that Dafydd had seen it? Ronan cleared his throat. "What makes you say that? What have I said or done to make you believe that I would want Bryn ap Gruffydd?"

"Well, nothing," Dafydd admitted. "But he's watching you. You have not seen him watching you?" Ronan's eyes had widened. "You mean, you have never noticed him, eating you alive with his eyes?" Dafydd almost snorted. "Camulus! I'd have thought even you must notice! He stands in the trees, yonder, by the smithy, watching you exercise with the swordmaster!"

"Watching lustfully?" Ronan asked doubtfully. "Or amusedly, hoping to see me cut off my own foot?"

"I. . .don't know," Dafydd admitted darkly. "But why else would he watch you, save out of desire for you?"

"He might watch me," Ronan suggested, "because I am his keenest rival, and he would like to see me make a complete fool of myself, even maim myself!" He pounced on Dafydd then, bowled him over onto their cloaks, which were spread by the hearth to dry after they ducked inside out of the persistent rain. Dafydd wriggled under him and Ronan kissed his mouth teasingly. "Want Bryn?" He demanded. "How could I possibly? My gods, he would tumble me like a hapless wench and my pride would be wounded beyond hope of healing! Bed with a chieftain or his son? Don't be a little fool, Dafydd. The only bedmate in Derventio I want, and the only one I have ever *really* wanted, is you." He put his head down and kissed the boy's soft, yielding mouth once more. "And I have you, haven't I?"

"Oh, yes," Dafydd whispered, breathless and ecstatic. "Oh, yes."

Satisfied, Ronan's arms and legs embraced the boy, and their limbs tangled comfortably together.

6

The little roan stallion had mellowed but Cullen was still oathing lividly about him. He believed the animal hated him — or was the shade of his late wife reborn in the horse to punish him for his misdeeds? Ronan simply ignored the bonded groom, which infuriated Cullen, though he kept his silence, and the horse ran for the joy of it. Red never needed to be urged or encouraged, he never felt the sting of the whip, but he would be civil for few men. Gruffydd only laughed. All the animal had to do was run like the wind at Catreath.

The chief had two old Roman solidas for Ronan the morning after he bested Brock, and he leaned on the paddock fence for a time, watching the horse go through his paces. The races at Catreath were a little more than a week away; the weather promised to be fine, and the lookouts along the coast from the tidal mouth of the Ambri to the Tees estuary saw no sails out across the Narrow Sea. Gruffydd rubbed his hands together expectantly, and as Ronan brought the little horse to a prancing halt right before him they shared a knowing grin. They were bound to bring home the prize.

That afternoon, when Ronan went in search of the swordmaster for his lesson, Cuddy had a set of weapons laid out on the bench. A good steel sword in a leather sheath on a studded baldric; a bossed, iron-banded shield, almost identical to the one he had trained with; two light javelins, two spare blades; a battleaxe; a set of whetstones, oils and rags, rawhide thonging, an awl and a thick steel needle.

The axe fascinated Ronan the most. He had cut timber often enough, but this was no small-bladed woodsman's tool. This was a weapon, heavy, on a short, leather-bound haft, with a single broad, curved edge that had been honed like a razor, and a backspike that would be as lethal as the blade. He took up the weapon, experimenting with its balance, and as the curving blade began to slice the air Cuddy whistled for the youngest of the blacksmiths.

A young giant came out of the smithy, half naked and glistening with sweat that made him seem to be oiled. He seemed to Ronan to be equal parts human and oak tree, and over his shoulder was a long steel bar. Ronan regarded the smith's apprentice with a dubious expression and the swordmaster whispered, close by his ear, "Let him get too close to you, and he'll likely wrap that thing around your neck. He has no idea of his own strength yet. But don't you dare hurt him. His father is the master swordsmith. I once saw him kill a man with a hammer, and I'd not like to see that again. Nick the lad, and you'll be tied to the gatepost having the back scourged off you, so take care."

Ronan blinked, first at his teacher and then at the swordsmith's son. "Then, what do you want me to do?"

The old man gave him a wrinkled, gap-toothed smile that might have been meant as encouragement. "The best you can," he said. "That's a battleaxe. Not for novices, nor for boys, and you're neither of those things now. It will fell a tree if needs be, or stop a man coming at you with a hammer — or a steel bar. It's not a sword, nor it is like one, and you can't learn to fight with it by swinging it at a wooden post! To learn, you must stop talking and *do!* How you do it is your concern, but watch out for your hide, Ronan, and for his. You're not out to kill each other for the sake of a lesson."

From Cuddy's lips it all sounded reasonable, but Ronan wondered if he had bothered to tell the young smith where his duty lay. The steel bar was as formidable a weapon as any Ronan had ever seen, and it was swung by more muscle than Ronan would ever be able to best, no matter how hard and limber he had become. He shifted the weight of the axe in his hands, searching for its balance, grappling with its strangeness.

No, it was not a sword, nor even like one, as Cuddy had warned. It was strange, foreign, uncomfortable. And then Ronan had no more time to even think about it, for the other youth was coming at him and death was a hand's span away, every instant. Ronan sucked in a breath as the steel bar came up, and the free end swung in a short arc. For the moment he was sure of only one thing. He must not allow this to become a wrestling bout, for if it did he would be snapped like a fresh carrot.

For the first time the new axe rang like a bell as it met the smith's unlikely weapon, and Ronan began to learn. The two circled, their manoeuvring taking them out into the paddock where the cavalry horses had cut up the grass and the ground was treacherous. The bar swung again, but Ronan was nimble and fast. He ducked under it and grinned at the smith's son.

"What do I call you, friend?"

As the weapon arced up once more the youth shook out his long red hair and said in a deep, resonant voice, "Call me Matthew. I've been watching you. Cuddy's given you a hard time. Harder than he gave the other lads." He swung the bar and the axe chimed as Ronan retreated a step. "You're very good. I heard Cuddy telling my father, you could be the best, when you're blooded." The next swing passed Ronan's face close enough for him to feel the air rush on his cheek.

"If I live that long," Ronan retorted. "Don't knock my head off, Matthew!"

"Sorry." Matthew's grin widened, showing sharp white teeth. "My father said you could be as good as Bryn, and Bryn is the best."

Ducking under the swinging steel bar, Ronan took a better grip on his own weapon. "Don't let my lord Bryn hear you say that."

Matthew chuckled. "He heard the two old men chattering! He'll have a thing or two to settle with you, by and by. He was always the best of the young swords. Until you came here. He'll not enjoy losing the laurels."

The curved blade of the war axe fluttered like a steel butterfly, chasing and striking Matthew's weapon repeatedly, until it was the smith's daunting son who fell back a few steps. His massive chest heaved, his skin gleaming in the sun as he went onto the defensive for the first time. The axe was heavier than the sword, Ronan mused, different, but not more difficult. He had simply to think in different ways, and he was more aware than ever of every move he made, every step he took, and the way the muscles in his arms and back and shoulders pulled as he learned the new weapon.

On the bench by the smith's shed, Gruffydd sat down with his old friend, and they shared a wry smile. The swordmaster tapped his grey temple with a gauntleted forefinger as he glanced sidelong at Gruffydd. "Watch him. You see? He fights with his head, not his heart or even his hands. From here, he'll teach himself all he needs to know. Tomorrow, he can train with the warband, they'll not injure him now." He cocked a brow at Gruffydd. "Though your son and heir might like to lop of his balls!"

"Bryn?" Gruffydd was surprised. "What's between those two? Some kind of rivalry? Or are they tangling each other's sheets by night?"

"Not that I know of," Cuddy said with a growl of quiet

humour. "No, it's just rivalry, like two whelps out of the same litter trying to prove who is the stronger."

"Then let them have their heads," Gruffydd counselled. "They'll make each other sharp."

"Or kill each other," Cuddy added.

Gruffydd gave him a hard look. "Then you keep them apart. I don't want my son maimed."

"And what of Ronan?" Cuddy asked pointedly. "It was you yourself who took him out of the village and put a sword in his hand. Bryn could maim him as easily as Ronan could do the damage."

"Keep them under your eye," Gruffydd said bluffly. "Mind, they're your responsibility, like all your bucks. If Bryn comes to harm, on your head be it, Cuddy." But he put a hand on Cuddy's shoulder, an expression of trust, and sighed. "And I don't want to be flogging Ronan for the crime of injuring my son, since you and I both know that Bryn would have stirred up the hornets' nest himself!"

"All right." Cuddy huffed and shrugged. "I'll separate them, keep them apart." And then, "Ronan will need a horse of his own."

The chief hoisted his big frame up off the bench. "He will, but I'll get service enough from those young limbs to repay me thrice over. Send him to the stable when you're done with him here, we've spare nags he can pick from."

The steel bar no longer swung close to Ronan, and the axe flew like a silver-grey bird in his hands. He was grinning as he realised that he had begun to find its measure, and moreover, he had discovered the skill within himself. Like a good-natured bear, Matthew was still determined to get the better of him, possibly just as well-temperedly breaking his bones in the process. Ronan's wrists had grown strong enough for him to take the repeated shocks, but new muscles in his forearms and back felt the intense effort while the smith seemed impervious. Ronan was panting, his skin prickling with sweat, but he drove himself on. If this were a battle he might have to fight on for hours. His body was a constant reminder to him of how far he still had to go before he was ready for that.

They circled, exchanging chiming blows for a long time, and then Cuddy roared at them. "Enough is enough! Come on, Ronan, finish it!" And 'finish it,' to the swordmaster, meant *win*. It was a test, he knew, a test he was honour-bound to pass. His grip tightened on the leather-bound haft and he took a quick breath. He could not match muscle with muscle, and he was not permitted to hurt Matthew. Yet, 'finish it,' Cuddy said, and Ronan saw only one way to do it.

A moment later, when the axe blade slithered around the steel bar again, he turned it a little so that the backspike locked like a lever. Ronan wrenched up and back so suddenly, Matthew, whose grip was light, never saw what was coming. The bar tore clean out of his hands and thudded into the grass, and they heard Cuddy's rude laughter.

"Bright lad, bright lad," he shouted at Ronan as he paced out to join them. "A man's wrist is the weakest part about him, aside from his balls. And since gelding your mate is hardly the most friendly way to finish a match, you take him by his wrists!" He slung his arm about the young smith's wide shoulders for a moment. "Well done, Matthew, you helped him learn a thing or two."

Resting the weight of the axe across his right shoulder, Ronan laughed breathlessly. "He almost killed me! Now what, swordmaster?"

"Clean your gear, oil your sword, go and run the impudence out of yourself before I box your ears. And then take your gear to the cavalry stable. Gruffydd says you're to have a horse. Choose which you want."

Ronan physically recoiled. "I could never afford to buy a horse from him!"

Not unaffectionately, Cuddy dealt him a cuff. "A warband's warriors are paid in coin and in kind, rascal. The chief will have the nag's worth out of you in blood and sweat, make no mistake. And how can you take your place in the cavalry without a horse under you? It's not your thanks Gruffydd wants, or your money, it's your service."

"And he shall have it." Ronan set the axe down with the shield and buckled on the leather baldric, with its heavy scabbard. He adjusted the weight of the sword at his left side and gave the old man a nod of gratitude. "Aye, my lord Gruffydd will have my service, and my blood if needs be, but you'll have my thanks, swordmaster, for as long as I live. Time was, I thought you'd be the death of me! But it's been worth the work and sweat."

"Rascal," Cuddy accused fondly, though he knew Ronan was not trying to beguile. "Well, then, you'll be thanking me for a long, long time, because I've taught you well, and you've the knack, the *way* with the tools of your trade. You'll live, Ronan of Whitestonecliff. You'll see the end of many a bloody day that others don't live to see. Now, be off with you and see about this horse Gruffydd promised you."

But before he went to claim the horse Ronan looked for Dafydd. His left hand clasped about the hard, spherical pommel of the sword, the very symbol of status, the mark of what he had become. Dafydd was in the kitchen, on hands and knees and grey with soot as he raked out the big cooking hearth. He looked up as Ronan appeared, and his eyes widened as he saw the sword. Ronan reached down to wipe away the smudge of soot on his nose, but Dafydd fended him off.

"You'll be blacker than me, Ronan!" He hauled himself up onto a bench by the fireplace and admired the weapon. "You're finished the training, then."

"Part of it. I'm to go to the stable now," Ronan told him. "They have a horse for me, I'm to join the cavalry tomorrow." He swept Dafydd up in his arms and swung him about, kissed both his cheeks, and Dafydd laughed in delight.

Only as he turned did Ronan see Bryn, standing in the door-way, overtly studying him, with a displeased expression. Ronan let go the boy and lifted his chin. He waited for Bryn to speak, but the chief's son said nothing and at length Ronan began defensively, "Your father is quite satisfied with me. I'm to train with the warband now, we shall meet at practice, tomorrow."

Bryn's dark head cocked curiously. "Most interesting it will be," he said quietly. "You've more ambition than is good for you, Ronan. Soon enough, you'll wish you were back in that rat-hole village of yours."

"Why should I?" As Dafydd returned to his work at the hearth, Ronan swung about to face Bryn squarely. "I've had the same training as you, cut for cut and blow for blow. Ask Cuddy!" His voice dropped to a rasp of a whisper. "But you don't have to ask Cuddy, do you? You've been watching me."

A flicker of surprise showed for a moment on Bryn's face, and then was swiftly hidden as he looked Ronan up and down. "Who told you that?"

"Matthew, the smith's son." Ronan's left hand clenched about the hilt of his sword until his knuckles were bone white. "What do you want from me, Bryn? What have I done to irk you? I've not said a word against you — or *to* you! Or is it that I won't bow and scrape? Why do you want to beat me bloody?"

"And who said," Bryn asked in a deep, sensual purr, "that I want to do that? You're dangerous. Let one upstart rise above his station today, and the whole rabble will rise next season. You're more dangerous than a Saxon raiding party marching out of the south."

"But —" Ronan began, only to fall silent, caught without an argument, since he could seen Bryn's point all too clearly. Bryn lifted one curious brow at him, and without a word stalked out of the kitchen. A tide of anger took Ronan by surprise and he swallowed it fast. Anger would avail him nothing. With a sigh, he sat on the bench at the hearth and pulled Dafydd closer. "Is he right, Dafydd? He hates me, doesn't he?"

"Hates you?" Dafydd echoed. "I think he might be more fearful than hateful." The words were muffled against Ronan's chest. "Truth is, if a hundred lads out of the villages had your kind of ambition and courage, Gruffydd would have no ploughmen and shepherds left."

"But he would never give permission for a hundred to come here and be trained," Ronan argued.

"If he forbade them because of their common birth, there would be ill feeling in the village." Dafydd looked up at him, brow creased in a frown. "Bryn may be right. The rabble might rise up. You should see yourself! I've made you sooty. I knew I would." He stretched over for a cleaning rag and began to brush Ronan's tunic.

Ronan stroked the boy's black hair gently. "Never you mind about that. Will you come to me tonight? Please."

"Of course I will. I'm so pleased for you, Ronan. It's a great thing you have done, Bryn be damned!" Dafydd's eyes sparkled, and they kissed deeply for a moment before Ronan left him.

The horses that were unspoken for carried the chief's brand. They were bred for the battlefield, big, muscular animals, even-tempered and patient. Ronan chose the iron-grey gelding with the white face and three white stocking feet — the horse that came to the fence to rub its bony nose against his tunic. Its velvet muzzle searched for treats but Ronan had none, and he petted the beast, spoke softly to him, instead. A black sheepskin saddle, and well used but well mended harness, were provided with the young war-horse, and Ronan's name was written on the leather by Gruffydd himself. Gruffydd was the only man here who could read or draw the Latin letters that spelt a name.

The sun was low in the west, striking warmly from between the dense layers of a bank of dark cloud. Beneath the inky overcast, Gruffydd's rich farmland was momentarily painted with a wash of gold, but the wind was from the northeast and cold. Bad weather ran on its heels.

The roan racehorse stood in the middle of the small paddock

where he had taken his own training, and his nostrils flared as he scented the breeze. He heard Ronan calling from the fence and broke into a skittish canter to join him. Ronan hoisted himself up onto the sun-worn timbers and stroked the horse's bony face, but was too intent on his own achievement to notice the animal's un-ease until the sensitive ears lay flat, his eyes showed a rim of white and Red danced restlessly from foot to foot.

He had never liked loud noises or wild weather. Ronan looked into the northeast now, and saw that Red was right, a bad night was coming. The sky was dark already, though the sun was still bright on the oily wings of a flock of ravens overflying the pad-dock. "The stable for you tonight, you old coward," he admonished. "And a few more lessons, to teach you not to fear loud noises! Perhaps I shall get Matthew to beat a drum till you learn, there is nothing to be afraid of."

The paddock was on the very edge of the chief's land. Beyond its perimeter at one end was the town, and at the other, a chequerboard of fields where spring crops greened the riverbank. A few other nags grazed there, unconcerned about the weather.

At the beat of approaching hooves Ronan turned away from the skittish little horse for a moment. Bryn was coming up along the fence, mounted on his favourite white cavalry horse, striking in a black tunic overwrapped with a heavy green cloak, fastened at the left shoulder with a gold brooch. He grinned mockingly at Ronan as he drew rein, and gestured at the new sword.

"Will you swing that against me on the practice field tomor-row?" The wind whipped at his voice. "Will you ride that grey nag at me? It will be interesting to see how an artisan's brat matches up against warrior men."

Was he trying to rouse Ronan to fury? Anger rose hotly in Ronan's belly and he choked it back. "You mean, against *real* war-riors? Say what you mean! Cuddy is satisfied and so is your father, satisfied enough to grant me leave to stand up and fight beside you when the Angles come!" *As your equal, damn you!* he thought, though he swallowed the bitter words into silence.

"Hold your temper on a shorter leash," Bryn advised in a mild tone that mocked all the more as he gathered the leather reins be-tween his fingers. "You have a place now, and if you learn to stay in it you might well prosper." He dug his heels into his horse's sides and the milk-white animal reared for a moment before it plunged into a canter and was gone.

Ronan glared after the billow of Bryn's green cloak. It was wrong to swear vengeance, and yet the oath was on the edge of his tongue. Bryn was the heir of a chief, and Gruffydd had shown Ronan more generosity than he could ever have expected. Still, vengeance was a tempting thought, and Ronan revelled in it for a moment before he returned to the little racehorse with a sigh.

"He hates the very blood in my veins," he said to the animal. "You saw that? What have I done to make him hate me? Ah, gods damn him!" Ronan spat into the grass, as if to seal a pact with Sian's old gods. "A few sessions on the practice field will tell!"

At work, under Cuddy's supervision, rank meant nothing. The old man would brook no nonsense and everyone answered to him, armourer and warrior alike. There, Ronan could have it out in mock-battle with Bryn, and no harm done. No *real* harm, he amended angrily. He slipped his fingers into Red's bridle, hopped down off the fence and urged the horse to follow him with a gentle tug. "Come, let me feed you and put you in a warm stall. You'll be happier there, won't you, while this storm blows through."

* * *

Twilight was still hours away and Bryn did not hurry the horse. He settled into an easy pace, heading west from Derventio, where the thick forest had been cut back to clear the way for crops, and for the village of Brevic. It was a small settlement, a cluster of wooden houses about a chieftain's long, low hall, on the shoulder of an east-facing slope.

Nothing and no one of importance was to be found in Brevic, but it had one single flower, a wild rose named Eamon, who was everything Aemilia Duratius was not, and more than enough to bring Bryn out on a stormy evening.

If Eamon had boasted so much as a drop of noble blood, Bryn would have brought the boy to Derventio and flaunted him before his father and the whole town. Derventio's Christians would have scorned and spurned his open affection for a male, but the Christians were in such a minority, Bryn disregarded them.

The warrior kind had always taken lovers among their own ranks. Bryn could neither read nor write, but he had heard every ballad, every story of the old tribes of Albion, of Rome and of Athens. If he loved a man, he only followed a very ancient tradition. But Eamon, beautiful as he was, was as much a peasant as Dafydd, the kitchen boy — Dafydd, who was mooning over Ronan of Whitestonecliff.

As Ronan crossed his mind, Bryn's mouth compressed. That lad was trouble. Oh, he was beautiful, lovesome, tormenting, tempting as no other Bryn had ever seen. But he was *trouble*. Bryn's first impulse was to leap into competition with Ronan, but what a waste of time and effort that would be. Bryn had much better things to do than skin his knuckles and graze his knees in stripling rivalry. Gruffydd and Cuddy thought highly of Ronan, which only irked Bryn further.

But what irked him most of all was that Ronan was good. He had a natural skill, and he would get better with time, and yet he could lay claim to no drop of noble blood. Where was the advantage and privilege of being born the son and heir of a chief, if a common artesan could sire an Iron Hand warrior? Bryn swore into the wind as he caught sight of Brevic.

And yet Ronan was so very beautiful. Since he had come to Derventio, Dafydd had eyes for no other, and Bryn was disturbed to find that his own pulse raced with the same beat as the kitchen boy's as Ronan passed by. His feelings for Ronan thrust him into the herd of the bonded people, and Bryn was irked, confused, discomfited.

Brevic stood on a chalkstone hill, high above the riverland. The wind whipped in from the sea, and Bryn tugged his cloak higher about his ears as he climbed up the eastern trails, and all of Gruffydd's land, and the wild reaches of the moor toward Whitestonecliff, spread out before him under the dark, sullen sky.

A few sessions on the practice field, he thought. A bloody nose, a gash or two, would persuade Ronan of his foolishness. The peasant would learn his place, stay in it, and all this nonsense about ambition would be quashed. Privilege and rank were for those who were born to it, or where was the purpose of birthright?

As he swung up onto the narrow, deep-rutted wagon track that lead to the settlement, the first brilliant fork of lightning skewered the horizon. Thunder rolled ominously out of the angry sky, shockingly close at hand, and Bryn glared at the storm front, wondering if he would make it to Brevic before the rain began.

A last slender finger of sunlight cut like a lance across the moor from green, mountainous Cumbria, but the wind had an edge like a knife. Bryn lay flat across the horse's withers and urged him to a fast canter. Up ahead, Brevic's cookfires were already burning.

7

Lightning crackled again, more vividly as the storm barrelled nearer. Gruffydd's roan stallion ran, ears flat against his skull, and his eyes rolled to white. The geldings and mares sharing the paddock gathered beneath the ems to shelter, but Red would not join them. His coat flecked with foam as his hooves churned the ground.

Then, a voice he did not like, singing raucously. It was Cullen, the worse for his ale. He had collapsed by the gate and was destroying a lovely old song as only he knew how. The horse turned, bolted along the fence, and when the thunder crashed almost overhead he began to rear. His hooves thrashed at the old, warped timbers, and planks broke away. He plunged through the gap in a tangle of falling wood and scrabbling legs, then he was out. Before him was the open country, behind him, the Roman town and the rumbling bass voice of the storm god.

With the first crash of much closer thunder, Ronan lifted his head from his work in the stable. He was preparing Red's stall, forking in straw, filling the feed basket, and although he was working as fast as he knew how, he realised that the storm had beaten him. The stable was crowded with grooms, servants and slaves. Dafydd was there, fetching a meal to the bonded people who were standing by a foaling mare.

"Can't it wait?" Dafydd asked as Ronan brushed his hands off on his leggings and made to leave. "It'll be raining in a moment."

But Ronan shook his head. "I'll have to catch the horse, and fast. Red is a coward and runs like a hare in this. He's sure to hurt himself." He touched Dafydd's face and gave him a smile. "Mull some wine for us, and we'll have it together. I'll not be long."

"I will," Dafydd promised, cheeks pinking like roses under Ronan's touch.

It was almost dark now. The rain had not yet begun but the air was sullen, heavy, damp. Ronan broke into a run, his left hand cupped about the hilt of the sword, which swung against his left leg. He quartered the paddock with narrowed eyes, and swore lividly, for a whole span of the fence was down, and the horse was gone.

Ronan's fists clenched in a moment's bitter frustration before he hurried back to the stable, for swearing would accomplish nothing, and there was only one thing to do. His own horse was saddled in moments, his gear lashed into place, and he hauled himself into the saddle with a grunt of aggravation.

An angry wind moaned before the storm, and as he slammed the stable door a cold, stinging rain began. The warhorse protested but Ronan quieted him as the reins became slick between his fingers. Red could not have gone far, and with luck he could be caught and back in the stable in an hour.

With luck. Some instinct in Ronan's breast counselled that nothing was ever so easy. He was hungry, cold, but he felt a stab of guilt. He should have stabled Red before the storm was on top of Derventio. The fault was his own. He had been so preoccupied with the new sword, the invitation to practice with the warband tomorrow, that he had been negligent, and Gruffydd would have been quite within his rights to deal Ronan a fair flogging.

It was his duty to go out and stay out until the mishap was redeemed, no matter his personal inconvenience. And if Red was hurt, it could still be a matter of a back whipped bloody when Gruffydd learned what had happened. Ronan was far from happy.

A shape detached itself from the gloom of the paddock and reeled toward him through the thickening mist of rain, and he heard Cullen, shouting at him. "Where are you going, gods damn your hide?" the drunken labourer bawled furiously as he tried to snatch Ronan's bridle.

"The horse is loose. Get out of the way, you fool!" Ronan snarled as he pulled the grey around the man. "And get someone out there to plank up the fence, or we'll lose the rest before morning, and I wouldn't be you when Gruffydd gets home!"

He was gone before Cullen could find a barbed retort, leaving the property by the same route Red had taken, out along the boundary fence where the corn was knee high and blue-green in the gathering twilight.

The little stallion had cut a swathe through the new crop. It would be easy to follow him at first, but soon the last of the dusk would be gone. Ronan's teeth clenched as he urged the grey to a canter, heading west, away from the river and the rambling town.

Soon Derventio was far behind and the moor was dim, blue, cold. The warhorse slithered to an uneasy halt as he reined back, and Ronan's eyes roamed the distance for any sign of Red. Nothing moved. More than likely he had run northeast, but the light was gone now, only a magician would read tracks before dawn. The rain was not yet heavy, and Ronan crossed his fingers, praying for it to stop, or those tracks would be washed out altogether by dawn. Gruffydd's fury would be boundless, and the skin of Ronan's back crawled.

The warhorse made heavy going of the sodden turf. For a time

Ronan called Red's name, but it was useless, and well he knew it. He hugged himself against the cold and twisted in the saddle to look back. How far had he come? As the moon broke through a gap in the overcast he realised that he had little hope of finding a landmark before dawn. A stand of alders offered a meagre shelter from the wind and he nudged the horse toward them.

Under their canopy it was still dry. The gale roared with the voice of an angry animal among the branches, and though he rolled himself in his cloak and bedded in the cradle of tough roots, Ronan did not sleep. All night he watched the storm slide by to the south, and pictured himself in the morning, dragging himself back into Derventio like a drowned cur, without Red, only to be tied to the gatepost and flogged by Gruffydd's own hand. Cullen would laugh at him for a week. The warhorse stood with his head down in the shelter of the trees, and Ronan spoke to him softly, the best he could do, when the animal was as cold and restless as he was himself.

Before dawn was more than a glimmer in the east he was glad to move. His body was cramped and his belly growled. He slung the saddle up onto the grey, gathered slick leather reins into his right hand and stepped out from the alders. The wind had died to a restless whimper and a few stars showed. Not far in the northeast, smoke curled upward from the hearths of a village that must be Brevic, for it stood on a chalk hill and looked east into the rising sun. Now, Ronan knew where he was.

For an hour he searched the turf for tracks he could recognise, but the earth was so sodden, he was wasting his time. Sighing, he rubbed the grey's bony nose and asked of the horse, "Where would you go, if you were a coward and fleeing before a storm?" The animal blew noisily through his nostrils. "Would you run to Brevic? No, it would seem to you that you were running upward, right into the storm. And the thunder was all behind you, in the north-east. You would run away from the noise, wouldn't you? And that means south."

He mounted up and scanned the brightening distance, hoping to see his quarry. "Come on," he coaxed his own unhappy horse. "Maybe we can find the coward before noon, and then it's hot food for you. . .and a whole skin for me, gods willing. It's not so wet today, at least." The grey snorted as if in scorn, but came to a stiff trot that jarred Ronan's every bone.

They passed the Brevic trail unseen, before even the slaves were about. Where the farmland sloped up to the moor, Red would have slowed his pace for the ground was treacherous with burrows and potholes. Red would pick his way more carefully and soon, Ronan hoped, he would come upon fresh tracks. But once Red got onto the moor's spring heather there would be no tracks at all, and from that moment he was hunting by sight.

The sun was up now, and he had begun to worry in earnest. Soon the uproar would begin in Derventio, if it had not already started. Was Cullen sober enough to remember what had happened? Ronan guessed not, but Gruffydd was no fool. A broken fence, a missing horse, the storm and Ronan's abrupt disappearance would speak clearly enough. At least he hoped they would. The evidence could be read another way — and Cullen would be happy to read it so. Brazen theft. Ronan oathed by every god he could remember and passed on, splashing through one of the many cold, clear streams that criss-crossed the moor.

To the south was Cua's Forest, and in the north by a few miles, Bogside. Two shepherds' hamlets lay between, but it was obvious at a glance that Red was not tethered there and Ronan passed by without more than a nod of greeting to the sole farmer who saw him. He kept to a narrow sheep trail for a mile more before entering woodland, where the ground was jumbled with the prints of deer, wild ponies, goats and boar.

There, he slid down to peer closely at the mud. He would know Red's iron horseshoes, if his prints were anywhere in this confusion, but from this point on the hunt was a puzzle and he would be on foot. Morning was already wasting.

He covered another mile slowly and painstakingly before he left behind the dripping trees. Ahead was a cluster of ramshackle buildings known to locals as The Potter's, for the craftsman cut his clay and kept his kiln beside a shallow stream. A scant few miles beyond was Whitestonecliff itself — Ronan saw the smoke of its hearths rising over the trees. He was almost home.

It was a full minute before he realised, he could see far too much smoke. Something was burning in the village. Had a roof gone up? How could it, in the rain last night? Then, a lightning strike? His heart tightened, but he told himself he was a fool. They would only be burning off their refuse.

He was so intent on the smoke that he flinched in surprise when the horse cried out shrilly, calling not to him but to another horse. A wild one? Many wild ponies roamed these moors and woods. Ronan swung back up into the saddle as an answering cry came from beyond the trees, and his heart squeezed as he recognised that voice.

It was Red. Diverted from the drifting column of smoke from

Whitestonecliff, he urged his grey cavalry nag into the last margin of woodland. A small herd of wild ponies, thin and shaggy, dozed in a glade there; its stallion patrolled between the sturdy, short-legged little mares and Red, who pawed the mud fretfully beneath a young oak, eager to join the group but reluctant to fight for the privilege. Ronan looked him over nose to tail and murmured a prayer of thanks. He was muddy, skittish, but unhurt.

Softly, he spoke Red's name. Several of the wild ponies put up their heads, and Red's ears twitched. Again, very quietly, Ronan called to him as he teased a rope halter from his saddlebag. Red knew him and called in answer, but the wild ones were stirring at the intrusive human voice, and for a moment Ronan was sure they would run, sweeping Red away with them. Red gave the mares a longing look, but the wild stallion was young, fierce — and angry.

Clearly judging it time to leave, Red came to Ronan and accepted the halter. Ronan sighed over him, scolded and petted at once. "You old coward," he accused fondly as he led the way out of the sodden woodland. "I'll wager you're as cold and tired and hungry as me! But I know where we can get warm and dry. Come with me. Whitestonecliff is poor, but they'll feed us."

The smoke was not so thick now, but it was an odd colour. More than refuse had been burned, and Ronan frowned at it as he tugged both horses forward. Red tossed his head, anxious, blowing through his nostrils, and Ronan was about to accuse him of cowardice again when he too heard the commotion at The Potter's.

It was a clattering and banging, and as he coaxed the two horses along the slithery clay bank of the stream, where the big kiln was cold and idle, he heard the rumbling squeak of wagon wheels. A heavy wain was being backed out of the cluster of tumble-down buildings, and Ronan came to a halt to watch the old potter. Crook-backed with age and the ill of the bones, he struggled to get his team into harness while his wife and children ran back and forth between the wagon and their heather-thatched house. They seemed to be fetching out, piece by piece, every possession they had.

A heavy black iron cauldron slammed into the bed of the wain atop the potter's tools, and the horses jumped in fright. The old man was on his nerves too, and Ronan moved closer. "What's the trouble, Potter? You're in a hurry."

His whole frame was twisted, his hands were gnarled, like the roots of old trees, and his temper was surly. He gave Ronan a sour look, tugged at his sheepskins and hauled himself up onto the wagon. "What's the trouble? We must get out of here, and so would you, if you had a shred of sense!"

"But why?" Ronan looked back at the smoke. The land was far too wet for there to be any danger of the fire spreading. The season was too young, the heather too moist to catch alight even if sparks escaped the bonfires.

"Angles, you young fool!" The potter's eyes were like red-rimmed saucers. As his young wife and children clambered onto the wain he shook out the reins and slapped them on the horses' backs to urge them. "The smoke, are you blind? The smoke is from Whitestonecliff, and they'll not finish there! They marched across the moor in the night, came up the Tees beyond Iarum, unseen, and there'll be no stopping them now, not without a battle." The horses threw their weight into the harness, struggling against the grip of the mud, and the wain creaked under its load as it rolled forward. "Get out! Get out while you can, lad. Whitestonecliff is finished, save yourself. Come with us to Eboracum." But the potter did not wait. The laden wagon rolled by Ronan as he shouted, its wheels already caked in clay, and it would be in Gareth Iron-hand's stronghold before it stopped.

Disbelief churned in Ronan's gut, but instinct sent slivers of ice threading through his marrow. His heart slammed at his ribs like a hammer, physically shaking him, and as the potter left he turned toward the pall of smoke that sullied the morning sky. His limbs were numb, frozen for some time, and then he forced his feet to move.

A moment later he was in the saddle. The grey warhorse splashed through the stream and he hurried the pace, dragging Red along behind, up the trail toward Whitestonecliff. Even now, when he was no longer a child, Ronan's ears were as keen as those of a fox. He picked up the noise long before the saw the commotion, and hustled the horses off the open trail. Red's halter knotted into the grey's harness, and he left them hitched in the woods, out of sight of the village. . .or of where the village had been.

Then he was running. Doubled up, he covered the last of the way along the muddy sentry path, and at last he was down on knees and elbows, snaking through the covering of undergrowth right below the village. From the lee of the great pile of firewood, he saw them.

The raiders were everywhere, big men, warriors, clad in battered, stained leathers and all heavily armed. Many were blood-spattered. Their chieftain was the stout, big-armed figure in the burnished helmet, and as Ronan watched he stood in the mud, shortsword in one hand, shield in the other, surveying his prize, evaluating it stick by stick.

The village where Ronan had grown up was beyond recognition. How long he lay behind the wood pile, barely even breathing as he watched the Angle raiders, he did not know. He saw no Britons on their feet, but he counted twenty bodies dumped haphazardly in front of what had been Ewan's hall before the fire gutted it. Ewan's was one of the bodies he recognised first. Others were too battered for Ronan to tell who they had been, and his heart choked him.

Was anyone left alive? Had they not even left the children? Where were they? He needed help, he must fetch a warband here to challenge the Angles, check them before they marched on, but the nearest help was Derventio, almost a day's march away. Every freeman, slave and lord alike, would have fled the moor after the carnage here. They would all be headed for Derventio in the east and Catreath in the north.

If any of them had made it out alive at all. Ronan knew he was simply lucky to have kept his freedom and his life this long. Derventio was too far away, and he was on his own.

Had anyone survived the slaughter at all? He held his breath as he watched more bodies dragged into the scene before the tumbled, charcoal ruins of Ewan's hall. Numbness had a way of robbing a man of his ability to think properly, and Ronan saw only the faces of his family and friends, felt only the sick fear that they were all gone.

Get out, the potter had told him, *get out while you can.* But he could not. For some terrible time he could not find the strength or will to move a muscle, and then, when he had control of his legs and might have taken to his heels, his heart would not let him. Surely someone must be alive, held prisoner in the village, locked away, perhaps chained with the animals. He had to know for sure before he could think about running; he could be leaving his brothers. His mother.

Very carefully, he retraced his steps, crawled back the way he had come, and when he had caught the horses' reins he took stock of the situation. He must get into the village in broad daylight, and alone. In those moments he was too blind to see the foolishness of it, and he had circled the village to enter from the rear, where the sheltering trees were thickest, before he began to think properly again, to think and react beyond the animal instincts that had served him when nothing else would.

He heard Angle voices, shouting, but the language was strange. No steel chimed now — the battle was over. No voices screamed, for the injured had all perished. The fight here had been over for long enough that the bodies were already cold.

Three buildings large enough to house prisoners had escaped the fire. They had been store huts, where grain was kept through autumn and winter, and this early in the season they had been almost empty. Ronan passed each in turn, listening for any sound that would betray the presence within of live prisoners, but no whisper or breath rewarded him. Nor were there guards at the doors, and Ronan retreated into the dimness of the woods, blind, deaf, dizzy with fatigue and shock.

As thought and feeling seeped back into him, the pain began. They were all gone, all dead. The Angles had taken no prisoners, and even if Ronan had arrived sooner, what could he have done save fight alongside Ewan and the others, and die with them? Grief consumed him like a fire in his gut and brain. Fury coloured his vision scarlet and acid tears burned his eyes. His mind screamed to understand *why*, but there was no reason, no sense in it, no way to redeem any part of it. There was only the truth, and a sense of futility that weakened his limbs and made his head throb.

He put his shoulders against the rough bark of an oak, slid down until he sat at its bole with his head on his arms, and lost track of time. He did not move until his whole body cramped, and then blinked foolishly at the sky between the branches. It was noon, or later, but he had no will to move. It was too late even to try. Boyd and Brian, Camilla and the sisters, his parents, all would have been here. All would have watched Ewan and the men go out and fight, only to be scythed down like corn.

He should have been one of them.

The guilt tormented Ronan like a hot iron. He should have been here. If he had not been at Derventio, he would have been as dead as the rest of them.

Derventio. His thoughts were blurred, and the potter's voice whispered to him indistinctly. *There'll be no stopping them without a battle.* It was too late to save Whitestonecliff, but Gruffydd's Roman town stood twenty miles in the east, perhaps unsuspecting. If the Angles had come up the Tees, marched over the moor from Iarum, as the old man believed, then Gruffydd could not know that Iarum and Whitestonecliff had fallen unless someone got out to bring the news. If no one escaped, Derventio itself would be horrifyingly vulnerable, easy prey.

Fear squeezed his heart now, and he forced himself up onto shaking legs. He felt heavy, as if he carried a stone in his chest. *One* had got out. It might mean nothing to the people of Whitestonecliff, but Ronan could take the news to Gruffydd, the warband could be massed to save Derventio, and perhaps Whitestonecliff's dead would watch, and know that one of their sons was alive, that a vestige of their honour survived,

He dragged his sleeve across his eyes and pushed away from the tree. By themselves, his feet found the trail that would take him back to the horses, but before he had gone a dozen paces instinct checked him. Animal reflexes brought up his hackles, and his right hand clawed for the new sword as he grabbed a breath.

Someone was coming.

Like a shadow, he stepped into the lee of an elderly oak. His sword ran out of the scabbard without a sound and he held his breath now, not wanting even that sound to betray him. The footfalls he had heard paused. Had he been seen? He must have been! So he must fight, here and now.

This was his blooding, for better or worse. This was the moment when the boy became the man, when the student became the warrior, or gave his life in the attempt. Ronan lifted the weapon, his right fist tightening about the grip until his knuckles were white as bones, and beyond the tree he saw the sun glint on the oil-sheened surface of an Angle sword.

He held to the tree, slipped about its curved trunk, maintaining the advantage of surprise, but fury seethed in him like a boiling cauldron, and all at once impulse overrode sense. Ronan stepped out, the tip of his sword arcing about like summer lightning.

Steel rang on steel with a bright, clear sound of bells, and Ronan let loose a flurry of blows that were barely blocked by the Angle. The man was squat and burly, thick with muscle — not a youth. With the experience of many years he met the sudden savagery of the challenge, but he turned aside the blows with nothing to spare. Ronan was wild, more animal than human, and anger drove his limbs with a power beyond his scant years and experience.

Still, the Angle was good. He had outlived his youth, the proof of his skill, and he tested Ronan with every trick he knew until only the boy's agility and fury made the difference between them. The blood sang in Ronan's ears, but his head was clear. It was as if his body had become a mechanism; he had no sense of time as he answered the Angle cut for cut, feinting and weaving in search of a breach in his defence through which he could thrust a killing blow.

When it came, he saw it on some instinctive level, and made a scything cut, like a striking snake. It was Ronan who cried out as the man toppled, pitched forward and sank to his knees. Blood surged redly as Ronan tore out the sword, twisting it as he had been taught to render even a shallow flesh wound deadly.

He had never killed a man before, despite his training, and if he had expected vengeance to taste sweet or satisfying, he was disappointed. It was sour as old ale, rank in his mouth and gut. For some time he stood gazing into the dead face, and his first kill etched itself into the roots of his memory. If he went on from this day, this moment, to win the rank and name of Ironhand, he would never forget this hour, when the last possible kind of virginity was stripped away from him. Should he have felt exhilarated? Ronan felt sick.

At the sound of voices his head snapped up. They were angry, shouting voices — the ring of swords must have been heard, and a whole patrol was coming.

Ronan ran. Since he had been old enough to walk, he had hunted through these woods, and he knew every nook, every trail, every fallen tree. He plunged into the green dimness with a certainty no one in the world could match today, and kept up his pace until he was well away. He listened for the baying of hounds, but none came. He was alone, with his whirling, crimson thoughts, the breath that scorched his throat, the heart that pounded and squeezed in his chest. The blood of his enemy that was darkening on his hands, staining his skin.

He went back to the horses in a great arc, circling the whole village, and by the time he found his way back to the glade his thoughts were his own again. The cavalry horse stood like a statue, immovable, but Red was tugging violently at his halter, showing the whites of his eyes again. Did he smell blood, smell death about Ronan? The warhorse was accustomed to it. Panting, Ronan took the grey's reins and pulled the two animals into the woods to wait and watch like a trapped fox.

The Angles would probably be on foot, since their only horses would be animals stolen along the way. Once he was clear of Whitestonecliff, Ronan was safe. They could not hunt him down.

Voices still shouted in the strange foreign language. Ronan heard only their anger. The men were thrashing about in the woods behind him now — had they found the body? Two men ran out into the open trail, one an archer, the other armed with several light hunting javelins, and shaded their eyes to search the moor visually.

They saw nothing, and Ronan began to breathe again. Afternoon was already hours old, and still he waited, unaware of time. Memory sent his family to him, and he thought that he should have wept. Instead, grief chilled him to the center of his bones, made him tremble, but no tears came. The horses blinked uncomprehendingly at him until from somewhere he summoned the strength to gather his wits and move. He must reach Derventio by nightfall.

The bellicose Angle voices quietened as they went to search for him on the moorland side of the ruined village, and as they softened with distance Ronan mounted up.

8

The hut was still dark but it was late. Bryn had slept until noon was long gone — he knew this as soon as he began to wake, when the soft sounds of the chickens pecking along the wall, and the women singing as they worked outside, would no longer mesh with his dreams. He smiled ruefully before he even began to stir. He had missed the morning's cavalry practice, which would infuriate Gruffydd and Cuddy, but it was not surprising to Bryn that he had slept so late. He had spent most of the night awake and working hard.

But for himself and the chickens, the hut was empty. Daylight streamed in through gaps about the door and sparrows were scratching in the thatch above. He yawned, stretched, rubbed his back on the smooth, soft sleeping skins. No linen here, no bath, no well-schooled bondsmen to run his errands. But Eamon more than made up for what other comforts Brevic might lack.

As Bryn sat up the door squealed open on pivots that needed oil, and he blinked in the sudden brilliance. The door banged shut again a moment later, and Eamon laughed rudely. "So you're awake at last. I wondered if you'd died! I've brought you breakfast."

He was as dark as Bryn, tall and leggy as a colt, in a blue shirt and tight britches. His long hair was loose about his shoulders, still pillow-tangled and inviting Bryn's fingers as he set the wooden platter on the bed beside Bryn and sat at his feet, just out of reach. He tucked his legs under him and cocked his head thoughtfully at Bryn.

"That's a disapproving look," Bryn ventured, yawning.

"Your people will be wondering what's become of you," Eamon observed.

Bryn finished half the cold ale Eamon had brought in one draught, and shrugged. "So let them wonder." He gave the lad a wicked smile. "I'm old enough to look after myself."

"Not so old they couldn't whip you," Eamon said doubtfully.

"They?" Bryn made a face. "Who's *they*? Old Cuddy? I should like to see him try. Gruffydd might threaten, but he'd not actually do it." He reached for the boy and Eamon giggled as he was tugged into his lover's arms, smothered with a series of kisses, each deeper and more profound than the last. Bryn's hands ran lightly over the slender, long-legged body, and then he sighed. "But still, I must go."

Eamon bit his shoulder. "But not yet."

"Not. . .quite yet," Bryn agreed, and held him lest Eamon bite again, for his teeth were sharp. Desire flickered through him like a live fire, and he said against Eamon's smooth cheek, "What will you give me, if I stay with you a little longer?" Eamon twisted, and kissed his mouth. "Very nice," Bryn admitted, "but I can have kisses anywhere." He patted the boy's round backside suggestively.

"You had that last night. Twice!"

"And I want it again before I go." Bryn nuzzled about the lad's mouth, and his wilful cock gave a throb and got up hard. "Give it to me, lovely boy. To remember you by till I can return."

"Wicked, my lord," Eamon groaned, but he had already wriggled down his breeches and Bryn tugged them right off. He had not yet bathed, and after the night's amusement he was still a little oily. Bryn's fingertips stroked deeply into him and Eamon sighed as he rolled over onto his belly. "Do you know, a monk told me that I shall burn in hell forever for doing this," he mused.

"Where is hell?" Bryn spread Eamon's long legs and could not have cared less where hell was to be found. He knelt between Eamon's knees and positioned himself. A nudge, a push, and he was inside again, making Eamon shiver deliciously.

"They say hell is somewhere in the earth," the boy moaned, as if his thoughts had begun to spin. "And I said. . .I said. . ."

Bryn rocked slowly into him. "And you said?"

"I said, take the cavalry and root out this place," Eamon went on in a soft, breathy whisper, "where they burn people for making love." Eamon tossed his head on the pillow as his voice failed him. "But they said it's their God who burns people, and you can't attack hell with cavalry." His words were slurred, one into the other, and he breathed hard, like a horse, as Bryn's rhythm pleasured him again.

Resting, Bryn brushed a drop of sweat from his eyes and seized on this question of gods and underworlds and punishment as a diversion, for Eamon was hurrying him too fast along the road to his coming. "They say their God loves people," he argued in a hoarse whisper. "Her doesn't do cruel things."

"He doesn't love sinners." Eamon eased his hips and spine.

"Sinners?" Bryn gasped as Eamon moved and held himself on his palms, looking down at the pale, slender body beneath him. Eamon's back was like perfect white velvet, the shoulder blades like wings. All this talk of hell, and Eamon made a man think of angels, especially when he was like this, rapt in love and spread wide against the sleeping skins. "Don't be a little fool," Bryn chided. "What is sinful here? I'm only making love to you."

"Are you?" Eamon squirmed again, and Bryn was almost lost. "Then why have you stopped?" Another wriggle, and Bryn swore, and turned to his duty with a will.

Afterward, he rolled himself and Eamon in the skins and they shared the food and ale. He would have explanations to make when he got home, but Bryn was not anxious. Cuddy had stopped scolding him a year ago, ad Gruffydd had never really scolded even when Bryn was a child.

The swordmaster would shake his head over Derventio's heir, tell him he would be dead in his first battle if he did not apply himself more diligently to the warrior's arts, but Bryn turned a deaf ear to the old man. He was quick, strong, had the natural ability to keep pace with the warband with a minimum of practice, and his time was his own.

Such thoughts reminded him of Ronan. He looked down the length of Eamon's beautiful body and wondered idly what pleasures were to be found in Ronan of Whitestonecliff, who was red-haired and wilful, lovesome and wild. Too wild to ever accept the favours of a chief's son? And if an invested chief were to offer Ronan those favours? Bryn pondered on this as he dressed and left Eamon with a kiss and a little purse of coins. Gruffydd would not last forever. After the pyres had burned out and grief was spent, life would go on. How could Ronan refuse the summons of a chief? Bryn felt the wicked grin on his face and lectured himself about caution.

It was mid-afternoon when he slapped a saddle on his horse and bade Brevic farewell. He turned east toward the river and did not hurry the pace, for Derventio had little to offer him. The rain seemed to have gone, though the sky was still heavy with clouds, but Bryn saw nothing to warn of more rain before morning.

He was on the deep-rutted wagon track and the shadows were long before he heard the sounds of another traveller, coming up behind in a hurry. He turned in the saddle, eyes narrowed against the sun, and swore in surprise. It was Ronan, urging his two tired horses along, and Bryn drew rein, blocking the trail to stop him.

Ronan had seen Bryn from a good distance away, and his teeth were bare in a snarl as he drew closer. From the look on his face, Bryn decided, he was in no mood to brook taunting, no matter what his 'impudence' cost him later. The grey warhorse was tired, though not yet spent, and Ronan himself was filthy and stooped with fatigue, and yet driving himself on as if a pack of wolves was baying at his heels. The racehorse tugged at his left side, tossing its head, and Ronan wrapped the halter around his hand to hold him.

"Where in Camulus's name have you been?" Bryn demanded.

"Chasing your father's precious nag." Ronan's voice was brittle and sharp, like bits of broken pottery. "I chased him most of the way to Whitestonecliff. The Angles are there, Bryn. They burned the village, everyone is dead. My family, the chieftain, no one is left. I have to warn Gruffydd. Let me pass. Let me pass!"

Bryn's heart gave a squeeze and every extremity was of a sudden clay cold. "All dead? Are you certain?"

"Of course I'm certain, damn you!" Ronan dragged his right hand across his face. "I went into the village to look for survivors, but there wasn't one, Bryn, not even a child."

For some time Bryn frowned at him in silence, almost unable to comprehend what Ronan was saying. His eyes lowered to the blue tunic then and his fists clenched tight. "Ronan, there's blood on you. Are you hurt?"

But Ronan's tousled head shook. "It's not my blood," he said tiredly. "I killed one of them." He met Bryn's eyes levelly, and Bryn saw shadows in Ronan's face that had not been there before. Bryn had not yet killed a man, and Ronan knew it. But the battle would soon begin, Bryn could feel it in his marrow. And then would come his own blooding. "Let me pass," Ronan was saying, tightening the reins. "They came over the moor in the night from the river, so the old potter told me. They could be anywhere, everywhere by now. They'll only wait for nightfall before they strike, and it could be Derventio,"

"Or Catreath," Bryn added as he watched Ronan struggled wearily with the horses. "What about Catreath?"

"It's out of our country and none of our concern," Ronan spat. "Gruffydd can send a rider, if he chooses, but Catreath could have fallen nights ago for all we know. I owe your father a great debt, Bryn, and now I'd like to repay a little of it." He kicked the warhorse to a canter and swung about Bryn in a wide arc.

A pace behind him, Bryn urged his own animal to a canter and drew level. The wind caught at his words, almost snatching them right off his lips. "Look at the sky, Ronan. It's growing overcast again, it's almost dusk now. We'll never reach Derventio before dark."

There was no answer Ronan could offer to that, and he seemed to cling to the tired grey, barely aware of Bryn or the trail or the fading daylight.

Fear was a curious emotion. Seldom had Bryn felt it, it should have been a stranger and yet it had a familiar feel, like a distant cousin with the looks and voice of a brother. Dread was a slab of ice in the belly, a sour taste in the mouth, a sweat that prickled the skin and stung the eyes, made a man drive himself when his limbs were begging for rest and his mind had begun to demand any respite, even wine or prayer. Beside him, Ronan was just as white-faced, with wide, hollow eyes, and Bryn was aware of the uneasy kinship between them.

They need not have driven themselves. Even then, haste was unnecessary. Dusk thickened quickly into night, and from miles out they saw the thick black smoke of the fires that consumed Gruffydd's old Roman town.

Still they pressed on, and swung around to approach Derventio from the woods to the south, where they would pass by like thieves. The wind in the trees was like the voice of a wild thing, screaming taunts out of the darkness, as if goading them to throw away their lives on the blades of Angle spears.

They stood together between the horses, under the tossing branches, and watched the blaze that raged along the banks of the Dervent. For a long time they were silent, and then Bryn said quietly, "They'll be fighting."

Ronan's dark head shook. "It's over. If the Angles got close enough to torch our thatches, they got into the town. The fighting is over, Bryn. There's nothing we can do now, and all we'd have done if we'd been here is die with them."

"Rather die like a warrior than stand here like a coward!" Bryn snarled. "Look at the fires. By Camulus, my family is among that! I have to go and find them, I must be able to find them,"

"You can't," Ronan shouted over the wind, but Bryn had the reins of his frightened horse in both hands and was swinging up into the saddle. "You can't, Bryn!" Ronan caught his bridle and put a hand on his leg to hold him back. "It's no good, we're too late, can't you see? You'll just get yourself killed in there!"

"You talk like the peasant you are." Bryn's eyes were red in the fire glow. "Aye, and a coward. If you were more than that, you would go yourself and lend your sword to the chief who took you off the farm and put you on the battlefield."

Anger twisted Ronan's face and his arm lashed out. The flat-handed blow struck the left side of Bryn's head, and he fell from the saddle as the horse side-stepped. The impact of the ground against his shoulder and hip almost shocked Bryn back to his senses and he looked up dizzily at Ronan, who glared down into the shadows where the chief's heir lay.

Ronan's voice shook with fury. "That is the last time you will speak those things to me, ap Gruffydd. I'll take no more of it. My own family is dead, and all my village. My chieftain, my friends, lover, teacher. I have nothing left to lose now but my honour, and I won't let you take that from me."

Slowly and carefully, Bryn clambered back to his feet. He rubbed his stinging ear, acknowledging the force that had rattled his brains. "I shall settle with you later for that. Don't doubt it. But only fools fight in a burning house, and ours is well ablaze." Bryn pulled both hands across his sweating face and dragged his shoulders back, swallowing on the sickness that churned in his gut. "I have to know if they're dead or alive, if they fought or are in chains."

"If they were fighting we would hear it," Ronan reasoned. "Listen! The only sound you hear is the wind and the fires. Even the screaming has stopped."

It was true. Bryn's blood may have been ice water at the thought, but surely he would have heard screaming if anyone was alive in the inferno. Now, there was just the noise and the stink of burning timber and thatch and rope. Ronan's hand was still on Bryn's bridle, and not until Bryn sank back against the bulk of a tree did he release it and knuckle his eyes.

"Still," Bryn whispered, full of a coldness he had never known before. "I must know."

"Go on foot if you must," Ronan said tiredly, "and go quietly, carefully, or you will die tonight as they died. Only you die without honour, for you waste the last of your father's blood without sense or need."

For a moment Bryn hesitated, one part of him wanting to strike out at Ronan, and then he snatched off his cloak and flung it over the saddle. A pulse pounded like thunder in his ears as he swung on Ronan. "Don't you dare seek to tell me the meaning of honour," he growled, fists clenching and stopping just short of delivering the blow. Ronan let it pass, as if he expected the outburst — as if he could feel some fraction of Bryn's pain.

And then Bryn slipped into the rank embrace of the darkness and was alone with the smoke and the windmill of his thoughts, the hammer-beat of his heart. The air was so thick, he could barely breathe it. It caught at his throat and almost blinded him as he doubled up and ran the length of the field of spoiled corn. If he was swift enough, he knew he would pass by unseen, and he dived into the darkness between the elms, within shouting distance of the town itself.

From there he saw the thatched roof of his home. Half of it was ablaze, the other half smouldering, a deep red colour like a kitchen hearth. The wind blew full in his face, fetching every sound, but he heard no swords, no voices crying in pain, fear or anger. Ronan was right. The battle was already over — and it was lost. Bryn sank to his knees and put his face into his hands, unable to think at all.

His mind spun like a top. Just that morning the world had been an untroubled place where his future, his inheritance, was assured. And now? His head seemed to be filled with the reeking smoke, his thoughts like wraiths. What was left for him now?

From down in the town came strange voices. Angle voices. They were looting, and he knew they must have taken prisoners. Bryn pushed to his feet, edged on between the trees and coughed on the smoke as he hunted for some way to get among the blazing Roman houses. Most of them had gone up, Derventio was ringed by a curtain of yellow and orange fire, but at last he saw a way in. A narrow, crooked little alley snaked between tumble-down huts, and by blind chance the thatch had not yet caught.

Doubled up, choking at every breath, he plunged the length of it and flattened out against the last warped timber wall. A little way on was the courtyard wall of his father's house, and no one barred his way. Bodies lay everywhere, warriors, tradesmen, servants, women, all dead. Bryn saw nothing alive, heard no Angle voices close enough to be dangerous. They were finished here, finished and gone.

He went over the wall like a cat, lifted himself up and let himself down by handholds he had learned as a boy. The length of his scabbard scraped over the jagged top, and then it was like jumping into a furnace as he dropped into the courtyard.

Everything was ablaze, the house, the stables, outhouses, and the bodies strewn in the yard told of the fight that had taken place here. The men of the household had fought to the last, they had died with their honour intact, no quarter asked. Yet they were dead, and save for the animal roar of the fire Bryn heard nothing.

The wall of heat held him back, and Ronan was right, gods damn him. Bryn was wasting his time here, and if he got out safely he would be lucky. He turned, reached up and set his hands on the top bricks, ready to pull himself up. As his chin rose level with his hands he heard voices, and his belly churned. They were coarse, Angle voices, belonging to two men, making their way up the very alley by which he had come into Derventio.

A moment later he saw them, lit by the bloody, lurid firelight. They were unsteady on their feet — injured, dazed, or else drunk on looted wine. For the moment Bryn could not tell. They staggered along the alley that led out of the ruins as if they had no fear of the fire, but as the muscles in his hands cramped Bryn let go the wall and crouched at its foot.

Blind, coughing, dizzied by the heat, he knew he could hide there only moments, and his heart was noisy in his ears. He cast about like a trapped bear, searching for a means of escape. He had two options: back over the wall, where he must cross swords with two drunken raiders — and risk their calling up a whole pack of sober friends. Or past the inferno of the house, and along the riverbank.

He might get out that way, if luck was with him. Bryn stood and wiped his sweating face on his sleeve. Bitterly, almost unthinkingly, he conceded that Ronan was right again. Ronan was no fool. The last of Gruffydd's blood should never have come here.

The riverbank was his only way out, and he pushed away from the wall. Skirting a mound of smouldering thatch, he hurried past red-hot, warping wreckage that had been Gruffydd's house, and it was like walking into a solid wall of heat. He felt his eyes smart and his skin seemed to wither, and he plunged on, knowing that only swiftness would get him through.

If he could get down to the paddocks where the warriors trained . . .had once trained. He could get out that way. He could make it to the water. . .the water. His mind seemed to have broken into a thousand fragments, like fireflies dancing above a bonfire, and he pushed on, gasping for breath, and prayed.

As he came out into the open his belly heaved, for the paddock was a litter of broken bodies. Men, horses, dogs, scattered in a mess of limbs and blood and stinking gore. Was this the reek of a battlefield? Since he was a child, Bryn had heard of if, but how could he have imagined the reality? He swallowed his sickness and moved on, never quite knowing where he was putting his feet, nor what he was stepping over, or upon. Once he looked down and thought he recognised the face that lay in the grass. It might have been Cuddy, but it was difficult to tell, since half the skull was gone, and the rest of the body lay some distance away.

Swallowing a white-hot wave of sickness, Bryn pressed on

toward the river.

* * *

Waiting in the woods was a kind of torture. Though Ronan had time for tears now he still could not find them, and he sat hugging his chest, wrapped in Bryn's cloak, listening to the sounds of the night and watching the inferno light up the sky with a hellish, crimson glow.

Pain knifed through him, and he realised dully that it was hunger. It was difficult to remember the last time he had eaten, and he felt weak. Beyond that, grief numbed all else and he barely thought at all. He merely waited, marked the time, and every moment believed that Bryn was dead too. He was gone so long that Ronan was on the point of leaving, and at last the stirring of the bushes close at hand, the sudden movement at his side, brought his skin out in a cold sweat. He half drew his sword, his fist clenched tight about the hilt, as the shape dragged itself out of the darkness and flopped down.

Ronan's nostrils flared. Bryn smelt like death, as if he had been wading in a butcher's midden heap. He reeked of smoke too, but the stink of death was stronger on him. Ronan stared bleakly at him, and when Bryn did not seem about to speak, nudged him.

Smoke-rough, Bryn's voice shook. Ronan heard a knife's edge in it. "It's all finished here. If the Angles took prisoners, I cannot say. There was no way into the town to find out. Derventio is too big, and it's all burning, roasting, like the Christian bad magic place. There's no more fighting."

They were silent for a long time, each consumed by the chaos of his own thoughts, and at last it was Ronan who forced himself to stir. He peered at Bryn's dark, hunched shape. "What will we do? Come dawn they'll send out scouts. They could already be hunting."

"They're drunk with victory," Bryn whispered. "Drunk on ale that my father bought from a Roman merchant not a week ago."

"But we can't afford to be here at daylight," Ronan argued. "We must get out of Gruffydd's country."

At the sound of his father's name Bryn's breath caught. He rubbed his eyes savagely, as if tears scalded them, and flung back his head, glaring at the sky. "And where do you propose that we should go?"

"Somewhere," Ronan said between clenched teeth, "where

there is a strong warband. The Angles won't stop here."

The anger surging through Bryn fetched him to his feet. "Gruffydd had a strong warband! What good did it do him? What use was it? I went through the paddock where we used to train, and they're all dead there. Brock, Cuddy, the smiths, the armourers. My father will be with them somewhere. I didn't have time to search. He turned away and for a moment seemeed to swallow his stomach.

"Bryn," Ronan began, well able to imagine what Bryn would have seen, and how little prepared for it he had been. Neither of them had seen or smelt a battlefield before. The last time the Angles raided this part of the coast, they were children. They had been sent to their mothers, kept well back from the fighting, and had only heard of it from the bards later.

I'm all right." Bryn fended him off as Ronan tried to lay a hand on his shoulder, perhaps for comfort. "Oh, they made a fight of it, but the bastard Angle curs must have torched the thatch before any warning could be given. Gods damn them all!"

A cold wind struck through to the marrow, and Ronan's joints locked like those of a man thrice his age. He felt his aches keenly as he forced his feet to move. "We have to think for ourselves now. We can't go north, obviously. If they came down from Iarum, the north is Angle territory now. To the east is the sea. What of Cambria? I've heard tales of a great chief there, Artos, son of Uther Ben, the Corishman who was the student of the Druid sorcerer. Artos is always recruiting cavalry. We could go there."

Bryn was dragging his fingers through his knotted hair. "Go where you like. You're a freeman, no one orders you."

His disdain struck like a dirk at Ronan. It would have been easy to bid him farewell, walk away from Bryn without a word, but Ronan felt a tight sensation, and knew what it was. He was afraid, and it was a dread of being totally alone. The fear stopped him. Tonight at least, he and Bryn were kindred, and Gruffydd's son was the last man alive to whom he was not a stranger. "And what of you?" Ronan asked under the sough of the wind.

The rawness of Bryn's voice betrayed his pain. He swallowed on his dry throat several times before he could speak properly. "I ride south. Gareth Ironhand keeps a warband at Eboracum that has fought against the Angles and won more than once. Perhaps he could use another sword. He knew my father well, and knows me by sight."

"But Eboracum is too close to Derventio," Ronan protested. "If the Angles march again they could be there in a day!"

"How many Angles cane?" Bryn asked hoarsely. "Enough to fight three times? More? Iarum, Whitestonecliff, Catreath, Derventio, the other villages across the moor? The men of each village would have put up the best showing they could. Can the Angles fight again so soon? No, I say they're spent for now. They'll stop here, build fences and guard them. But next season? Let them come to Eboracum!"

"Aye," Ronan mused. "You may be right. And then again, if they could march on Ebracum in a day I would count it my duty to ride to Gareth Ironhand with the news." He nodded, knuckled his eyes, dragged his cuff across his face. "So we go to the stone city on the Ambri," he said softly, "as soon as we have light enough to ride hard. yes?"

"Yes," Bryn growled bitterly, and even then was looking east in search of the first glimmer of dawn.

Sunrise was grudging and unlovely, and before the grey light had found its way to the riverbank they were moving. Under cover of the last shroud of darkness they crept like thieves away from Derventio and into the farmland to the south. When the sun showed, several miles already lay behind them, lookouts would have been posted, scouts would soon be dispatched in every direction, but for the moment they were out and running, with a good head start.

On a high slope they stopped to rest the horses and looked back on the burned-out town. By daylight Derventio looked like an open wound that had been cauterised by the hot iron. Only the recent rains had contained the extent of the blaze; but for the storms that had come across the moor the day before, the crops might have burned, or the woods.

Dawn fetched another shower, and as they looked down on Derventio they saw that the fires were doused. Where the town had been, now Bryn saw just a scar in the earth, and the north wind reeked of death and defeat. The Angles were as drunk on victory as he had seen. If they had posted lookouts at all, the men were lax in their duty.

No scouts patrolled to the south, and when Ronan led the way down from the high ground they slowed their pace. The horses were tired; as for himself, Bryn felt bruised from head to toe. The river carried blackened debris downstream, and sometimes the bodies of men and horses floated in the turbid water, half submerged, already beginning to bloat. Bryn began to count them but soon stopped and looked away. He would grieve for the dead later — much later, when he was sure that he and Ronan would not soon be among them.

They were on a shepherd's trail, so old that it must have been worn into the earth long before the Romans came. It wound through the woods to Eboracum, took them well out of sight of Derventio and into the comparative safety of the forest. They rode in silence while the morning warmed, but when the little racehorse began to protest Ronan reined back with a soft curse. Bryn watched as his companion slid down to examine the animal's slender legs, so delicate by comparison with the warhorse's.

"Is he lamed, Ronan? Badly?"

"Badly enough." Ronan straightened. "Enough to make this a slow journey. You'd best go on without me. I'll catch you up if I can."

Still mounted, Bryn looked about in all four directions, and shook his head. "This country has become dangerous of a sudden. I'm seeing Angles behind every tree. We're safer travelling together — two pairs of eyes to see, ears to hear. Two swords if they're needed. You just look to the horse."

Ronan regarded him bleakly, clearly weighing the wisdom of Bryn's words. They had been spoken in a tone of command, but Bryn was well aware that he had lost the authority to issue orders and have them unthinkingly obeyed. At last, and not to Bryn's surprise, Ronan made negative noises. "You look to the horse," he said shortly as he secured Red's reins to his own saddle and un-buckled his baldric. "I'm going to find something to eat. It's days since I've eaten properly."

With that he slipped out of the glade before Bryn could utter a word. Swearing under his breath, Bryn slithered down from the saddle and grunted as his feet hit the ground. He thought of Eamon and of Brevic as he led the three weary horses into the concealment of a thicket of briar and tethered them there. Had Brevic fallen? Had its people seen the Angles coming, since they commanded the high ground, and had they fled? With luck, the Angles would have captured an empty village, and beautiful Eamon and his family would be a day's march in the west by now, seeking the shelter of some other chieftain.

The sun was high. Shafts of gold speared down through the canopy of the forest, and Bryn heard the chatter of a tiny brook that sprang out of a knoll beyond the briar. He washed his face and hands, drank deeply, and set his back against the bole of a young oak to wait.

Ronan was gone long enough for him to begin to worry, but since when did a peasant woodsman come to grief in the forest? Sure enough, just as Bryn's belly began to prickle with anxiety,

Ronan returned with several wood-pigeons, plucked out of the branches by those throwing knives. He gutted them deftly while Bryn watched, and when Ronan's green eyes gave him a hard look, he cast about for dry kindling that would burn smokelessly.

When the birds were spitted on a sharp rod and propped over the makeshift hearth, Bryn and Ronan settled on opposite sides of the fire and glared at each other. Bryn rubbed the left side of his head, which had received the flat of Ronan's hand the night before, and could be starting to bruise.

"You struck me. I've yet to settle with you for that."

The corner of Ronan's mouth quirked in scorn. "Did you want me to let you ride into the midst of the Angles and the fire like a fool? Next time, please yourself. I can't say that I care." His chin lifted, a little expression of defiance. "Do you think you're going to lord it over me now? Why should I endure that, when you're no more a chief's son and heir than I am? I told you last night, Bryn, you'll not rob me of my honour."

"I've seen stable lads flogged bloody for less than that," Bryn snapped, but it was as if he were a spectator, sitting outside his own body, listening to his own voice. He heard the words, and the sound of anger, but all he felt was emptiness, and a terrible sense of dislocation.

"I'm no stable lad!" Ronan retorted. "And who is going to whip me? You? You're welcome to try! I've a sword of my own, and I'll use it!"

Resentment smouldered in Bryn's chest as he watched Ronan's eyes sparkle. Beautiful eyes, green as malachite in the sun, and the more angry he became, the more beautiful he was. Bryn was sure Ronan had no awareness of it. "You give yourself too many airs and graces, scullion," he accused. "Like as not, you need a lesson before you'll mend your ways. A painful lesson."

"A lesson taught by you?" Ronan laughed shortly, a harsh, unpleasant sound devoid of any humour.

"Perhaps." Bryn looked into the fire and listened to the confusion of his thoughts. "The gods know, you've given me reason enough to see you thrashed." He saw his right hand then, saw that his knuckles were so white, they looked like lumps of bone knotted about the hilt of his sword, and yet he could not feel the burn of that grip in his palm. Odd, Bryn decided. Most odd. Ronan was speaking again, as if from a great distance away, and he forced himself to listen.

"I've had reason enough to deal you the same thrashing. Your rank stopped my hand and my tongue a dozen times, ap Gruffydd.

But, the Angles. . .the Angles have made us equals. From this day on, I'll have no more from you."

It was as if a spring released inside Bryn, and all at once he was on his feet. Colours were too bright, lurid, like the light shining through transluscent gems, and he was filled with a frothing mass of anger. It was fury at the Angles, at the Fates, the gods. Rage at the futility of his father's plans and schemes for defence, burning resentment for all he had lost, his birthright, his nobility. But all of it became focused on Ronan, whose pride and tenacity and beauty were suddenly like salt rubbed into wounds, and Bryn wanted only to strike out.

"I've been too patient, too long," he snarled. "Up with you, on your feet, scullion, or will you be the peasant's brat that you are, and sit still for chastisement?" And he drew his sword with the hissing, serpent voice of steel on old, oiled leather.

Infuriatingly, Ronan regarded him cooly. "If you're trying to kill yourself, do it somewhere else. The sound of swords will fetch an Angle scouting party here faster than we could run away. Where are your wits, Bryn? Bring them back from wool gathering! Your grievances with me will have to wait a while, till we're out of harm's way."

He was right, which only fanned the blaze of Bryn's fury. The sword whined back into its sheath and he crouched across the fire, glaring broodingly into the flames as Ronan tried the pigeons. They were half done, edible, and he slid one off its spit. Almost as a gesture of mockery, he offered it to Bryn, but Bryn's belly was so knotted, the meat would have sickened him. He shook his head and looked way, slamming a shutter before the chaos of his thoughts.

So Ronan ate alone, and if he saw Bryn's black looks he ignored them. A runaway from a rat-hole in Whitestoneciff had no rank to lose, and would take his loss easily, Bryn thought sourly. Ronan wore a surly face as he chewed mechanically on the meat, but Bryn saw a strength about him today, a tenacity and defiance that went beyond mere stubbornness. He was not about to yield to words. The red hair was tangled, his face was smoot-smudged, his mouth was sullen, sultry and tempting as he ate. Bryn almost wanted to reach out and brush away the soot, run his thumb across Ronan's lower lip. Ronan was as beautiful as Eamon . . .or more so. Eamon was a boy, and Ronan was a man now, and Bryn felt the lick of pure lust, a sensation that astonished him. He had believed himself too near dead to feel anything good or pleasant or positive ever again, yet here was Ronan glaring at him with wide, bruised green eyes, and here was the pulse throbbing in Bryn's throat like life drizzling back into him.

Weariness had a way of soon smothering rage, and Bryn slumped down, needing to rest while Ronan ate. He closed his eyes but did not sleep, listening for the sounds of movement as Ronan kicked out the fire and knelt to examine Red's leg. The fetlock was swollen but the horse was not yet entirely lame, and they had to travel. Every second they tarried was danger.

Bryn hoisted himself to his feet, unhitched the cavalry horses and led them around the briar to the spring. They drank, and while Red also drank his fill Ronan went down on hands and knees and put his face into the water to slake his own thirst. Like an animal, Bryn thought dizzily. Like a lean, healthy, vibrant young colt, filled with life, eager to be off the halter and running free. And then Ronan looked up at him, face wet, mouth open, eyes wide and feverishly bright, and Bryn felt heat rise in his cheeks.

"Move yourself," he said sharply, as if Ronan was deliberately wasting time, "or we'll find our freedom forfeit."

It was a statement of the obvious and Ronan accorded it all the consideration it was due. The barbs slipped by like loosely aimed arrows, and a moment later he was back in the saddle. They were out of the safety of the glade moments later, and now the shepherd's trail wound up onto an open hillside on its way south to Eboracum.

In a mile they took to the forest once more, too anxious to show themselves openly for long. But the woods made for slow, heavy going. Bryn was numb. He felt nothing now, not even grief or anger or resentment. He was too tired, his senses too battered, and it was little comfort to him to watch Ronan, see his slumped shoulders and the shadows on his face, and know that Ronan felt the same pain.

Did all warriors feel this? Was it a private madness that all suffered, and somehow transcended so as to survive and fight again? Bryn was surprised to find that some corner of his mind was still thinking. How often had Cuddy said that Bryn was his own worst enemy, for he would not work, 'knuckle down to discipline', practise enough to become a swordmaster in his own right. Bryn was a lover and a gambler, not a born warrior.

And Ronan? Bryn's eyes were on Ronan's back even then. Ronan was born for this. There was a strength in him today that Bryn could not find within himself, and envied. Cuddy had said much that was wise, and Bryn could remember barely a fraction of it. Now that Cuddy was gone he treasured every word. Cuddy would surely have died well. He would have fought beside Gruffydd and Sian. They would have protected the women, the bonded people. Dafydd, the beautiful boy from the kitchen, Sian's last born.

They would all have fought in the end, since the only alternative was slave irons, the Angles would never have let them go free. Their only escape was through the mist into the Otherworld, and Bryn prayed that they were safe there, at peace. These were Gruffydd's and Sian's convictions, a tradition as ancient as the island itself. Bryn had heard the stories over and over from the woman's lips, and she had heard them from the last Druids of the Deer people of the Brigantes.

It was past noon when Ronan led the way to a shallow stream overhung by the boughs of an old, twisted oak. The horses put their heads down to drink and Bryn followed Ronan down from the saddle, stiff, sore, cramped and grateful for respite. Ronan stooped to work at once, bathing Red's swollen leg, and Bryn stood rubbing his hands, watching and waiting.

They had not spoken three words since morning, and Bryn was sure Ronan was trying to ignore him. The silence was brooding, uneasy, like the last hour before a thunderstorm, and it could not continue. Bryn cleared his throat and Ronan looked up at him, already on the defensive, as if he expected the promised whipping to be delivered here and now.

"Where do your loyalties lie?" Bryn asked. "Once, you would have served me. If your loyalties don't lie with me, then where?"

Ronan returned to the horse's ailing leg. He splashed cold water over it, massaged the strained tendons as he said, "I don't know. For the moment my only loyalty is to myself, for I'll be no man's eager servant. To escape that fate, which I was born to, I let Cuddy take me apart, bony by bone, and remake me. He thrust me into the furnace and forged a warrior. I'll serve in the stables no longer."

"Warriors can't be made." Bryn was only quoting a time-worn belief, and it had begun to sound shallow, hollow, to his own ears. "They must be born of warrior blood," he added, looking anywhere but at Ronan.

"Cuddy was satisfied with me." Ronan was on the defensive again. "You set yourself up as a better judge of fighting men than the swordmaster?" He let go the horse's leg, stood and dried his hands on his thighs. "Aye, and you've already forgotten, Bryn. I'm blooded. I've spilled my share of Angle blood. You have not. Strictly speaking, that makes *me* the warrior, not you."

Bryn felt his face grow taut as a mask. "This impudence is unbecoming." Pushing, pushing, looking for a chink in Ronan's armour. Trying to needle him.

"So sweeten your temper," Ronan suggested drily, "and speak more civilly. It would make for a more pleasant exchange."

It had to come to this. They had both known it from the beginning. Two young males, fighting for dominion with locked horns — it must come to some kind of resolution, or they killed each other. It never occurred to either of them to question it, and they had drawn their swords, dropped into fighting balance, before there was even a moment to consider the foolishness.

A fleeting acknowledgement of futility licked through his mind, but Bryn's blood was drumming in his ears and his sword seemed to be swinging itself. It was time to fight. The blades rang, bell-like and clear, as Ronan met the first blow, blocked it with all the strength and skill Cuddy had instilled in him, and returned it. Bryn swung again, listening to the pulse in his ears, feeling the drumbeat of his heart. . .oddly, feeling rage pare away with every swing of the sword, every beat of the blood in his veins.

Where was fury? The match was more of a ritual than a challenge, something that had to be done, because it had always been done, this was the way of things, and though Ronan could irk Bryn as few other men could, Bryn *had* no desire to injure him. Between them, they were all that survived of Gruffydd's heritage.

Sunlight caught the upswung blades and refracted as they circled. Boots splashed in the shallow water as they hunted for footing on the smooth, polished pebbles in the stream bed. The quick, hot temper that had come between Bryn and his judgement cooled with the old, old ritual of male battling male for dominance, and as Ronan blocked his cuts with an ease and grace Bryn envied, fury gave way to weariness.

Tired right through to his marrow, he fell back, and back again, and one foot slithered as a rock turned under his heel. He met the water with a livid curse and was up again in an instant, expecting Ronan to seize his opportunity to finish it. Ronan's right hand shifted on the grip of the sword, it would have been so easy to send Bryn sprawling, to make him the victim of his own wilful pride, but for some reason Bryn could not imagine Ronan stayed his hand with a faint, humourless smile.

Grunting with effort, Bryn clambered to his feet and gave Ronan a quizzical look. "You could have killed me."

"I could have." Ronan's shoulders lifted in a shrug. "But in the gods' names, why should I want to kill you? I'd sooner you were my friend."

"Your friend?" Bryn echoed. His right hand clenched on the sword and the shining, oily blade arced up again.

"Your friend," Ronan repeated warily, mindful of the beautifully crafted blade, which Bryn kept honed like a razor. "I'll not call you my master, ap Gruffydd."

Temper surged again but spent itself even before Bryn could find his voice. For a single moment he felt poised to launch a flurry of killing blows, but before even one was made the spirit seemed to bleed from him, as if his life's blood coursed from an open wound. The sword went down, his chin fell onto his chest, he had barely the strength left to stand. At last, even his fingers loosened on the hilt of the weapon and it fell with a dull, flat sound into the stream's soft bank where they stood.

His voice was a hoarse whisper, and he would have sworn it was no more than an echo from the hollowness inside him. "Will you kill me? Quick and clean. Do it now. You're stronger than I am, Ronan of Whitestonecliff. Stronger than I shall ever be, for I can't go on. Camulus, why am I left alive? They're all dead, all of them! I've no right to be alive. Look at you, damn you, sullied with Angle blood. Your own kin are avenged while mine are likely howling for vengeance they'll never see. I have no right to be alive." His voice almost choked him. "Kill me now. I haven't the courage to go on, and haven't the courage to take my own life. Kill me, damn you. Kill me!"

Bryn sank slowly to his knees and put his face into his hands. How many years was it since he had wept? Tears were difficult, painful. A warrior lived in honour or he died in it. Perhaps Bryn ap Gruffydd had done neither. This was cold as a winter's wind in his mind as he waited for the blow to fall.

Yet Ronan barely moved. The tip of his own sword traced a gentle pattern on Bryn's wide shoulders, but the blow that had been demanded never came, and Ronan's voice was low, thick with emotion. "I don't yet understand the warrior's creed fully," he said softly, "but I know a little. You ask me to kill you to save your honour. You want me to send you to the place the others are now."

"Please," Bryn murmured, eyes squeezed shut. "Just have it over with. One blow, you know how to make it kind."

"Where is your arrogance now?" Ronan asked, and although the words could have been a taunt his voice was very gentle. "Was it a shield between you and pain?"

"Kill me, gods damn you," Bryn muffled as his head began to throb.

"Your shield is broken now," Ronan said in the same quiet tone. "You made me fight just now in the hope that I would murder you. Didn't you?" And he knelt beside Bryn, one hand moulded about his shoulder. "I'll not do that. It's not each other we should be fighting, it's the Angles." He shifted closer and touched Bryn's dark hair. "The gods let us live, Bryn. I don't know why, but they would have taken us if they wanted to. We are alive today because they will it, and that means they have no need of our dying. Swear vengeance for your household. I swore vengeance for my family — one dead Angle is not enough to pay for them all!"

The words seemed to catch in Ronan's throat, and when Bryn looked sidelong at him he saw the pain, raw and naked in Ronan's eyes. Tears streaked his cheeks, and only then did Bryn realise Ronan was filthy as a mudlark. He was blind, too, gazing at some vision only he could see, and his fingers had clenched into Bryn's tunic so tightly, the linen might have ripped away.

"Ronan." Bryn lifted his head and blinked dizzily at him. In all their lives, they had shared nothing at all before this moment. Bryn had seen Ronan a hundred times on the road, in the stables, but aside from noticing a wild youth's red-haired, green-eyed beauty, he had spared little attention for him. Now Ronan was a man, and of a sudden he was Bryn's kindred. Grief, loss, the hunger for vengeance, made them one.

Kin. Closer than brothers could ever be. Bryn looked levelly into Ronan's eyes — green as a cat's in the sunlight, they flayed the flesh from his bones and he swallowed his heart. "You'll never call any man your master, will you?" Bryn asked hoarsely, and Ronan shook his head, slow and sure. Bryn's right hand rose unsteadily, fingers splaying about Ronan's dirty cheek and finding it coarse with a man's beard. "Do you know, I wanted you."

"I knew." Ronan licked his lips. "You were watching me, while Cuddy taught me. Dafydd saw, and the smith's lad, Matthew. They saw you watching me."

"Did they?" Bryn sat back on his heels. "Sometimes I wanted to beat you bloody, to prove that I could. I was wrong." He tipped his head back, closed his eyes and gazed at the red glow of the sky through the sealed lids. "You're stronger than I am. I admire that."

"I'm just more knocked about," Ronan said gently. "Where were you when Cuddy was wearing me to a wraith? In some fellow's bed, I'll wager, the same place you'd be when I was out on the moor before dawn on mornings as black as pitch, training horses, or working by lamplight, shovelling out your father's stables. All that time, you'd have been warm and coddled by some man, some boy, and I'd have traded places with you in a moment, if I'd got the chance."

Bryn drew in a deep breath, held it, let it out slowly. He opened his eyes, almost surprised to find that the sky was blue, the trees were fresh and green. And that Ronan was close beside him, filthy and tired and beautiful. He traced the shape of that face with all ten fingertips, and Ronan's lips parted slightly. "In the baths that evening, I thought you wanted me. You remember?"

"I remember." Ronan's cheeks flushed faintly as the disturbingly gentle caress touched some raw spot deep inside him that needed to be soothed. He moaned soundlessly and turned his face to Bryn's leathery palm.

Perhaps he had never realised how much he needed the comfort of love, or even of an embrace, Bryn thought. "Ronan?"

"I might have wanted you that night at the baths," Ronan said self-mockingly, "but I would never have gone to you. Not to the chief's son. If I had, I would have acknowledged you as my master, even in bed."

"And you would never do that," Bryn whispered. "You're more prideful than a peasant has any right to be, Ronan."

"I am a warrior." Ronan pressed his lips to the sword calluses in Bryn's palm. "And so are you, and it's all you are now, Bryn. You have nothing else left."

For a moment Bryn was frozen, and Ronan's eyes widened as if he was waiting for something, an eruption, long overdue. Bryn was on the knife's edge, and he had to fall. It could be fight, flight or surrender, and even now Ronan was poised, clearly not knowing which to expect.

And then Bryn leaned closer, caught Ronan's body in his arms and pressed them together. Ronan cried out as he felt his ribs crush in the desperate embrace, and did not seem aware that he was crushing the breath out of Bryn's lungs.

How long did they cling blindly together, on their knees by the stream? Bryn did not know. He might even have dozed, for he jerked back to awareness as he felt the brush of lips on his cheek, the rasp of whiskers, and he opened his mouth as Ronan's fingers threaded into his hair to hold his head. Their tongues met, and they froze again, eyes wide, and then it was Ronan who pressed the kiss home. His hands clenched into Bryn's hair as if he were terrified that Bryn would try to escape, or spurn him. Instead, Bryn took hold of Ronan, pitched him into the damp grass and pinned him there while he ravaged his mouth until he tasted a drop of blood.

They lay pressed together in the grass for a long time, too exhausted to move. Physical desire was impossible. It was the closeness, the warmth of another's body that Bryn hungered for. Ronan

97

was watching the horses grazing along the stream, waiting patiently for him to speak, and at last Bryn stirred and found his voice.

"Can you call me your friend, when once I would have had you taken out and whipped for speaking your mind to me?"

"You were a chief's son," Ronan said easily. "You were born to it. I would have taken a whipping without protesting much, if I had earned it. That's what I was born to."

Bryn buried his face in the warm, hard curve of Ronan's shoulder. "I shall have to curb that arrogance in future. I can't trade on Gruffydd's name now." He lifted his head and looked into Ronan's face. "You're very beautiful. I always thought so. But I knew you would never bed with me, so I never really approached you. I believe I was insanely jealous of Dafydd — imagine, a warrior madly jealous of a crippled kitchen boy."

"Dafydd must be dead," Ronan whispered. "My gods, Bryn, what is to become of us?"

For some time they were silent, each bound up in the whirl of his own thoughts, unaware even of the rush of the forest around them. Then Bryn forced himself to stir and dragged his fingers through the tangle of his hair. "Where are we going?"

"Eboracum, as you said." Ronan came stiffly to his feet. "You said you know Gareth Ironhand."

"Only a little," Bryn said dubiously. "He might recognise my face, he might not. I never spoke to him directly, but I was with Gruffydd when he went there on warband business." He watched Ronan whistle for Red, and catch the little stallion by the halter when he came. "Who I am. . .who I was. It's not much to wager on."

"It's better than what I was," Ronan said drily as he caught the reins of his cavalry horse and swung up into the saddle with a grunt.

Discovering himself bruised and shaking, Bryn retrieved his sword and called for his straying horse. "We'd best be moving. Who knows how far the Angle scouts may have come?"

"They may be near already," Ronan mused. "Where are our old gods?"

"Can you believe in gods, anyone's gods, after what we've seen?" Bryn mounted up with a supreme effort and turned the horse back toward the shepherd's trail. "We run today." He gave Ronan a smouldering look. "We won't run again, and when next we meet with Angles, we leave no drop of blood unshed." He looked up, eyes narrowed against the sky. "Do you hear me, you useless, misbegotten gods? It is an oath!"

The wind tossed the trees as if in answer, and Ronan nodded.

"An oath of vengeance," he agreed quietly. "Oh, yes. They do hear."

Revenge was not enough to salve a man's heart, but it was a beginning. Bryn touched his heels to his horse's flanks and they moved off slowly, at Red's pace. Their silence now was companionable, and Bryn saw himself mirrored in Ronan. Haunted, stricken, but alive. He watched Ronan now with the eyes of a lover, and felt a shiver as Ronan looked at him with the same dark, prideful eyes.

What kind of lover would Ronan of Whitestonecliff be? Bryn fancied that he would find out soon enough.

9

Rome's old city on the Usan river stood beyond the forest and farmland. They crossed the frontier country unnoticed, holding the the woods, for Gareth Ironhand would surely have an army of scouts on the trails, and if they were seen they would be challenged.

By late afternoon Red was limping badly, and their pace was slow. For a time Bryn considered loosing him to fend for himself, but he was shrewd enough to realise that Red was an asset. Neither he nor Ronan had any money, nor anything worth trading, except that horse. In Catreath, Gruffydd had haggled over his price with a trader, and in the end had paid a considerable sum for the wayward animal. Red could be sold again for a better price, now that he was trained, and there would be money for Bryn and Ronan to begin again.

The shadows were long when they left the tangle of woodland and entered a chequerboard landscape of tiny fields. Beyond the young, green crops they saw the river, where the sun cast a sheet of brilliance from the surface of still waters. Bryn hunted for his bearings now, and pointed west. Ronan turned his face to the setting sun, shaded his eyes, and a moment later murmured as he saw it.

The old Roman walls were not far now, and through a gap in the hills they glimpsed the ramparts of Eboracum. Mutely, wearily, they moved the horses onto the wain-rutted road, following a dry stone wall that bordered a barley crop. Farmers tended cattle in the meadows running down to the river bank, big men, Ronan observed, each armed with a warspear longer than he was tall. No man here was simply a farmer; and they had seen the strangers already.

A boy abandoned his geese and ran to a cluster of huts. Two words passed between him and the chieftain of the hamlet, and a moment later hooves drummed on the road. Ronan heard the jingle of harness and turned in the saddle to look eastward.

"We've been seen, Bryn."

"They're not blind," Bryn said quietly. "And you don't just ride into another chief's lands, unaccounted for. We knew we would be challenged."

Trespassers often came to blows, and Ronan's pulse quickened as they reined back to allow the chieftain and his three men to approach at their own speed. They would speak with Gareth Ironhand's authority here, if not his specific orders. Ronan lifted a brow at Bryn, who suggested,

"A polite smile may be in order."

The chieftain was a man old enough to be Ronan's father. His face was seamed and lined, his eyes nested in creases. Broadsword and Roman shortsword slapped at his thighs, and behind him, clad in deerskins, leathers and coarse linen, rode a smaller man, of an age to be Ronan's elder brother. His face was wide, pleasing though not handsome, and he at least seemed friendly. His hair was a mass of loose, dusty brown curls, long on his shoulders, and he alone greeted the intruders pleasantly.

The chieftain spoke in a voice roughened by the barley spirits. His grey eyes, narrowed suspiciously, examined Bryn first, and then Ronan, head to foot before he demanded, "What's your business here?"

Ronan and Bryn shared a tired glance. They were not a sight to inspire confidence, and they knew it. They were battered, dirty, smoke-blackened, and Ronan's tunic was dark with another man's blood. They were windblown, days overdue for barbering, and Ronan knew they must look like fugitives, perhaps like criminals. He watched as Bryn nudged his horse forward a pace and raised his right hand.

"We come from Derventio, to warn you. Angles attacked in the night. The town is in ruins, did you not see the smoke? I don't know if anyone is left alive. I am Bryn ap Gruffydd, the old chief's eldest."

The chieftain's suspicious look did not waver. He looked at Ronan now, saw the warrior's weapons — and the stains of old blood. "You fought? Where?"

"I fought at the village of Whitestonecliff," Ronan said, gruff with tiredness. "The Angles are everywhere. I was told they marched over the moor from Iarum, on the Tees. We were taken unawares, we have lost everything, and the most we can do is warn Gareth Ironhand."

The message seemed too terrible to accept. For some time the chieftain stroked his chin, glaring at the two battered strangers as he weighed up what they claimed. He cocked his head critically at Bryn. "You're Gruffydd's eldest? Gareth will know if you are, and if you're lying you shall toil your days out as his bondsman."

"Why would I lie?" Bryn demanded, a sharp edge of anger in his voice.

"Why would you?" The older man gave a disdainful sniff. "I don't trust either of you, but it's for Gareth to decide, not me." He snapped his fingers and the cavalrymen moved up. "Bind them. Let the Ironhand sort this out for himself."

The curly-haired young man with the friendly face brought his horse up. "You're as bad as a three-legged old fox, Ceard. You were caught once, and now you'll never trust another man as long as you live. Good gods, do they look dangerous?"

"I told you to bind them," Ceard barked tersely. "Do as you're bid, ill-mannered whelp."

The young man's mouth compressed but he took a fistful of thongs from his saddle and slid to the ground. He moved, Ronan saw, like a lithe young animal. He came to Ronan first, and shrugged his apologies. "He's a stupid old nanny goat, but he's the chieftain, gods only know why," he whispered. "Let me tie your wrists. Gareth will soon untie them again, and feed you while you tell your story. I'm Kynddelig, from Danum. You didn't say your name."

As his wrists were thonged loosely at his back, Ronan told his name and his village, and Kynddelig gave him a smile that might have been welcome before he went on to secure Bryn's hands. Red's halter was tied to Ronan's saddle, and Kynddelig led Ronan's and Bryn's horses forward by the bridles.

"There, Ceard, are you satisfied?"

"Aye, I am." Ceard regarded his prisoners hawkishly from beneath straggling brows. He stabbed a blunt finger at Bryn. "If you're who you say you are, ap Gruffydd, Gareth will know your face. Woe betide you if you're a poxed liar."

"I am Gruffydd's son, damn you," Bryn growled, too tired to be civil any longer. He looked down at Kynddelig, who was knotting the reins together to lead the horses. "How far is it? These bindings are already chafing me."

"Not far." Kynddelig mounted up and took the mass of reins in his left hand. "But we'll make slow time. Your little horse is lame. We'll travel at his pace, if you want to get him to Ebor without damaging him. Upon your order, my lord Ceard."

"Get along, get along," Ceard said dismissively, as if he suspected that Kynddelig was mocking him. Perhaps Kynddelig was.

He set a slow pace that Red could easily keep, along the twisting road that led to the gates of Gareth Ironhand's town. Ronan had never seen it before, and not even weariness could quell his astonishment. Rome had left a mountain of stone on the banks of the Usan. Much of the legionary fortification endured, though the troops had left the northcountry long ago. The walls were massively thick, built of grey stone. Ronan thought they would stand forever. And along the ramparts were armed guards, hard-faced men at whom Kynddelig shouted and waved, until their glares became smiles. They knew him, and the party passed by unchallenged. But let a stranger show his face here, Ronan observed, and it could easily come to blood.

The sounds and smells were new and fascinating, and Ronan's nostrils flared. Bryn had been here several times before and ignored much that made Ronan's eyes widen as they were led in through the open gates. A priest of Mithras was preaching just inside the gate, in a bass voice that made Ronan's hackles rise. Gaudy whores flaunted their wares from a tavern doorway opposite, and a girl blew kisses at Ronan. In the marketplace to their right, a merchant with the look and accent of Rome was peddling silks and spices, a cockfight had drawn a crowd of raucous gamblers, and a pair of half-naked wrestlers were mock-fighting for the entertainment of an audience that threw coins at their feet.

Crooked alleyways led off in every direction. The buildings inside the walls were mostly wood and wicker and thatch, just like those of Derventio, generations away from the original Roman houses. From the tavern came the pungent aroma of beer and coarse wine, and Ronan heard the rattle of dice, the bawdy songs of guardsmen. He licked his lips, aware of the dryness of his throat, as they were led about the marketplace and at last Kynddelig brought them to a halt outside a long, low timber hall, newly thatched with green heather.

Woodsmoke prickled the nostrils, and wolfhounds lay panting in the late afternoon sun which pooled at the front of the hall, where steps led up to wide double doors. Spearmen stood guard here too, black-bearded, fierce, and their warspears were dressed in fresh feathers, the blades so newly honed that they still shone.

From within the hall came the sweet sounds of harp and flute, and a mournful, passionate melody. Kynddelig slid to the ground and whistled for a boy to take the horses. Bryn and Ronan kicked out of the stirrups and Kynddelig beckoned them up the steps, by the growling hounds and watchful guards. A word to the dogs and they were quiet.

The hall was dim, smoky. Daylight shafted down from a hole in the thatch, over the hearths. Two score warriors and women lounged about, talking and drinking as they watched servants quarter a roast boar. Halfway down the hall, on the right, a broad bench draped in black and white sheepskins, faced the main hearth, and the man sitting there wore a scarlet cloak, the brightest colour, the only red, in the hall.

His body was thick with muscle and half-clad in brown leathers, and he wore his swords even here. His arms were heavy with ornaments, bronze and gold, and on a heavy chain about his neck hung the amulet of a chief. Gareth Ironhand's grey eyes were on the strangers, and he paused, wine cup halfway to his lips, as Kynddelig fetched them closer.

For one so respected, he was young. Ronan had expected a man of Cuddy's years, and was astonished, for Gareth could be no more than twenty-five summers. He was tall — taller than Bryn, broad shouldered, almost burly and yet as sleek as a hunter. His skin was smooth and nut brown, and as they drew closer to the firelight Ronan saw that he wore many intricate tattoos. His hair was black and cropped very short, in the Roman fashion, framing a face that some would have called handsome and none could have called unkind. To Ronan's eyes, Gareth did not have Bryn's rich beauty, but his looks were fine enough to turn a man's head, even when Ronan was so intent on Bryn.

As Kynddelig approached Gareth lifted a hand in greeting. Kynddelig inclined his head for a moment and looked up again with that ready smile. "Well met, Gareth. You have visitors, and the news is dire." He beckoned the prisoners forward. "They come from Derventio. . .or where Derventio *was*. The Angles came in the night. The smoke we saw was the whole town burning, and Gruffydd is dead. Ceard had me bind their hands out of suspicion, but by your leave, Ironhand, I'll cut them loose."

"Aye, and quickly." Gareth's voice was light, almost boyish, and yet compelling. He stood as Kynddelig retrieved his thongs, and came down into the firelight. Bronze rings gleamed in both his ears, and as he turned his head Ronan saw that his temples and jaw were tattooed with coiling blue serpents. He gestured for his visitors to sit and summoned a steward. "Bring wine and meat. These two have a starved aspect about them." Gareth fixed them with a hard look. "You fought, this I can see. There is no mistake about Derventio?"

"Mistake?" Bryn echoed bitterly as he sank down onto a bench. "I wish there were. My whole family is dead. Do you not know me, Gareth?" He turned his face to the firelight. "I'm Bryn."

For a moment Gareth frowned deeply at him, and then he swore by several gods who were strange to Ronan. "So you are. Gods be damned! You're cheated out of your inheritance, then, Bryn ap Gruffydd."

An elderly bondsman shuffled toward them with a pitcher of wine, and Ronan gulped his cup to the lees much too quickly. His head fogged and he surrendered to drowsiness, listening with only half an ear as Bryn told what he knew. Startled, horrified chatter rushed about the hall's warrior contingent, and at Ronan's shoulder Kynddelig said quietly, concernedly, "Are you injured, Ronan? You look unwell."

"I'm tired," Ronan confessed. He looked up eagerly as the old servant returned with a platter of pork, almost too hot to handle.

"You were lucky to get out of there alive," Kynddelig observed.

"Was I?" Ronan was already eating, teeth tearing famishedly at the meat. "I suppose I am, but my heart says I should have died fighting. I was hours too late. It was over before I arrived, and where's the honour in that?"

"Yet you're bloody." Kynddelig gestured at the rust-brown stains. "If that's not your blood, one Angle at least has his veins opened in vengeance for your family. You're half starved! Eat that, I'll send for more."

For an hour, Gareth Ironhand listened to every word, all they could remember, and he and his captains exchanged bleak looks. It was likely that some among the Angles who had razed Derventio were the same rievers who had attacked Eboracum weeks ago. That time, they had failed. An early warning was flashed up the coast by the old Roman signal towers and the cavalry had massed to stop them, miles from these walls.

"So they take Derventio this season," Gareth said thoughtfully. "For a year or two we shall have peace and quiet here, but they will be back, and Ebor will be next. Every spring, when the seas lighten and the east winds grow warm, they come at us again." He shook his head. "Many chiefs have been slaughtered. How long before they come at us again? We are a rich prize for an Angle captain."

"Grim thoughts, my lord," Bryn said. "Will you march on them, Ironhand? We could drive them back to Iarum, and to the sea, be rid of them. You have the numbers and the weapons to do it with."

"We've fought already this season," Gareth mused. "Some of us are still licking our wounds, and we have many of our own dead to remember from our last fight. What say you, Kyn?"

"If you told me to fight, I would fight," Kynddelig said drowsily. He sat by the fire, hands around a cup of wine, and he had been drinking steadily for an hour. "I'm half healed and my lover is as yet unavenged. I lost Fergal almost at the end of the battle, and I saw the scar-faced, whoreson devil who killed him. I pray every day to see that face again. Aye, Gareth, I would fight."

"And like as not be slow enough, still, to be killed by Scarface before Fergal is avenged!" Gareth rubbed his palms together and frowned at Bryn. "We're not yet ready to fight again. Next season, perhaps. I'd count it a pleasure to knock some empty Angle heads together, but this year... Look around you, Bryn. We're still weeping for our own dead, as you'll weep for yours." He paused, looking Bryn and Ronan over, two young warriors, tired and battered. "You live, and you hold up your heads after an Angle storm," he said slowly. "That proves your worth. But what now, for the two of you?"

Ronan had been gazing into the fire. The wine thickened his head and his wits were dull. "I could ride on," he said, thinking aloud. "I've never travelled far before, and I'd like to. Or I could ask if you need an extra sword here."

"We always need extra swords." Kynddelig smiled at him. "Especially after a battle."

"Are you any good?" Gareth leaned forward, firelight dancing in his eyes.

"Cuddy taught me, and told me that I am," Ronan said softly. "Did you know the swordmaster at Derventio? He taught me all his art and trickery, at Gruffydd's bidding. There is an Angle raider lying dead in the woods by Whitestonecliff, to mark my blooding. I learned my trade the hard way, Ironhand, but test me if you must."

The chief grinned, boyish and disarming. "Good enough. I'll not dishonour you by questioning your word. And you, Bryn?"

"Cuddy taught both of us," Bryn said simply. "Gruffydd's warband would have been mine to command one day, and I was schooled to lead it." His voice caught and his head bowed. "Forgive me, Gareth. My heart still refuses to believe what my head knows to be true."

"Aye." The Ironhand sighed. "We mourn our dead with every new campaigning season. New friends and kin replace the old, fill the empty spaces, but the lost ones are always with us, never forgotten." He spread his hands in a gesture of welcome. "You will have a home here, and a place in our cavalry. This is the best fortification left in the island. We've ships on the river, Angle slaves till our fields, and Ebor's cavalry horses are descended out of the royal Iceni and Brigante stables. Call this place your home, raise your swords for her. Or go your own way if you wish. You're freemen in my land."

The offer was vastly generous, and Bryn seemed barely able to grasp it. At last it was Ronan who made the decision for them both. "Where would we go?" he asked as Bryn blinked at him, foolish with the wine. "We can't just wander on and off the land of strange chiefs, even with friendly intentions. We came here with news, Ironhand, and that chieftain of yours, Ceard, had us bound by the wrists in a moment! No, I believe we'll stay. For the time being I've come far enough. I'm tired to the marrow of my bones. Bryn?"

And Bryn agreed. "No arguments from me, Gareth, You're more than generous, and I'm not so mindless as to refuse you."

"Good enough, then." Gareth slapped his thigh. "Kyn, look to their needs. Settle them in quarters and see that they're well armed."

"Count it done." Kyn smiled up at Gareth and then offered his wrist in greeting, first to Ronan, then to Bryn. "Welcome among us. One day we shall break angle heads together."

"One day soon," Bryn agreed.

"You may break a few Angle skulls sooner than you think," Gareth told him ruefully. "We must move swiftly, no later than tomorrow, to secure our northern border against the raiders. Let them settle in Derventio, burn their dead, lick their wounds, in a month they'll be *here*. We'll be pitching them off our own walls. We must secure them where they are, make sure they come not one step further south. We'll need a warband to guard the frontier, and it must ride out tonight." He shook his head emphatically as Bryn opened his mouth, obviously to volunteer. "Not with you, ap Gruffydd, not yet. Rest. Time enough later for your vengeance! It will be all the sweeter if you come home alive to enjoy it!"

It was twilight when they left the hall. No stars showed through the thick overcast, and rain was on the air. Eboracum — 'Ebor' as its people called it — was quiet now, the market abandoned, and lamplight shone from the cracks about a door here, a window shutter there. Kynddelig was yawning as he led the way from Gareth Ironhand's hall, turned left by its north corner and ambled through the darkness with the ease of one who knew this place intimately.

A cat mewled as they passed. Its eyes reflected some little light escaping from the house across the way, and Kyn spoke softly to it by name. "The barracks are full," he told Bryn, who was a pace on his heels. "But a friend of mine was killed in the fighting and his house is still empty. You can stay there, at least until you decide for yourselves where you want to be."

"Fergal?" Ronan whispered. "Was it your lover's house?"

"No. Fergal lived with me, quartered between the barracks and the stable." Kyn spoke with a tone of deep sorrow. "Fergal died well, for what it's worth, but I wish. . ." He shook his head. "Come this way. Don't worry about your horses and your belongings, I shall send for them in the morning."

He had brought them to a low, thatched house built of planks on stone foundations which were still blackened by the fire that had demolished the original house. Those were Roman foundations, and this might have been the home of a legionary commander or a rich merchant, Ronan knew. That house was gone now, its stone and brick replaced by timbers logged in the forest not five miles away. Pivots squealed for want of oil as the door opened, and they waited, watched, as Kyn struck flint to steel.

Tinder caught alight in the hearth, and they saw that the house was just as Kyn's friend had left it. Blankets were stacked in a corner, a calf hide lay on the bench by the hearth; half-cut thonging, a scatter of tools and utensils littered the floor. A basket of firewood stood by the door, a knife was jammed by its point into the scarred old table, and strings of onions hung from the rafters.

Kyn lit the wicks of three brass lamps and picked up a stone jar, still full of ale. "Whatever is here is yours. The food will be ruined, so come to the hall and eat with us. No one has laid claim to this house. I think we all see Connor here, in every shadow, every corner. But since you never knew him. . .well, if you like the place, be at home here. I think Connor will sleep the sweeter, knowing that his house and his things have passed into the care of young men with all their lives before them." Kyn smiled wistfully. "He was alone, never wed, the last of his house, and no children to come after him, you see."

"It's a nice house," Ronan said thickly as his eyes prickled, for he was thinking of Dafydd then, and all the simple things the boy had wanted. Dafydd would have loved this little house. It would have shone, would have smelt of baking bread and been warm and welcoming as any home. He forced his thoughts back to the present and found Kyn looking strangely at him. "Thank you, Kynddelig. Just let us sleep, and I'll wager we'll make better sense tomorrow."

"Sleep well, then. I'll introduce you to your sword brothers in the morning."

The door slammed behind Kyn, and Ronan stood numbly at the fireside. It seemed he had come a thousand miles since morning, and aged a hundred years. He looked across the fire at Bryn's tired, dirty face, and saw not a rival but an ally. "We're lucky. I was half afraid that Gareth wouldn't know you. It must be some time since he's seen you, and he might have remembered you as a boy. You're a man now, and there's. . .quite a difference."

"I know." Bryn rubbed his face. "I was anxious, I knew it could go badly for us — that chieftain told the truth. Gareth has strangers in irons, fast, and it takes months to earn freedom. There's no trust here, no one can afford it. It's all a matter of defences, Ronan, they don't mean anything by it. No one trespasses here."

But Ronan's brow creased. "They saw the smoke, so Kyn said. They knew something had happened at Derventio. No matter who we were, we had the same message to give." His words were slurred with weariness.

"Come here." Bryn held out his hands, and Ronan went silently to him. Bryn took both his wrists, clasped them rightly. "You're stubbled, you're dirty, you smell like a horse, and I want to go to bed with you."

Ronan smiled faintly. "Once, you would have spurned me for those things."

"Once, I was a fool." Bryn took a breath, held it. "Will you go to bed with me, Ronan? I promise you, I'll not be the arrogant bastard you expect, for I've nothing to be arrogant about now." He touched the stain on Ronan's tunic. "You're the blooded warrior, not me."

"Not yet. Soon." Ronan came closer, moved against him and set his head down on Bryn's wide shoulder. "Does it unman me if I confess, I wish you would hold me."

"Only if I am unmanned by the same feeling." Bryn's arms went about him. "That bed looks soft as goose feathers. Lie down with me. Don't fret, for I'm too tired to take advantage of you!"

"More's the pity." Ronan drew back and pulled his tunic off. "My gods, I stink like a pig. Blood and smoke and sweat and horse." He yawned deeply. "Then again, so do you." He undressed quickly and spread his clothes out in the hopes they would air and smell fresher in the morning. Only when he was done did he realise that Bryn had not moved, nor taken his eyes off him. He felt the heat flush in his cheeks, felt the pulse in his throat. "What is it, Bryn?"

"You." The wraith of a smile tugged one corner of Bryn's

mouth. "You are as beautiful as any young man I have ever seen. When I'm rested, I know I'll want you in every way you can imagine. If it offends your damned pride, tell me so before we go any further."

"Flatters me, rather," Ronan corrected. He looked down at his own body with a critical eye and gave a self-mocking grunt. "Cuddy put these muscles on me. Two months ago, I was a scrawny boy."

"You are a man now," Bryn whispered. "And a most desirable one." But he yawned too, and tipped back his head, worked his neck to and fro. "And I am — a eunuch! As a rule, my loins would be ablaze at the sight of you like this, but I seem to be gelded tonight." He glanced pointedly at Ronan's lax genitals. "And you?"

"The same." Ronan stretched, artlessly sensual as a cat, and investigated the bed. "It's straw after all, but the mattress is well packed and the skins smell clean." Thick white sheepskins cushioned his back as he stretched out and he groaned. "Oh, my spine never thought to rest again." At the rustle of clothes he opened his eyes, watched Bryn undress in the firelight, and smiled. "How do you want me? And what will you give me?" His eyes roamed from Bryn's smooth breast to his groin where his cock was thick, even in repose. Ronan shivered as he imagined that spear haft inside him, for he knew what Bryn must want.

The mattress dipped as Bryn eased himself down. "What do you want from me?" He turned on his side and pulled Ronan against him with rough tenderness. "You know well enough what I desire!"

"I want the same," Ronan murmured. His lips followed the line of Bryn's collar bone, his nostrils flared at the pungent, male smell of him. "But I imagine you, a chief's son, have never submitted to that. Will I be your first, or will you refuse me?"

To his surprise Bryn made soft sounds of rueful humour. "I've been sundered already, and it was years ago. A glass merchant in Catreath had me. He hurt me a lot, which robbed the act of pleasure, but I know you'll be more patient. I know how much delight a man is supposed to reap from his own ravishment, and I've waited for the right lover to pleasure me, instead of hurting me again."

"And I'm the one?" Ronan was astonished, and deeply gratified. "Days ago, you threatened to have me taken out and flogged."

"Did I?" Bryn kissed him. "That was in another life, another world. All I remember is that we fought on the bank of a stream, and I saw you with a sword, your clothes filthy with a dead man's blood, and a look of scorn on your face as you turned aside my sword with tricks Cuddy once taught me. You were blooded, and I. . .when my family was being butchered, I was out bedding a lad. I felt worthless, shamed. I bent my neck and asked you to kill me. And instead, you held me."

"Oh, Bryn." Ronan held him again. "I would not have killed you, no matter what you thought of me. Once, I'd have relished the chance to bloody your nose! But, kill you? You are too beautiful. Perhaps I wanted you all along, but could never have you. And now?"

"You can have me," Bryn murmured. "Now, all we have is each other," he continued, so softly that Ronan struggled to hear him. "And it's enough. Gods help us both,"

They said no more, and soon Ronan realised that Bryn was asleep. He pulled up the sheepskins and settled, eager for rest, but as soon as his eyes closed the dreams began. A dead face looked accusingly at him — his sword snapped like a twig when he raised it, and Bryn's voice cried hollowly out of a shallow, unmarked grave beneath the elms in the paddock where Gruffydd's warband had once practised.

Ronan jerked awake in a cold sweat, with his heart slamming painfully against his ribs. Beside him, Bryn was too exhausted to stir and he forced himself down onto the sheepskins again, praying for blind sleep, if not for pleasant dreams.

10

A banging at the door woke them, and Bryn was out of the bed before he was half awake. His heart beat at his ribs, urging fight or flight, but it was only Kyn with a basket of bread and meat and pastries for breakfast.

To Bryn's astonishment it was already mid-morning. He ate hungrily, eyes following Ronan as he slung a kettle over the fire for hot water and searched through some other man's things for a razor. The house was just as Connor had left it. His shaving knives were sharp, his combs and linen were clean, everything they could have wanted was to hand, as if they were the guests of a generous host. Perhaps they were; but their host was dead.

Methodically, carefully, Ronan razored his jaw, and passed the shaving knives to Bryn. His cheeks were smooth as a young boy's, deserving of kisses, but he ducked Bryn's advances and raked his nails through Bryn's stubble. With a grunt, Bryn picked up the razor and was almost finished when Kynddelig arrived from the barracks with their belongings and a basket of oddments.

"Clothes," Bryn observed as he rummaged and found clean tunics and linen.

"You're starting out with nothing," Kynddelig said thoughtfully. "You got out with your lives, and were lucky at that. You'd be surprised how many of us here at Ebor arrived as fugitives, dirty and famished, desperate for Gareth's protection.

"Even you?" Ronan asked.

"Even I." Kyn gave him a smile. "You slept well?"

"Well enough." Ronan looked away. "I. . .dream. How much do we owe for all this, and to whom?"

"Gareth, I suppose," Kyn said offhandly. "Not that it matters. You'll be well paid for your service to the warband. I don't know that Gareth keeps any particular accounting."

"We've a horse to sell too." Bryn lifted a brow at Ronan. "Red would fetch a handsome sum."

"The little stallion with the lame foreleg?" Kyn seemed surprised. "Why don't you race him instead? You could make more in one scurry, what with the purse and the betting, than you'd get from his sale."

"Run him?" Bryn sat back on his heels by the hearth and watched Ronan pour three mugs of the rich, apple-sweet ale. "We could, Ronan."

"Your decision." Ronan handed the mugs around. "It was your father's nag, I only trained him. I'll jockey him for you, if you like, but Red belongs to you, to sell or race as you decide." He looked over at Kyn. "Mind you, I'll be in Gareth's debt for this house, the clothes, even this food, until I'm paid. As you said, Kyn, we got out with nothing save our lives. Best tell Gareth this. I can turn my hand to many jobs, if I ought to work. Horses and harness were my work before I was taught the warrior trade."

"I'll talk to Gareth for you," Kyn promised. "But for now, come and meet your fellows. You're the talk of Ebor since last night."

Brass lamps and three hearths lit the cavalry barracks, a long, low building constructed of whole trunks and thickly thatched in fresh heather. Men and boys lay dozing on the cots ranked along the wall, and several were drinking by the main fireplace as Kynddelig made quiet introductions. *Cavalry*, Bryn thought as he saw the saddles, leathers, smelt the unmistakable scent of horses and harness. It was a familiar, comfortable smell that made him feel at home. Gareth's whole establishment was much more regimented than Gruffydd's, but the company was more than congenial.

Kyn had a ready smile and unfailing good humour, and his friends were quick to offer their hands in greeting.

By the hearth, a tall, fair-haired youth raised his cup, and tossed an empty mug to Kyn as he appeared. His right arm was bound tight to his chest, bearing out Gareth's remark that some among Eboracum's fighting men were still licking their wounds.

"Yon one-armed one is Taran," Kyn told them. "Taran, from Cambria."

"One-armed, is it?" Taran had the sweet, singsong accent of the far westcountry. "We'll see about that when I get these bandages off! And these two are joining us, Kyn?" He gave his good hand to Ronan. "We need all the new blood we can get."

"The fighting was so bad?" Bryn took the man's hand as Ronan released it.

"It was." Taran and Kyn sat by the fire, and Kyn slung his good arm around his friend's shoulders. "We held them off, but it was savage work. But for Gareth's thinking we might have lost out. Ebor could be an Angle stronghold today."

"Gareth is young, for a war leader," Ronan mused. "I'd expected a man much older."

"Oh, he's old enough." Kyn topped up his cup from an earthen pitcher of spring water. "Hereabouts, we measure a man's age not in his years but in his battles. And by that measure, Gareth us very old indeed. He was blooded at thirteen, when the Angles raided up the river, more than a decade ago. His sister swung a sword beside him that day. I was only a child. It's right and fitting that Gareth should command here. He's earned the name of Ironhand time and again. Now, tell us your story. Every man in this barracks wants to hear what became of Derventio."

Rain pattered on the thatch as, once again, Bryn and Ronan told the story. Much of the time, Ronan sat listening to Bryn, for Bryn had a way with words, and then Bryn would fall silent as some shade possessed him and Ronan would take up the tale. Raindrops splashed through the smoke hole and sizzled on the hearthstones; Ronan whispered that the sound reminded him of home, that he could not hear it without the memories flooding him. He leaned heavily on Bryn's shoulder and was grateful when Bryn's arm went around him.

"Are you lovers?" Kynddelig asked quietly, when Bryn paused for breath. Just then, Eboracum's fighting men were preoccupied, remembering their own dead.

"Not quite. Not yet," Bryn admitted. "We never found a way before the Angles came, and have been too tired since. Last night we bedded together for the first time and went right to sleep."

"There is always tonight," Taran teased. "It's best for warriors to take warrior mates, don't you agree? Gareth thinks so. He'll have no wedded men in the warband, did you know that? No husbands and fathers leaving widows and orphans behind. The Christian folk don't like the arrangement, but they know better than to challenge the Ironhand. And among us, you two are welcome." He sat with his good arm around Kynddelig's waist and, like a big cat, rubbed against him. "Some of us are friends, some are lovers, all are sword brothers. It's just as well that you're not eager for wives and children. If you were, Gareth would tell you to hang up your swords."

Surprised, Bryn's brows rose. "This is an unusual place."

"Only since Gareth's time." Kynddelig stirred and rubbed his left thigh. "The wound is paining me today, Taran. All this rain does me no good."

"I'll rub you, if you lie down," Taran offered, and Kyn was pleased to accept.

He stretched out by the hearth, head on his lean forearms. Taran sat beside him, his good hand working on the cramped, aching limb. "Gareth was taught to read," Kyn went on drowsily. "He learned Latin and history. He'll tell you of the Greeks and the barbarians, and a Sacred Band of warriors in a city called Thebes. I don't know where it was, but it was far away from this island. The Sacred Band was made up of lovers." He shared a smile with Taran at that. "This band of ours is not quite so distinguished, but we have our battles to fight, and Gareth is right. We leave no widows and orphans behind us. Brother Peter gives us dirty looks, but holds his tongue!"

"A monk?" Ronan accepted a cup from a boy with wide blue eyes and freckles.

"The confessor from the monastery." Kynddelig stretched under the welcome treatment. "A fat-bellied young sod with a little shaved patch on the top if his head that goes pink in the sun, a big book in one hand, and a wicked knotted rope in the other. He said the devil will burn us for our sins. Gareth said no gentle god would ever allow a demon to torture the souls of men who died fighting to protect women and children. Brother Peter had no answer to that."

Bryn frowned, for he was thinking of the merchant, Marcus Duratius, and his daughter, Aemilia. "You're not a Christian, Kyn?"

"Me? No." Kynddelig sat up and tousled Taran's hair in thanks. "If I pray, which I seldom do, it's to Cernunnos, the horned one, or perhaps to Mithras, who was a warrior's god. There's no Christian in the barracks that I'm aware of. A few fought with us, once, but were killed years ago. Killed honourably, mind, which is better than a half-life in Angle slave chains."

"But Gareth said you keep Angle slaves, for labour," Ronan said pointedly.

"Just as the Angles keep Britons for labour," Taran said almost indifferently. "It is the way of things. As a warrior, you know that. You fight, you take your chances."

He was right. Bryn looked into the fire and acknowledged the chill that prickled through him. Taran was a stranger who looked at him and saw not a child, not a youth, but a man grown, and a professional fighting man at that. Youth was over, swept away. Bryn closed his eyes. Among these people, he was a warrior. Ronan had no peasant past to live down, and neither of them had a point to prove or a score to settle, no debts owed, save to Gareth Ironhand himself. Bryn sighed, pleased when Ronan's arm wound more securely about him.

But it was a woman's voice that whispered into the darkness of his mind, and Bryn was thinking of Sian. Fey Sian of the Deer people, who had been taught by the last Brigante Druids, and who spoke with the voice of ages past. She would tell the stories of the years before Rome — and even then tribe fought against tribe. The stories were blood-soaked, feuds and raids, great loves and great hates. The Romans and the Angles had not fetched war into this land; the tribes had never been at peace. No matter when he and Ronan had been born, Bryn knew, this would have been their destiny.

He was quiet for so long, preoccupied with his thoughts, that Ronan leaned closer and murmured, "Are you sickening?"

"No." Bryn's hand moulded about Ronan's knee. "Haunted, Listening to dead voices that speak of other times. . .or perhaps they speak of the future."

Kynddelig stood and stamped his foot. "My thanks Taran. The ache is almost nothing now, I am whole again. Now, I'll speak to Gareth for you, Ronan. Perhaps he wants you to work, but I doubt it. More likely, he'll bribe you to ride with the cavalry. And in any case, you can run your little red stallion in a fortnight's time, if his leg is mended. Some of the fastest horses between here and Danum will be running."

"And that horse is like lightning," Bryn said smugly, "and Ronan is the best jockey you're likely to see in Ebor for a long, long time! Talk to the Ironhand, though. Already we're in debt.

Like Ronan, I've no taste for it.

"Then I'll go now," Kynddelig decided, and took a cloak from the rack by the door, since the rain was still falling.

They waited an hour for his return, and Ronan half expected to be working before the day was out. His resigned grumbles made Bryn exasperated, and as Bryn had guessed, he was wrong anyway. Upon his return, Kynddelig placed several silver coins in his hand, and several more in Bryn's.

"What's this for?" Ronan wanted to know, though he was quick to accept the coins.

"Bribery, as I told you. An advance against what you'll be paid when you ride with us," Kyn told him. "Gareth knows that freemen must be wooed to stay here, or he'll lose you both. There are rich pickings in Cambria for men who have the courage to answer the call to arms."

"The great war leader, Artos," Bryn mused, counting the coins with a sense of satisfaction.

"Artos," Kynddelig agreed. "He's raising cavalry in old Caerleon, to chase the Saxons back to the sea and drown them there. Gareth loses men every week as more and more ride west to join Artos and that great archdruid of his, the one with magic enough to turn back the tide and pluck the stars out of the sky." He cocked his head at Bryn and Ronan. "Is it in your heart that you'll go west and join him?"

"One day, perhaps," Ronan admitted. "Who hasn't heard the stories? But not yet."

"Our fight isn't with Saxons," Bryn added, "but with Angles." He gave Ronan a speculative look. "With money in my hand, I've an itch to spend. Will you go marketing with me? We need a good many things."

Despite the rain the market was busy. They threaded among the stalls, shouldered for space between Eboracum's common people, and haggled for leathers and linen, whetstones and olive oil, without which even a fine sword would dull and rust away.

But the olive oil made Bryn look thoughtfully at Ronan, and Ronan blushed as if he knew full well what Bryn was thinking. When Bryn slipped his arm about Ronan's waist to urge him back to their house, Ronan did not protest.

The door closed and bolted, the shutters were secured, and three lamps fluttered to life in the thick, companionable dimness. Bryn had dropped their purchases by the door, but he gave the phial of oil to Ronan, who held it to the lamplight with fingers that trembled just a little.

"You know I want you." Bryn's voice was deep, almost a purr. "And you know how. Kyn and the others took us for lovers. It's not true yet, and it ought to be. Gareth is right, men with women and children have no place in a warband that is fighting constantly. If you and I died tomorrow, who would be the poorer for it? Only ourselves, if we were unloved. . .and who else will love us?"

The stopper lifted out of the phial. The oil was thick, viscous. Ronan's throat bobbed as he swallowed, and he pressed a hand to his middle as if his belly fluttered with last-minute apprehensions. "Is that what you want from me, Bryn? Love? I thought you hated me, once."

"I never hated you. In another life, I resented you. A life in which I was an arrogant young idiot, riding for a fall." Bryn's hands closed on Ronan's upper arms, he leaned closer, laid his cheek against Ronan's soft hair. "Are you thinking that I'll hurt you for the sport of it?" Ronan looked up almost guiltily. "Trust me," Bryn said softly. "No matter what you may think of me, I've never hurt a lover, not even to bruise him."

From somewhere Ronan produced a faint smile. "Then show me. You're not my first, you know. Did you want to be?"

"It doesn't matter." Bryn kissed him as he slowly, deliberately undressed him. He dropped his own clothes carelessly, and pressed Ronan onto the bed. As Ronan sprawled back, Bryn explored every hard contour and curve of his breast with teasing lips. "Who was your first?"

"A woodcutter." Ronan held Bryn's head to his chest as his nipples were gently bitten. "I can't say he hurt me much, for he was quite small and I was very excited. . .and there have been others since then. A shepherd, a warrior from Catreath. I had some younger boys too, who wanted me to do to them what the older men did to me. I've always loved to be with men or boys. And you?"

"The same. We're more alike than you know." Bryn rested his cheek on Ronan's flat belly and considered the hard young cock, an inch from his nose. "I think I know every touch that would bring you alive." He moved down that inch and his lips encircled Ronan's shaft. It was hard as a lance wrapped inside of smooth, hot velvet, it smelt musky and tasted of salt, it was hot and its veins pulsed on his tongue, and Bryn loved it. He closed his eyes to savour the taste and sensation as he took Ronan into his throat and bobbed his head.

Breathless, Ronan could barely move or think, and he mocked himself. "Every time I imagined your love," he whispered, "while I lay with Dafydd, I saw myself tumbled in the hayloft and spread wide, used carelessly and then discarded. How wrong could I have been!"

Bryn lifted his head, replaced his lips with his fingers and swirled caresses about Ronan's swollen balls. "Or would the arrogant Bryn ap Gruffydd, before the Angles came, have used you roughly, to teach you that you were just a stable boy?" he murmured. Ronan did not answer — had probably not even heard — and Bryn put his head back down once more to suckle and cherish.

At last he moved up, covering Ronan's whole body with his own. Twin shafts nestled together and Ronan's arms went about him. Bryn was very much aware of Ronan's smaller stature, yet astonished by his strength. Growing excited, he almost lifted Bryn physically as his hips humped and thrust, and Bryn caught his hands, pinned them by his tousled head.

"I want you, Ronan. I want you so much. Please."

In answer, Ronan's legs spread. His eyes were hazed with some mix of lust and astonishment, his breathing was ragged, and he swore in a hoarse undertone as his legs were lifted up over Bryn's shoulders. He caught his breath sharply as two oily fingers slid into him without warning, but Bryn was gentle and patient, and Ronan seemed to will himself to be calm.

Heart pounding like a mallet, Bryn reined back on the impulse to take and use. Beneath him, Ronan was so trusting, and Ronan was the blooded warrior with an Angle kill to his credit. Bryn's fingers, deep buried, discovered the soft, moist heart of Ronan's body, and his cock ached to have that too.

Slowly Ronan relaxed. His head pressed back into the sheepskins, his eyes closed, and Bryn kissed his breast, his belly. "You're ready, aren't you?" An inarticulate murmur answered him. "I'll take that as your invitation." Bryn withdrew his fingers and moved up.

A wild little cry escaped Ronan's throat as he was pierced. Bryn growled like a hunting cat, for Ronan was tight as a fist, hot as an oven. Sheathed to the balls, Bryn rocked on him, into him, and Ronan's musk dizzied him. Bryn thought he would never forget the scent and the feel of Ronan at love, and he thrust hard, harder yet, not surprised when Ronan cried out sharply and came. The deep contractions racking his body demanded climax of Bryn also and, helpless as a boy, he surrendered.

How long they lay tangled and panting, they did not know, but at last Bryn forced himself to his senses and looked into Ronan's flushed face. "You were very pleasured," he said thickly, fighting

117

his tongue for the power to speak at all.

"Very pleased," Ronan echoed. "You were more patient than I could have imagined." His hands followed the curve of Bryn's skull, nape and shoulder. "You, who could have had a chief's daughter to wed. Why do you want me?"

Bryn's brows arched at the unexpected question. "I don't know, save that you're lovesome, and after all male, which I prefer to the other. Beautiful." Ronan's cheeks warmed with a blush once more. "And you're a warrior," Bryn added soberly, "of my age, and from a time and a place that are gone. You're the nearest to kin I shall ever have."

"I'm from the rat-hole of Whitestonecliff, remember," Ronan said drily. "I've not forgotten that."

"You must," Bryn sighed. "It's gone, Ronan, all of it. None of that means anything any longer."

"I know." Ronan arched his spine to ease it and looked up at Bryn with a curious smile. "You know what I want from you." Intent on his lover's hard breast, Bryn only nodded. "I want what you took from me just now," Ronan added, lest there be any mistake. "When I've had that from you, then we shall properly be lovers."

"Equals," Bryn guessed. "Make it soon, then." He kissed Ronan noisily and rolled up off the bed. "But not now. I want to look at Red's leg. He might run in their scurry in a fortnight, and he might win, if you ride him."

"He'll let no one else ride him," Ronan said scornfully as he washed swiftly and reached for his clothes. "Red may belong to you in law, but *he* thinks otherwise."

"Then perhaps he belongs to us both." Bryn's arms draped about Ronan's shoulders from behind, "If he wins, we share his winnings evenly."

"And if he loses, we share the loss." With his breeches back on, Ronan turned into Bryn's embrace. "I think I like sharing with you. Sharing all things." He looked at the rumpled bed and smiled. "Including that."

"Especially that." Bryn turned Ronan's face back toward him, cupped it in both hands. "You could have killed me, after we fought in the woods. I asked you to, and I was sure you would. Fear was in my marrow like ice. You touched my back and my neck with the tip of your sword and I thought, Camulus, this is the end of me! I prayed only for you to make it quick."

"Oh, Bryn!" Ronan began, exasperated.

But Bryn was not listening. "How does it feel to kill a man?

You're blooded. Tell me."

The question clearly startled Ronan. He puffed out his cheeks and seemed to hunt for words, or for the truth within himself. "Hot in the belly, cold in the chest. Fear and excitement, like a kind of sickness. Almost like being aroused, but not to sex, not to love. Your arms feel weak, your heart is wild with fear and excitement, and he seems so much quicker and stronger than you, and then. . .then you see his rhythm, you see your chance and you take it, and you feel surprised. It's as your teacher said. The sword is sharp as a razor, and it slides in like. . .like cutting fruit. His eyes bulge and he drops his weapons. When he falls to his knees the sword comes out, and it makes an awful sound. A horrible sound. Blood spurts from the wound, on your hands, everywhere. You smell his entrails, you smell death. It has a reek you won't ever forget, though you wish you could. His eyes become sightless as you watch, as if a light has gone out, and you realise that a man's life has ended at your hands." He started suddenly, as if jerking awake, and took a breath. "I can tell you no more, Bryn. I would not have killed you after we fought. I could not have."

"Yet I thought you would." Bryn stooped for Ronan's tunic and handed it to him, watched him put it on. "My time will come, both in that bed, and in battle."

"You sound eager." Ronan tugged the tunic down and buckled his baldric over it.

"Eager for one, Ronan, not for the other." Bryn swatted Ronan's backside. "Now, come and look at Red's leg. If we have any chance of an honest fortune in this place, he is it."

11

Big ships came up the Ambri with the tide. Most were Roman vessels, and the more shallow-keeled could skim the mud flats on the estuary. They were rowed up the narrowing, winding waterways and dropped anchor when the banks ahead became too close for them to turn about. They hailed from Karitia, in Gallia, from Africa, from Rome herself, and in the riverside taverns seamen told stories of a troubled land across the Narrow Sea.

Bryn sat over a cup of ale, listening with keen ears. The fighting across the water brought raiders and, worse, settlers to the island's eastern shores. As far away as the mountains of Cambria, the Britons were restless, watchful. Every year, the Saxon and the Angle marched inward — and often they fought each other, squabbling for land that had been stolen from chiefs like Gruffydd and Gareth a single season before.

Only a dozen miles north of Eboracum's walls, where the woodland had been hewn back for fields by generations of Derventio's farmers, Angle guards now patrolled with warspears, keeping vigil on the new frontier.

Two days after the burning of Derventio the first skirmish was fought. A hunting party came to blows before an uneasy truce could be called, but even a tacit agreement to respect the frontier did not contain the Angle scouts. They were in the forest to the south of the Derventio, they were seen and heard there, no matter that they denied it, and the security of Eboracum itself was precarious.

It was like keeping a bear in the stable yard, on a short chain with weak links, and the situation could only get worse. Three times, Bryn had counselled fighting before winter and, reluctantly, Gareth had to admit, he may be right. Ebor's warband would fight in the end, winner take all, as so many chiefs had fought to hold dominion over their vulnerable coastline.

The traders from Gallia and Rome spoke of coming west to settle, but Alba was little more peaceful than the crumbling remnants of the old Empire. Only in the far west, in Cambria, was there safety from the invaders. The Angles themselves were fleeing from barbarians who poured out of distant lands, far in the east, and not even Rome was safe. Bryn could scarcely believe the tale of the sacking of the great city itself, but three merchants told the same story independently, and he knew it must be true.

Overnight, after the burning of Derventio, the Angle slaves vanished to a man from the fields around Eboracum. The moment their guards' backs were turned, the labourers fled into the forest.

A day after they ran, the first raiding party skirted the forest and stabbed into Gareth's land. A few sheep were carried off, a few head of cattle and pigs, several horses. Gareth had expected no less and could afford the loss, but he was still angry. That morning, horns brayed across Eboracum, mustering the warband for duty.

The frontier was decided as a line from the hills to the sea. It passed through the camp at Dubgall, and a garrison was posted there. Every week, men went up from Eboracum to relieve their exhausted fellows, and men returning from 'the line' told of Angle warriors just across the no-man's-land, of the sun gleaming on drawn swords, and words shouted in a strange tongue, that might have been insults and taunts.

The season's truce was as yet undocumented, unspoken, but a

state of armed peace settled, and for the moment at least Gareth accepted it. Next summer, the summer after, they would fight again, but that was soon enough.

* * *

Rain fell for several days before the sun broke through and the wind grew warm. Red's leg was not badly lamed, and Ronan had him out on a leading rein every morning, before the routine cavalry practice. Bryn rode with him, and often they would stop to rest the little stallion, miles to the south of Eboracum, quite alone, and make love in the early morning sun. Each lovemaking brought them closer, and Bryn keenly felt his kinship with Ronan.

Red was fit and strong in a week, and Ronan rode rather than leading him. Even now the horse would allow no other rider. In the meadows along the river, Ronan gave him his head, encouraged him to extend himself to the limit in preparation for the coming race. Since Eboracum lay miles away no one saw his speed and agility; he would enter the event as an outsider and the wagering would go his way. Bryn and Ronan saved four silver coins to gamble. If he won, they would earn enough in an hour to live well for a year, and Bryn was sure Red would win.

The morning of the scurry was warm and humid. Ronan was bare-chested, already beginning to grow brown with the season. Bryn watched him with lazy appreciation as he worked the horse gently, enough to limber but not tire him, since he would race soon. He looked very good. And so, Bryn thought, did Ronan. Lust was a constant companion now. He could seldom see Ronan's body without wanting him, and Ronan was always eager for games.

Three times in the fortnight they had been at Eboracum, he had let Bryn enter his body. Often he said that he desired Bryn in the same way, but he had made no move yet, as if he was half convinced that Bryn would refuse him, and rejection would be more painful than never asking at all.

Bryn gave him a smile as he brought the stallion back up the riverbank. Both Ronan and the horse were sheened with sweat, and Ronan was satisfied. He slid off and sprawled out on his belly under the white willows at the edge of the water. Across the river, a shepherd called to his animals; white butterflies danced in the primrose, and swallows darted across the river's smooth surface. Bryn saw none of this. He straddled Ronan's slim hips and massaged his shoulders, his breasts, loving the feel of a young man's muscles. Surely nothing compared with this sensation, and Bryn was gratified when Ronan gave a pleasured squirm.

"We shall win," he said shrewdly. "I've looked over the other nags, Bryn, and they're good, but they're not good enough. And I've two silver coins to wager. You have the winner's purse, of course, since you own the horse."

"But I owe you the jockey's pay," Bryn added glibly, "and since I shall very likely lavish the rest on you in gifts, you'll finish the day with everything." He leaned down and kissed Ronan's mouth deeply. "And you will have another prize, if you win. So you *must* win."

"The money and gifts will suffice." Ronan's supple body stretched.

A thrill of delicious lust lanced through Bryn's groin. "The prize will be one of those gifts, then. And my pleasure to give it to you."

"Give what to me?" Ronan demanded.

Bryn took a breath. "My body. It's yours, but you've not claimed it yet. I've begun to feel cheated out of my pleasure."

Determinedly, Ronan rolled him off, turned over and propped his chin in his palm in the grass. "Do you mean that, Bryn? I thought long and hard about asking for that, and at the last decided not to." He huffed a sigh. "It has been no hardship to me to be mounted and ridden! But before the Angles came you were such an arrogant sod."

"I was," Bryn agreed. "But it seems half a lifetime ago. Camulus, is it only weeks? It might as well be a year. Kyn said, time and tears and kindness heal all wounds. He must be right."

"He is." Ronan captured Bryn's head to kiss. "I would sooner not ask for favours than ask and be denied. If I'm desperate to mount a willing body, I can find a boy from the cavalry stable who would oblige me."

"A boy from the stable?" Bryn sat up. "You would bed with another and betray me? You would *cuckold* me?"

"You sound outraged." Ronan punched Bryn's shoulder none too gently. "We never vowed fidelity, Bryn. And I would sooner mount a lad from the stable that be rejected by my lover."

Filled with exasperation, Bryn hissed through his teeth. "I have no intentions of refusing you. But if you cuckold me, Ronan, if you do that, I shall certainly be furious."

"You mean that, don't you?" Ronan turned over onto his back again and pillowed his head on one forearm. "You want me for yourself alone, as if we had vowed before a priest."

Heat crept into Bryn's cheeks, and he lifted his chin. "And if I do, what of it? You're mine!" And then, with boyish hesitancy, "Aren't you?"

"Yes." Ronan tugged him into the grass and pressed against him. "Then we had better promise to keep faith with each other, so long as we remain together. And I think I had better take what is mine, and soon." He slipped his hand about and cupped Bryn's round buttock. "I've longed for this, every moment, Bryn."

Bryn's eyes closed, squeezed shut. Through the clench of his teeth he whispered, "I love you." The confession seemed to be tortured from him, and yet as soon as it was spoken a sweet, familiar warmth coiled through his belly.

"How long have I wished to hear that, too," Ronan murmured. "A pledge of faith, then." He took Bryn's hand and placed it on his own chest, over his heart. "I shall bed with no others, nor kiss them, till we are separated by death, or we farewell each other from choice. Say the same to me, while you have the courage!"

"It doesn't take courage," Bryn muttered. He rested his cheek on Ronan's soft hair. "I told you, I love you. I don't want to go with anyone else when I love you,"

"That was not a pledge of faith," Ronan protested. "Say what I said!"

Bryn pressed his lips to Ronan's ear and whispered moistly, "I shall bed with no others, nor even kiss them, till death separates us, or else we farewell each other. Now, say you love me. I've not had that from you yet, and I want it once, even if you never say it again."

"I love you." Ronan rolled over in the grass and laughed. "My gods, it's not a lie, Bryn. I do love you." He laughed again as Bryn began to pluck dry grass from his hair. "Later, I will have what is my right and due, if you still want to give it."

A shudder of anticipation took Bryn unawares and he pounced on Ronan like a hawk on a hare. "You will have me, or I'll know why not!" He bruised Ronan's mouth with a kiss and then was on his feet in one fluid movement. "We shall miss cavalry practice if we don't run, and we'll have to pay that fine. I don't want to forfeit the money this morning, since we need it to wager on the race." Without waiting for a response from Ronan, he pulled his companion up to his feet and whistled for the horses.

The cavalry practised in the paddock under the old Roman walls. From the rampart Gareth could watch the whole session, and sometimes bawled scathing remarks. Shields were carried, but without boss-spikes; swords were wrapped in leather to blunt them, javelins and spears were bound with sheepskin to dull the points, but injuries still occurred.

As they took their place among the older men Bryn leaned closer to Ronan. "Be careful this morning. This of all days, don't let yourself get hurt. I can't ride than damned horse — no one can, but you."

"Don't you trust me?" Ronan had shield in one hand, javelin in the other, and was controlling his horse with his knees and heels.

"I trust you," Bryn retorted, but glanced pointedly at the men. "It's them I don't trust. They know you'll be riding against them in the race, and if they can put you down, injure you so you can't ride in the scurry, it means they'll have one less outsider to worry about!"

"This is true." Ronan bit his lip. "Then be my shadow. Fight with me as you would if this were a real battle, and my life forfeit if we fail. Don't let them have me."

Challenged, Bryn brought his horse closer, settled the weight of the round shield, which was made of wood overlaid with beaten bronze, and drew his sword. He looked up at the rampart and saw Gareth Ironhand, recognisable by his scarlet cloak — a Roman cloak, once worn by a cohort centurion. In his house, he had that man's helmet, shield and greaves too. He was one of the last officers to serve in Eboracum and was killed in the looting, in the chaotic days of the withdrawal of the Roman troops. The man looted until a merchant stopped him with a dirk between the ribs. The man who ended the centurion's career, Gareth swore, was his own grandfather, then just a youth. Today, that scarlet cloak tossed in the lively wind off the river, and when Bryn lifted his sword in salute Gareth waved.

Ebor's cavalry played very rough. Every morning, mock battle was joined in the lee of these walls, and every morning someone would be hurt, though dire injuries were rare. Gareth's men played harder than Gruffydd's ever had. Their mock blows came closer and the impacts taken on the shield arm were much heavier.

After every session Bryn felt bruised, but he knew that he had held his own against men older and battle-seasoned. His skills were growing sharper. Ronan also wore bruises, but he too was in better fighting condition after a fortnight working with a professional warband, men who fought for pay and earned their money the hardest way they knew.

The morning of the scurry, Bryn shadowed him and when a blow was swung, intended to unseat Ronan, Bryn took it across his own back. He spun the horse and without looking to see who it was thrust a counter-stike with his leather-wrapped sword. The man was flat in the grass before Bryn saw that it was Trenmore, who owned a fast little black pony, also entered to run in the scurry.

Trenmore was winded, gasping and angry. He lay clutching his belly and Bryn heard Gareth's laughter from the head of the wall.

"They are less green and raw than you suppose, Trenmore!" the Ironhand bawled. "He is wise to your plan and guides the jockey's back like a jealous lover!"

Trenmore had the grace to make his apologies to Ronan and clambered to his feet with a glare at Bryn and a lot of huffing and swearing. "A jealous lover, is it? It was a fair blow," he added defensively. "You can't say it was a foul thrust."

"A foul thrust on today of all days," Bryn said tartly, "when you know our chances here depend on Ronan." He swung the horse about again and came up to guard Ronan's back once more. "And you," he shouted at his lover, "take more care! If this were a killing field you would be dead by now!"

An hour later, sweating and dusty, they plunged into the river to bathe. Along the bank, the course of the scurry was marked out with banners and crossed spears. It ran a mile south, skirted the woods and doubled back, and Ronan had walked every foot of it, looking for slippery places or holes. The ground was well prepared.

Bryn hoisted himself out of the water and stood, naked and streaming, in the sun. "If I go now, I'll get good odds., Give me your coins and I'll make the best wagers I can."

"How fair you are," Ronan said dreamily, still floating on his back and looking up at Bryn. "Naked and fair, like an undine."

"A what?" Bryn had never heard the word.

"A water sprite." Ronan's eyes slid down over Bryn's body and came to rest on his groin. "Though I doubt any sprite was so well...proportioned." He mocked himself with a little husky laughter. "Pay me no mind. I would listen to Sian, when she would tell stories to the bonded people on cold nights. She saw an undine once, when she was a child. It rose out of the water by the reed beds and looked right at her, as sprites will never confront the adult. She said he was the most beautiful creature she had ever seen."

"Flatterer," Bryn accused, and gave Ronan his hand to pull him up onto the bank.

"For telling the truth?" Ronan rummaged through his clothes, found his black pigskin purse and searched it for the last two silver pieces he possessed. "Don't be greedy with the bet, though, or you'll ruin your own odds."

"Now, who's the gambling man, you or me?" Bryn demanded as he took the money, and he nuzzled Ronan's damp neck before he scrambled into his clothes.

With the coins safe, he tousled Ronan's hair and jogged away toward the course. When he ran now, he could hear Ronan's voice in his ear, words Ronan had said to him a week before. "You move like a young animal," Ronan had said. "Like a hunting cat. And you're mine." The possessive words had taken Bryn by surprise, and he cherished them.

Red was very fit. Ronan had groomed him until he shone, and borrowed Kynddelig's black harness for him. The farrier had checked his shoes, replaced one, and when he came up to the starting line with the others he looked their equal. Ronan held him on a short rein, and his eyes skimmed the crowd, looking for Bryn. At last they made contact as Bryn waved, and a hand signal passed between them. The odds Bryn had secured were ten to one.

Ten to one meant forty silver coins in their purse, as well as the purse for winning the race. Roan's belly fluttered, and he leaned closer to Red's ears to whisper, "Run like the wind. You must fly today, as if a thunderstorm is growling at your heels! Run for me, eh?"

He looked back at Bryn, at Kynddelig and Taran, who stood with Gareth beside the banners. And then a bondsman waved a yellow flag, and the horses sprang away. Some were small, stocky animals, of the old Brigante breed, others were longer-legged and white, out of the Iceni stables, while a few were the descendants of horses brought over from Rome. Of them all, Ronan could not tell which blood had bred Red, only that he ran as if every goblin out of hell was behind him and the god of horses before.

He was ahead before they had gone fifty paces and Ronan did not let his pace slacken. He chanced a glance over his shoulder as he approached the woods and saw his nearest rival, Trenmore's black pony. But the rider was already whipping him, while Red had the bit between his teeth and it would be a fight to *stop* him.

The most difficult task was to hold him on the course, make him turn about the fringe of the woods when he wanted to run on down the river bank, as he did every morning. He knew those meadows, and Ronan had to fight his head around, well aware that they were losing time as they fought. At last Red consented to go where he was told, but by then Ronan was hearing the drum of hooves right behind, and again he looked back.

The black pony was with him, several lengths behind. Foam flecked his chest and the rider was whipping him once more. Ronan leaned his weight over Red's withers and slackened the reins. "Come on, run! Run as you do when only I am there to see you! Pretend it's thunder in your ears and not the hooves of a fellow. Run!"

He felt Red snatch at the bit and plunge forward. Powerful hindquarters pistoned with a turn of speed that must leave the black pony behind. Gruffydd had paid a high price for Red in the market at Catreath, and he had a shrewd eye for horses. Had he seen Red today he would have been proud, would have been on his feet and shouting.

The wind sang in Ronan's ears as he brought the little stallion around the marker and gave him his head for the run back to the banners and home. Far off, he saw the crowd, the flags and pennants of chiefs and chieftains who had come to Eboracum to run their best horses. He twisted his neck to look back then, but Trenmore's pony was ten lengths behind, weakening, and Ronan grinned. "Gruffydd would pay money to buy you all over again," he told Red. "This is the race you and I would have run for him, and won for him. We were his gamble, you and I. And old Gruffydd is the winner today."

It seemed only Bryn was cheering as Ronan came to a slithering halt behind the starting marker. Most spectators wore rueful, even disgusted looks as Ronan slid breathlessly out of the saddle and Bryn caught him in a hug of victory.

"See their faces, Ronan! They have lost a fortune today — aye, and we've won one!" A boy from the cavalry stable took Red's bridle and Bryn tugged Ronan toward the Ironhand's people. "They gave me ten to one — mind, they won't give us odds like that again, now they've seen him run." He hugged Ronan tightly again. "Even Gareth lost a lot of money. I tried to tell him not to wager on that pony of Trenmore's. I whispered in his ear, but he wasn't listening."

"Then he'll listen next time," Ronan panted as he was hauled before Gareth.

The Ironhand wore a perplexed smile, and Ronan relaxed. Heart still racing, still breathing hard, he set one knee to the ground at Gareth's feet and cleared his throat. "My lord, Bryn said you lost a lot of money, I didn't intend that you should lose. Let me make up your loss somehow, if I can."

But Gareth only laughed quietly. "I wagered a good sum at three to one, on Trenmore's nag, but your mate whispered urgently to me. Put your fortune on the little red stallion, he said ...so I put a few coins on your Red, and won almost what I lost on Trenmore's horse. Now, if I had only listened to Bryn ap Gruffydd first!" He tossed a soft leather pouch at Bryn, who caught and kissed it. "Aye, won fairly, ap Gruffydd," Gareth said generously, "and you've your wagers to collect. Dine with me tonight, and tell me where you came by that little red devil."

Forty silver coins were counted grudgingly into Bryn's hand. The purse held ten gold, and with their pay and their winnings secure they withdrew to the sanctuary of the house. With the door locked and the window shuttered, Bryn divided the money and pressed ten silver, three gold coins into Ronan's hands.

"Your fee, for the ride, and for training him."

"No jockey was ever paid this much, Bryn," Ronan protested, but he took the money anyway and offered a kiss.

"And these," Bryn went on, adding two more gold coins to Ronan's palm, "are a gift, a little belated, to mark this morning's betrothals. You and I are mated like a pair of hawks or foxes. Even Gareth saw it, and called me your 'mate'. I liked the sound of that." He took Ronan's face between his calloused palms. "I liked it very much."

"I'll claim what's mine now, Bryn," Ronan whispered against Bryn's palm. "I want you as I always have, and now I can have you."

"You could have had me a week ago," Bryn said drily. He gathered up the phial of olive oil, which was kept with the whetstones for the service of their swords, and gave it ceremoniously to Ronan. Then he checked the bolt on the door, locked down the shutters, and in the sudden dimness stripped to the skin.

He was big with excitement, and when he dropped his breeches Ronan swallowed as his own body caught slight. Bryn stood by the bed, waiting, and Ronan undressed with shaking hands. He tumbled Bryn onto the sheepskins and held him down, hands knotted into his hair, knees between his thighs, his mouth ravenous. Beneath him, Bryn seemed to quiver like a startled horse, and Ronan lifted his head.

"Are you sure? Or do you shiver with dread? I cannot forget who was your father! I ask myself if I have any right to do this."

"I quiver with delight," Bryn retorted, "and am so urgent, I will disgrace myself with eagerness if you lay a finger on me." He stopped Ronan's hand as it reached for his cock. "Don't. Roll me over and sunder me, like a lad you would tumble in the fields for the sheer fun of it."

Ronan shook his head slowly. "No. Roll you over and make love to you, like the warrior you are." He sat up and gave Bryn's hip a push, and Bryn turned over onto his belly, both hands clenching into the grey sheepskins as his cock pressed into the bed. Ronan stroked his flanks and buttocks, so smooth, so white. "Will it be quick, Bryn, or will I be slow, as I would be with a virgin boy?"

"Quickly!" Bryn got his knees under him and tilted his hips, wanton and wild. "I've waited so long for this, too long. You have me mad!"

It was nothing like making love to Dafydd, and Ronan was dizzy as he made Bryn ready. His fingers were swallowed hungrily, and Bryn growled. He twisted them, and Bryn cursed. Dafydd had been just a boy, soft and slender, but beneath Ronan today was a man, hard and muscular, stronger than he was himself and yet spread in complete surrender. He withdrew his fingers and knelt between Bryn's lean, widespread thighs.

Once, he would never have believed this could happen, and the reality stunned him as he slid into the clench of Bryn's body. Bryn quivered and swore, but he was not in pain. A thrust, and he cried out, a sound as sharp as a skinning knife. His muscles rippled and once again Ronan was astonished, for Bryn had come.

"Are you all right?" He stroked Bryn's shoulders and cheek and took a calming breath.

"You touched something inside me," Bryn groaned. "I don't know what it is, but I could scarcely help myself. You can touch it again, whenever you please! You're not hurting me. Let me feel you move in me, come in me. You feel so wonderful."

It was a feeling Ronan knew well. He rocked deeply into Bryn, but it was all too overwhelming and he could last little longer. Climax burst through him, drained him, and he plunged into a muddle of leaden limbs and confused thoughts, only half aware as slipped out of Bryn's body, and Bryn turned over to hold him.

For a long time they said nothing. Outside, Eboracum was busy with ringing hammers, noisy traders, geese, goats, barking dogs. Inside, the house was as dim as a cocoon, and as peaceful. At last Bryn roused himself and looked down at Ronan with a fond, mocking smile. "It was me who was ravaged, not you!"

Ronan kissed his arm. "You were not ravaged. You were loved."

"I know." Bryn stretched his spine and growled. "You were patient, and I was grateful for that."

"You were pleasured," Ronan said quietly. "At least, I think you were."

"I came as quick and hard as a young boy!" Bryn said sheepishly. "Doubtless, I shall learn more stamina when I grow accustomed to *this*." He palmed Ronan's lax cock, stroked its whole length with his thumb from root to crown. "You were like a lance in me."

"You should have told me it hurt," Ronan protested quickly.

"I didn't say that it hurt." Bryn stooped and kissed Ronan's flat belly. "It felt magnificent. It was such sweet sin as would be worth a year or three in hell — supposing you believe in the place."

"Do you want to bathe?" Ronan got reluctantly to his feet and rummaged for flint and steel. He swung the blackened kettle over the fire and turned back to find Bryn looking broodingly at him. "What?"

"I should apologise." Bryn stirred guiltily.

"For what?" Ronan demanded.

"I was comparing you with a woman. With Aemilia Duratius, the one Gruffydd was trying to betroth me to."

"Comparing me with Aemilia?" Ronan stood with both fists on his hips, looking down the length of his very hard, very male, though still quite slender body. "And?"

"And I am lucky," Bryn said ruefully. "I escaped by the skin of my teeth, and got a better betrothal contract than I could ever have imagined." He slung his arm about Ronan's shoulders. "I wonder if Aemilia was in Derventio that night."

"If she was, she is dead." Ronan stroked his lover's back and patted his rump. "She was a Christian, wasn't she? Then her God and her Otherworld were waiting for her. That was her faith and her hope. It's time to lay old ghosts to rest, Bryn. You can do nothing for her. Come, let me bathe you."

* * *

That evening, when they went to the hall to eat with Gareth's household, the Ironhand raised his cup to them in salute and seated them at his right hand. Bards sang, one against the other, and dice rattled in the shadows. A pig was slowly turning over one of the hearths and the air was rich with the smell of herbs, bread and ale.

Gareth leaned back in his enormous, carved wood chair, between the banners of his tribe, his house, his victories. "You ride out tomorrow," he told Bryn as Ronan took a cup of wine from a bondsman. "You can ride up to Dubgall with Kyn. Taran has begged to go, saying he has keen eyes and a loud voice, and can stand watch, but he is forbidden to fight yet, since his arm is withered half to bone. Keep your eyes skinned for Angles. Listen for them in the woods. If the bastards break through, stop them if you can and if you can't, light the signal fires. You'll have the whole warband at your backs in half an hour, this I promise you."

A fist seemed to clench in Bryn's insides. So this was it — their marching orders. Every day they had known that this moment must come, and it was the duty Bryn had most hoped for. Ronan wore a shuttered expression and refused to comment on Gareth's orders until they were alone once more, but for himself Bryn was eager for the opportunity to strike for vengeance.

In bed, in the hour before dawn when they were waiting for the horn that called the cavalry to order, Bryn reminded him, "We swore that we would avenge our dead. We could soon have our chance. Has your heart changed?"

Still Ronan said nothing, and Bryn dealt him a shake. He took a deep breath and let it out slowly, "Vengeance, aye," Ronan said at last, "but not at the cost of your life. I don't want to be the one standing beside the funeral pyres, Bryn. Not for the sake of avenging men who are stone-cold dead. You're not even blooded yet. No one here knows that, they never asked. But I know."

"And you doubt my skills." Bryn said up in the darkness, and purred almost like a cat as Ronan stroked his back.

"I don't want to lose what I have just found," Ronan murmured. "I have had you so short a time. Must I lose you too?"

"So you do doubt my skills!" Bryn rubbed his face. "You could be killed as easily as I. Perhaps you don't realise it."

"I realise it." Ronan sat up and leaned against him, head on Bryn's shoulder. "I doubt nothing about you, love, save my own will to live without you. I'm being selfish, I know." He gasped as Bryn turned and crushed him in both arms. "Still, we will have Kyn and Taran, and we'll be back in Eboracum in a week or so. Our luck has held this far."

"Luck?" Bryn muttered. "What strange kind of luck cuts down a man's family and then denies him the right to vengeance?" He slid back into the bed and pulled Ronan down with him.

12

It was still early when they followed the old Roman road to the new frontier. This was road up which the doomed Ninth Legion must have marched, Bryn thought, and permitted himself a shiver. Everyone knew the story of how they vanished into the northcountry, a whole legion, and never returned. Despite the warmth of the morning sun that had made Ronan and Kynddelig peel off their tunics, he felt an odd chill.

He watched Ronan with hungry, possessive eyes. Ronan was sunning himself as he gambled idly with Kyn, a horse's length before Bryn. They were wagering on everything they saw, from the fall of a pebble to the flight of as butterfly. Beside Bryn, Taran rolled to the steady gait of his horse and exercised his withered arm. The scar was ugly, but the wound had healed cleanly and now he must strengthen it, rebuild the lost muscles, harden his hand for the hilt of a sword. Bryn did not envy him the task.

But Taran only laughed. "Listen to them." He nodded at Kyn and Ronan. "They would gamble on two flies walking up a wall!" Bryn made no comment, and Taran continued thoughtfully, minutes later, "from Dubgall you can almost see the rooftops of Derventio."

"I know." Bryn shook himself, banishing the old ghosts. "What does it matter anymore? The greatest kindness Ronan and I can do ourselves is to forget. I should have been the chief in Derventio, but what does it really matter? I do the same things now that I ever did, and I have Ronan. Before the Angles came, we were rivals, not lovers, you know. And I like Gareth. He's a better war leader than Gruffydd. Meaning no disrespect to my father, but an Ironhand he was not. He was a talker. And I have never seen talking achieve anything."

The old grief still punished Bryn as he spoke of his family, but he could bear to think of them again. Ronan was right. They had sworn vengeance, but if it was won at the cost of their own lives or limbs, the price was too high. Bryn was thinking this as he gazed so possessively at Ronan. The new leathers and boots looked good on him; he was mounted on a fine horse, his weapons were of the best quality, but all this could not be measured in terms of money. A horseboy from Whitestonecliff could never have earned enough in his whole life to buy such things. Ronan had come a long, long way from that village.

Bryn nudged his horse up alongside Ronan and caught his attention with a smile. "With a little luck," Ronan was saying, "we might get a proper fight out of this. His face was dappled by the shifting branches overhead as he watched the birds. "A proper fight, Bryn, not a vengeance hunting, for glory, that ends in your death or mine." He flicked a glance at Kyn, who was listening, and Kynddelig nodded soberly. "The Angles have a lot to pay for. Who better than us to collect what's due?"

"None better," Kyn agreed, "but we're not out to pick a fight, remember."

"Then we will be deathly bored for seven or ten cold nights,"

Bryn said drily.

Kynddelig chuckled. "What, the two of you can think of nothing to do? If you've grown tired of each other already, there's pretty girls aplenty in Dubgall. Though, like as not they've seen enough of the warband lately to last them a year. It's to be hoped *they* are not so bored!"

"You're a man for women, Kyn?" Ronan asked, surprised. "I thought you were like us. Your last lover was a man, and Gareth won't allow family men to fight."

"A wench is a way to pass the night without reminding myself of Fergal," Kyn said so softly that Bryn struggled to hear him over the breeze in the grass. "I have lain with Taran once or twice, but each time I wake in the dark, and a man lies against me, and I can't sleep for grieving. A soft, round girl is warm and welcoming, but nothing reminds me of Fergal. He forced a smile. "Sometimes they guess, when I talk in my sleep, but the men of Gareth's warband are well known hereabouts. Often as not, I'm cosseted rather than tossed out of bed."

The village of Dubgall was no larger than Whitestonecliff, or Cua's Forest, Elmgrove, or any of the other settlements that had fallen into Angle possession this season. It was swamped with spearmen, marching up from Eboracum, and if not for their presence it would have been abandoned by now, its people fleeing southward. The Angle fences were no more than a mile at most from the Britons' dry stone walls.

The peasant farmers of Dubgall had seen Derventio burn, had breathed its smoke, smelt its stink. Terrified messengers, on foot, stumbled into Eboracum a day behind Ronan and Bryn, believing their lands to be lost even then. Now they were back, labouring in the fields between Dubgall and the Dervent River — and cavalry from Gareth's warband rode among them, getting in their way and exchanging boisterous insults with the women.

Greetings were called out as the relief column appeared on the road. The farmers made way for the newcomers, something that was still so strange to Ronan that he shook his head over it and grinned sidelong at Bryn. Not long before it would have been himself on the roadside, standing back to let the warriors go through.

They reined in between a wain and a gang of labourers and a woman's voice called, with mock accusation, "You're late!" She rode with the cavalry, a sturdy girl with long black braids, clad in a scarlet tunic and leather breeches. A sword slapped at her thigh and two javelins rode by her right leg. She was broad faced, handsome rather than pretty, and good-humoured. With a white-toothed smile she lifted her hand in an informal salute before Kyn, who would be in command in her place when she had gone.

"We're not late at all," Kynddelig retorted, glancing at the sun. "In time to break bread and drink ale with you, I should say."

The horses turned about the laden wagon and ambled into the shade of the elms that skirted an open pasture. Ravens fluttered and called noisily in the tops of the trees, and Bryn gave the big, black, predatory birds a thoughtful look. Many men swore they were the harbingers of bad tidings. Often, they were shot before they could fetch in bad luck. Had they warned of the raze of Derventio, and had no one been listening? And what, Bryn wondered, did they warn of today as they fluttered and called hoarsely over Dubgall.

"Has there been any nonsense from the Angles, Cora?" Kyn was asking. "You've not fought these last days?"

The woman made negative gestures. "They've been quiet. Perhaps they've learned where their borders are, and that we will strike hard if they cross them. It's a pity, Kyn. A good fight would break the tedium of counting sheep every day."

The rank of old trees marked the edge of the warriors' camp. Boys ran to fetch food as they turned the horses loose to graze, and Ronan set his back against the coarse bark to gaze out, northward. Derventio was just visible, if one used his imagination to strip away the riverbank woodland. The distance was hazed, but with a squint the blackened walls and burned thatch could just be made out.

As Bryn handed a cup of wine to him he seemed to jerk back to the present. Cora sat on a fallen log beside Kyn, who was asking, "Do you see any slaves labouring in their fields?"

She frowned up at Bryn and Ronan. "No, we've seen no survivors. If there are any. . .and gods know, there must be. . .they keep them hidden from us, since they would be an excuse for a fight. I'm sorry, Bryn ap Gruffydd. I know how it feels. We all know. Many of us had friends in Derventio, and some of us had lovers, family."

"Thank you." Bryn gave the woman a look of some gratitude. Cora was several years older than himself, Ronan and even Kyn. She had shared many of Gareth's battles and the Ironhand trusted her as much as any of his men. Ronan sat at the foot of the tree and the woman came to rest beside him. Taran tossed her a cake of black bread, which she broke into two pieces. Half, she handed to Ronan.

Bryn cut deeply into a haunch of pork, and Ronan stuffed his bread with the meat. Across the fields, draught horses threw their weight into harness and a laden wagon creaked and groaned as it rolled forward.

"These labourers work with a strange determination," Bryn said thoughtfully.

"As if they expect each day to be their last," Ronan added.

"Perhaps they do." Cora drank a cup of ale to the dregs and wiped her mouth. "The old folk say it's to be a stormy summer, and everyone here is afraid of raiders. Angles often do their red work under cover of the storm, have you heard this? And people work faster when they are afraid." She held her cup out for Kyn to refill it from the skin he had appropriated. "Anyway, I *wish* the bastards would move against us. I've a few old scores to settle with their kind."

"Your mother should have told you," Bryn said, amused, "females are supposed to be gentle and soft, and stay at home with their children."

"My mother," Cora retorted, "was wilder than I ever was, and her mother before her. I was raised with a sword in my hand. I've no brothers, you see, they were all killed as children — Angles again. I was the last born. My mother put a knife into my hand when I was four years old, a sword when I was eight. In my fourteenth summer I rode to battle." She sniffed disdainfully. "You will find a few swordwomen left in the wild northcountry, and especially north of the wall, but one day I believe they will all be gone."

"A woman in Gruffydd's household told tales of the old Brigantes," Ronan told her. "Nights, I would sit with the bonded people at the kitchen hearths, listening to tales of the Deer people. I cherish those memories. Were the Deer people your tribe?"

But Cora's dark head tossed. "If my mother is to be trusted, we were Iceni."

"Boudicca's tribe," Bryn said, impressed.

"It's odd to fight beside a woman," Ronan said slowly, "there were none in the warband at Derventio. But Sian several times spoke of the warriors sisterhoods. Did you know her?"

"Of course I did!" Cora's teeth were white in the sun. "And aye, women fight here, they always have. Gareth's own sister swung a sword beside him."

"Until she was killed," Kyn added. "The loss of such women is the reason most men beg their wives and daughters not to fight. To lose your women in battle is too great a waste. Gareth thinks so."

But Cora only scoffed. "No greater loss than the death of a

boy. You, or Taran, or any of you. Good men are hard to find, and it's the best who are killed every time while the dregs escape." She shot a smile at Bryn and Ronan. "Not meaning any offence to you! Your day has yet to come."

"No offence taken," Bryn said quietly, intent on Ronan, who wore that haunted look.

The cavalry that had stood duty at Dubgall left in the afternoon, and Kynddelig's group settled into the same lodgings. The spearmen camped under the elms, but the cavalrymen were accommodated in a hut that had the dusty smell of stored grain. The spring wind blew warn, breaking up the clouds, and across the mile-wide strip of common land Angle farmers also worked, Angle spearmen also patrolled.

Between the new fence in the north and the crumbling stone wall in the south, only goats, geese and pigs grazed. The big, blond guards who leaned on their feather-dressed warspears did not press their luck.

Even they were not keen to fight again so soon? Bryn sighed. Were the Angles also counting their losses? Then, Gruffydd, Cuddy and the others must have made a fight of it, wreaking havoc among the Angle ranks. Bryn found a curious solace in that, and settled himself to wait for as long as it took. The vengeance would keep, so long as it was there in the end. The dead lived outside of time, so they could not be in any hurry for blood.

The longer the frontier was garrisoned, the more secure it felt. Ronan climbed up to sit on the northernmost part of the wall in the evening, while Bryn stood comfortably against his leg. Twilight would be long, and they were tired. The lights of Dubgall flickered like fireflies in the trees, and in the north similar lights marked the Angle frontier camp.

Yawning, stretching, Bryn stirred. "Seven days, and we can return to Eboracum. It's a good, friendly place, even if it is a great pile of Roman stone. Friendly people, as Kyn often says."

"Especially the little blond girl with the big brown eyes, who signs after Kyn," Ronan added. "She would have him in an instant, if Gareth permitted his warriors to take wives. You know the girl, the wheelwright's daughter."

"I know her." Bryn stroked Ronan's long, lean thigh. "But Kyn is still in love." He looked up at Ronan, who was outlined against the sky. A few stars sparkled, though it was not yet dark. "Just as I would love you, though you were dead." Ronan's hand cupped his nape and rubbed gently there. Bryn closed his eyes and sighed.

Where Derventio had been, lights beckoned through the trees, but they were not the welcoming lights of home. "Cora said they've seen no slaves in their fields by day," Ronan mused. "But who works in their halls by night? Answer me that." He looked down at Bryn and then slid off the wall into his arms. "I have said as much to Gareth, twice, but his hands are tied, I know that. If he fought now, it could only be a bloodbath, and no one in his right mind would want another slaughter so soon,"

"Yet our people may be wearing Angle shackle iron," Bryn added. "Perhaps even friends of ours." It was a goading thought, and Ronan looked searchingly at him. Bryn's heart turned in his chest. "Perhaps Dafydd." Ronan's eyes closed. "He was too beautiful to go unnoticed, you know that. If the choice was between death or bondage, and if he lived —"

"Sian would have killed him," Ronan said hoarsely. "She would never have allowed him to fall into their hands. And Dafydd would have fought, as they all did. No, Bryn, the only ones suffering in this are ourselves, with our imaginings."

"Perhaps." Bryn pressed him against the wall and kissed him, "But we should have gone into that town long ago."

"You did go," Ronan whispered.

"On a night of such chaos, even the Angles were not sure who had won the battle, who was alive, who had died." Bryn nuzzled his ear. "If it were you and I on the inside, Ronan, wearing irons, I would hope that someone would come and fetch us out. By gods, it makes me leaden with guilt."

The truth always struck a sore spot. Ronan rubbed his eyes tiredly. "But it's not for us to remedy this. Gareth ordered against it."

"So he did. But it's not Gareth's friends and kin who might be chained in there, and rotting, is it? It's not difficult to be detached when it's not your own people." He paused, and Ronan waited for him to work through the problem before he spoke again. "Perhaps I shall speak to Kyn about this."

"Kyn has no authority to order a raid across the frontier," Ronan said quietly. "If he did, it would be worth a whipping, if Gareth were the kind of commander to punish a man with a birch across his back." He slid his arms around Bryn's waist. "Come to bed and think clearly in the morning. Put your own life first, or put mine first. Where you go, Bryn, I must follow. Do you want to get me killed too?"

"What do I want?" Bryn buried his face in the mass of Ronan's hair. "You would blush if I told you what I want! But it will have

137

to wait, since we are barracked with a dozen other men. So think chaste thoughts till we are home."

"Seven nights," Ronan mocked. "I would sooner make love out here among the acorns." He tugged Bryn back toward the lights of Dubgall. "But not tonight. Let me seduce you tomorrow."

"Or shall I seduce you?" Bryn took Ronan's leathery hand and allowed himself to be tugged back to the warriors' music and laughter.

* * *

But every day for the week of their duty, Bryn sat on the wall and gazed out across the common land at the ruined town, and if Ronan allowed it, he would brood. With the tedium of a week's duty behind them they were to be relieved the next morning. Ronan knew, if Bryn were to make his move any night, it must be this last one at Dubgall. He had not spoken to Kyn, and no one save Ronan knew that he was so restless, so fretted.

It was fully dark when Bryn said quietly, "I have to go. Look for me at dawn."

"Don't," Ronan warned. "Bryn, please."

"I must," Bryn hissed. They were standing at the wall where they often lounged to watch the sun set, or made love in this little privacy. "If I don't, Ronan, I shall never sleep easily again as long as I live."

"Then don't go alone." Ronan checked his own weapons. He carried sword, dirk, the hunter's throwing knife in the sheath at his back, as well as the pig-sticker in his right boot.

But Bryn took his arm firmly. "One can pass silently, two would be heard."

"In that case, stay back yourself and let me go, since I was the hunter, not you! And suppose you were seen, and jumped?"

"Then I shall need someone on the outside, who knows where I've gone and cares enough to raise the alarm for me."

"Kyn would never sanction a raiding party to fetch you out," Ronan said sharply. "I would have to go in after you alone! It makes better sense if I go with you in the first place." Bryn opened his mouth to protest but Ronan silenced him with his hand. "No, Bryn. Either we both go, or neither. I'll not farewell you here, and mourn you when you're gone,"

"And supposing we're both seen and jumped?" Bryn demanded. "Someone must know where we went!"

Ronan took a breath. "I shall tell Kyn, and ask him to keep

faith with us. If we come back alive we can make our explanations to Gareth tomorrow. If we are caught or killed, it was our own decision to risk our lives. Wait here for me, Bryn." He moved away to run back to the barracks but hesitated a moment longer. "I mean that. Wait for me. If you go ahead without me, I shall come after you and the risk will be double!"

"I'll wait." Bryn groaned. "You have my word, for what it's worth these days."

Darkness swallowed Ronan in a dozen paces, and he jogged quickly toward the barracks hut. "Idiot," he breathed, angry, because he felt the sharp tug of guilt. Bryn was right to go, but Gareth was also right to warn against it. Yes, they should have made the foray a week before — but it was folly, too.

Derventio had been his home also. If his friends had lived, he had wished upon them an unnecessary week of bondage. Guilt prickled sharply as he ran back along the wall that girdled the south side of the common land. The spearmen on watch did not see him pass by. He heard the jingle of their coins, smelt their wine. In the eyrie, the rooks were restless and he paused as he heard their hoarse voices. Did they carry men's fortunes, good and ill? Ronan's mouth compressed as he lifted aside the weighted door skins and ducked under the overhang of the heather thatch.

Inside, Taran was poking at the embers while young John, who ran his errands, threw more wood into the brazier. Kynddelig sat drowsily with a red-haired girl in his arms, listening to the flute player and the bard from Lindum. The music was lilting, wistful, even sad. The drowsy girl did not see Kyn's tears, but Ronan knew where his thoughts were. Fergal was in his arms tonight, and Ronan wondered if Fergal had been red haired too. The girl would remind him painfully. Ronan waited impatiently for the melody to finish, and when the flute lilted into silence he said,

"Kyn, I must speak to you."

"Aye." Kynddelig rubbed his eyes as if they were merely smoke sore, set the girl aside and took a cup of ale. The bard moved closer to the brazier.

"Keep your swords by," Ronan said quietly, "and your ears open. Bryn is going into Derventio under cover of darkness to search for prisoners."

Disbelief silenced Kyn for a moment, and then he whistled through his teeth. "If he starts a fight and there is killing among our ranks, Gareth will have the hide off his back."

"Have him whipped for courage?" Ronan bridled, not believing it of the Ironhand. "Gareth is more likely to commend bravery than to condemn it."

"For deliberately defying orders!" Kyn amended. "Over two hundred hot-headed young bucks ride with our cavalry, and a lot of wayward mercenaries who are hard to control. If they get the notion that they can disregard a direct order, you'll have chaos in the ranks in a week. There is one law, Ronan, one law for us all. It's for our own good, but it will crack down on us just as hard."

Rubbing his face, Ronan nodded. "I know, and I can see the sense of Gareth's law. But it will have to crack down on me, too, Kyn, for I'm going with Bryn."

"No!" Kyn was on his feet at that. "I forbid it! You are going to be killed, the both of you!"

"I can't argue him out of it," Ronan said bitterly. "He is too determined. You know how he can be. And I can't allow him to go alone. I love him, Kyn, as you loved your Fergal. I have to go."

Kynddelig sighed. "I suppose you must. When shall I look for you, then? It's not far to Derventio, but you'll make slow time."

"Watch out for us no later than dawn," Ronan told him. "We will take every care and be back sooner than that if we can. Trust us."

But Kynddelig looked disturbed. He stroked the girl's long hair and closed his eyes. "If we hear baying hounds, raised voices, the ring of swords in the night, we will know the worst has happened. No one will come after you, Ronan. I can neither order nor even sanction it."

"I know." Ronan hesitated for a moment, aware of Kyn's accusing eyes on him, and then he slipped out of the house and ran.

Bryn was still by the wall, a shadow in the darkness, as good as his word. Ronan loped up and by, without stopping. The river lands were the old hunting ground of Bryn's childhood. He had grown to manhood there, first playing, later hunting over every mile, and Ronan let him take the lead. He moved quickly, like a wraith, through the tangled woods. Ronan had only to keep to his tracks.

On the north fringe of the woodland they stopped. Ahead were new buildings, new paths trodden by shepherds where none had been before. But the land itself was familiar, quiescent beneath the yellow face of the moon. Angle sentries were posted, but they were complacent on this side of the no-man's-land, and Bryn and Ronan went by like hunters.

They knew what to look for. If Britons were being kept as slave labour, they must be penned at night, herded and shackled. If women had survived it would not be so simple to find them, but even supposing they were found, Bryn and Ronan could do little. They would take the information back to Gareth, of who was held prisoner, and where. The decision to fight or not would not be made so easily.

Clouds slid silently across the hunter's moon, plunging the world into impenetrable darkness, and they were grateful for the cover it afforded. They smelt goats as they swung down toward the river, skirting a byre that stood where a field of young barley had been burned out.

Long, low boats were tied up at the riverbank, and they crept soundlessly by. From aboard, they heard the snores of men supposed to be guarding them, but every step from this moment on was an adventure in uncertainty.

The Derventio they knew was gone. The great walls, ancient and friendly, were piles of rubble, and the old Roman houses of Gruffydd's day had been razed to the ground. In their place was a new, ramshackle town of wooden, thatched houses, and about it, a fence of stout posts, each sharpened at the top so as to impale the unwary trespasser.

They crouched beneath the elms where Bryn had played as a boy, and looked back and forth along the stockade fence. Four men stood guard, and two of them sounded drunk. Their language was strange, but the words were slurred and angry. Bryn left his shadowed hole and doubled up, leading the way until they lay in the wet grass right at the foot of the fence. Then they kept quiet, waiting, listening. Still, they were unnoticed. Luck was with them.

Handholds in the stockade were not hard to find, but the timbers creaked and groaned as they climbed over. They dropped down into the darkness on the inside and listened once more. A wine jar smashed against the wood as sentries squabbled, and Bryn began to breathe again.

This was alien territory, and he led the way with extreme care, treading lighting, like a dancer or a thief. Ronan was tight on his heels, close enough to touch him. One wrong step could be the end of them, and they knew it. Or one hound who sniffed a stranger's scent on the air. Ronan had slackened the throwing knives he wore in his belt and boot.

They had made very slow time, as Kyn warned, and it was already late. The cookfires were cold now, and most of the Angles either slept or sat at the fires in the great hall, listening to the chieftains' improbable stories and the epic tales of their ancestors. Voices sang, laughed, protested, from inside, while overhead the sky was soft and dark as clouds masked the moon and stars completely. It would be raining in the morning.

The smell of stables drew them to an area a little apart from the houses. If slave labourers were held anywhere in this camp, they would be quartered with or near the other work animals. Ronan prayed only that what he smelt were not cavalry stables where they would meet warriors.

But Britons often gloated over the fact that the raiders — Angles and Saxons alike — were not cavalrymen. How many times had Gruffydd said that, laughing with that merchant, Duratius, who plied between the northeast shores of Albion and the ports of Gallia.

Horses moved about under the thatched roof, great shadowy shapes, just recognisable beyond the post-and-rail fences enclosing the stable. Bryn crept by, knowing the nags must have caught his scent, and Ronan kept even closer on his heels. If the horses took fright the intruder might be dismissed as a fox or a wolf. The hunting dogs might be turned out, and that would be fight enough, but if the Angle chieftain turned out his warband it would be a manhunt. It would end in death.

Beyond the stable and its barn, Bryn checked and poised in mid-stride. His heart beat hard at his ribs as he heard voices — and understood the words. They spoke in subdued whispers on the very edge of his hearing, and he drew Ronan closer to the rails of the enclosure. A sentry stood outlined against the sky, and a moment later they heard the unmistakable chink of chain mail.

Bryn and Ronan moved with a care dancers never learned. Their boots were noiseless on the earth as they edged sideways along the stable's rear wall. Ronan's fist clenched about the hilt of his sword as, a dozen paces from the pen, they dropped into a crouch and peered through the rails.

It was difficult to count the number of men and boys inside. Twenty, thirty, perhaps. The darkness was too thick for them to be sure, and they dared move no closer. But of one thing they were sure. These slaves were Britons.

Voices called from the gateway in the fence opposite, and the guardsman hailed his comrade. Bryn pressed his shoulders against the stable wall and held his breath. They heard the faint, fluid sound of a ceramic wine jug, heard even the sound of throats swallowing. These prisoners at least had survived the burning of Derventio — had others lived? Women, girls? Where were they?

Reason enough for Gareth to move against these Angles! They did take prisoners, they did keep slaves, and they were wise enough to keep them well hidden. Bryn glanced up at the sky and wondered where the night had gone, for it was very late. He looked at

Ronan's half-seen face, thought he glimpsed its grim expression. A wind was rising, a north wind, bearing the taint and tang of bad weather. The old people had foretold a gentle summer, but they were wrong.

"We have to get out of here," Ronan whispered. "Which way? If we don't get back out, no one will ever know these people are here."

The horses snuffled fretfully as they crept by, but it was the wind disturbing them now, not the intruders, and the drowsing Angle horseboys paid them no heed. With the quickening gale it was difficult to hear fine sounds. From here, Bryn and Ronan knew, it became much more dangerous.

They kept to the walls and shadows, and the night seemed full of eyes. Noise erupted from the hall behind them, laughing and shouting as some contest was won. Cold sweat prickled Ronan's ribs as he pressed against the timbers and let Bryn pull him in tight. A little light spilled through a crack between two massive tree trunks, and Bryn slid along the wall, set his face to the crack, as curiosity overcame fear. Ronan moulded to his side and pressed in close to see, and a pulse skipped in his temple.

His view was partially obscured by the warriors sitting at the hearth nearest to him, but between them he glimpsed down the length of the smoky hall. He saw bards, hounds, young men wrestling in a wide, cleared area, and several bonded people serving the freemen.

Dark-haired bonded people, with the black circles of iron slave collars about their necks. Some of them limped, all appeared cowed. Four of them were women, young, lovely, naked save for the swathes of blue paint decorating their skin with designs that were meaningless to Britons.

Finger to his lips, cautioning quiet, Bryn motioned Ronan a little further along the crevice, where the view was better. Anger knotted Ronan's insides as he watched the crude treatment the prisoners received, but the painted women disregarded it. By now they were accustomed to the hands that pawed them.

And then Bryn caught his breath and his hand clenched around Ronan's arm, drawing his attention to one girl in particular, who filled the cups of the warriors at the hearth halfway down the hall. Oh, Ronan knew her. The grime and paint could not disguise the beautiful, sullen face that was haloed by an uncombed tangle of raven black hair. Aemilia Duratis stooped to slop ale into the cups, and Ronan swore beneath his breath as he watched a man, an Angle warrior, put his hand between the legs of the woman who was once Bryn's betrothed.

She did not seem to notice the caress, and turned away as other voices called. As she moved away through the hall Bryn slid away from the crack between the timbers. He and Ronan stood in the lightless space between the posts holding up the overhanging eaves, and for the moment they were safe enough. Bryn pulled both hands across his face and Ronan moved closer to him. His voice was a soundless whisper.

"Bryn, that girl."

"You knew her?" Bryn murmured.

"I thought it was. . .Aemilia? Are you sure?"

"Of course I'm sure!" Bryn's whispers sharpened with a sudden sting of fury.

Ronan would have expected no less. To see the girl whom he might once have wedded, naked, tottering in paint and bruises, serving as a bonded tavern wench in an Angle den — how many men would not have been enraged? And she was a Christian, Ronan remembered bleakly. How prudish those people could be. He took a deep breath and held it. Whatever the treatment, the captives had survived this long, they would survive a little longer. Ronan forced himself to move.

"Which way out? Bryn! Which way?"

"The quickest way. Over the stockade fence," Bryn guessed. "The sentries are drunk, it should be easier getting out than in."

This time they knew the hiding places, the handholds to go over the massive fence. They were out much more quickly, doubled up and scurrying into the darkness. Behind them, the Angle settlement drowsed on, lights were doused, nothing moved.

It was not long before dawn as they found the familiar river bank and began to run. Now, dogs barked at the wind but they were too far away to be in danger of pursuit. Ronan's breath burned in his throat as they struck out across the wide band of common land, where the Angles grazed their pigs. He scrubbed his palms as they climbed the wall that marked their own border, and he and Bryn sat for a few moments in the coarse moor grass against the stones on the south side to get back their breath.

"They'll say we were mad," Bryn panted, "but you saw what I saw."

"Aye. And we *are* mad. But what to do about it?" Ronan raked his hands through his hair and peered toward Dubgall, where lights had begun to show in the cluster of houses. The full dawn twilight was still an hour away, but already the sky had that steely look, and he could just make out Bryn's features. "Kynddelig will likely skin us alive," Ronan added.

"And if he doesn't, Gareth will." Bryn clambered to his feet and gave Ronan his hand to pull him up too.

The wind shifted the thatch as they ducked back into the barracks. Most of the men were asleep, but Kynddelig was stirring. He slept like a cat, and in any case he must have spent the night listening for them. He was rolled in a black sheepskin, close to the brazier's last warmth. Taran, John and the bard from Lindum were sound asleep.

As the door skins swept aside Kyn rolled to his knees, his knife half drawn. He relaxed as he saw Bryn's face, and swug the knotted sheepskin about his shoulders. He came to his feet as Ronan closed the door and barred it. Kindling rattled in the brazier as he raked over the embers and blew on them to encourage a new fire, and then he held his hands to the heat and fixed Bryn and Ronan with a hard look.

Ronan sank tiredly down by the fire, and Bryn helped himself to a cup of wine. Kyn waited with cynical patience, for they were both drawn with fatigue and their faces were bleak. Kyn could guess what news they had brought. At last Bryn rubbed his eyes and cleared his throat.

"They're in there, Kyn."

"Who? How many?" Kyn rubbed his palms together as the wind tossed in the thatch and a dog howled, close at hand.

"A score, perhaps two, that we saw," Bryn judged as he held his cold hands to the heat. "They're using our warriors as labourers."

"But we've not seen them in the fields," Kyn protested.

"So they're too clever to display the blood prizes of battle so openly." Bryn sat down beside Ronan and closed his eyes. "They're not complete fools, Kyn. If they employed them, logging in the forest, how would we see them?" He paused, looking deeply into the fire as if the future were to be read there. "And they have women, too. I don't know how many, but we saw four serving ale in the chieftain's long hall. We looked through a gap in the timbers."

"Ah, damn." Kyn sat down by the hearth and out his face into his hands. "We expected it, but it still smarts." He paused as Taran was woken by their voices and sat up, but before he would give his companion the news Kyn pressed, "Were the prisoners hurt? The women?"

"The women?" Bryn shrugged. "What can you expect? They're on their feet, at least. Dirty, naked, and painted head to foot in patterns that mean nothing to me. Perhaps it's an Angle custom.

One of them is Aemilia."

For a second Kyn struggled, trying to place the name, and then his brow creased in a deep frown as he remembered. "I saw her once. The merchant's daughter. . .betrothed to you, so you told Gareth. She was with her father in the market, their ship had just come up the river from Karitia, and Marcus Duratius was haggling over the price of silver. She was beautiful, but when I smiled at her she turned up her nose and looked away. Who else is in there? Cuddy, do you think?"

"Or Matthew," Ronan said softly. "Oh, Dafydd. Not Dafydd. The old gods would not be so cruel." He frowned at Bryn. "What of Aemilia, then?"

Bryn's face was dark, brooding, but he admitted, "I sang no love songs for her, you know that. I did everything I could to discourage my father from making the betrothal! I'm not a man for women to begin with, and if I were, Aemilia was the last I would have chosen for myself! But that's of no consequence. She was gentle born, and a Christian. But, sanctimonious or not, a man's got the right to decide what he wants to do with himself, and so has a woman. None of our people should be in there. I ride for Eboracum in the morning, Ronan, and I'm going to tell Gareth what I did, and what I saw, even supposing he flogs me for it. There's no need to involve yourself in this. I wanted you to stay behind and wait for me, and I would be happy for Gareth to believe that I went in alone. No one else knows about this, only you and me, Kyn and Taran."

"Idiot," Ronan accused without heat. "If Gareth is of a mind to punish, let him punish us both. And we ride for Eboracum today," he corrected. "It's dawn already." He sprawled limply on the rugs and pillowed his head on his arm. "Get an hour's rest. Just an hour, Bryn, and they we'll go."

But rest eluded Bryn. When the sun crossed the horizon he was sitting at the door, watching Dubgall's many dogs and children, and Ronan stood beside him, eating a makeshift breakfast of last night's leftovers. Kynddelig had slept a little and was in a bitter mood as he buckled on the heavy, iron-studded baldric and tugged his tunic straight. He arched one cynical brow at Ronan.

"You are with him in this, I suppose?"

"Where he goes, I go," Ronan said levelly. "If he is to face Gareth's anger, I should face it too, since I was with him. And if he's to be outcast, or whipped, half the lashes should fall on my back, not his."

Mead swirled in the bottom of Bryn's cup as Taran refilled it,

146

and he glared at the frothy liquid as he heard Ronan's resigned tone. Kyn hooked his fingers into his belt and rested his chin on the leather collar of his tunic. "Well, Kyn, my friend?" Bryn prompted. "You have known the Ironhand since you were both boys."

"I don't know if Gareth will fight," Kynddelig said slowly, thoughtfully.

"You don't know? What choice have we?" Bryn was on his feet now. "Friends of yours are probably wearing Angle slave chains in that place!"

"I know, I know." Kyn rubbed his face hard enough to leave his cheek ruddy, and his fingernails rasped in the morning's stubble. "We could fight. We're not strong enough yet to be certain beyond any doubt of victory, but we *could* fight. It's for Gareth to decide, not us. Trust him, Bryn. He's as good a judge of men as I ever knew, and he's lucky, in war as in love."

Bryn drained his cup to the dregs. "Fair enough. I'll fetch up the horses. We can be out of here before morning wastes. Ronan?"

"Yes. Go," Ronan threw the remains of his meal to the dogs and brushed off his palms.

"Ride with him," Kyn counselled, one hand on Ronan's shoulder. "Speak for him. The warriors might find their hackles raised by your tales, and even if Gareth is given to caution he will give an ear to the men. We might get a fight out of this yet."

"We?" Bryn echoed shrewdly. "Then, you would fight?"

"I would. For Fergal." Kyn lifted his chin and his face was filled with that wistful expression of longing. "But then, I was always a fool where my heart is concerned, and I am still in love with him. If I was killed in this battle of yours, hunting for Fergal's vengeance, what would it matter to me?"

Before the sun was over the trees they were on the road and heading hard into the south. The wind was chill and the sky grew more sullen with every minute. Summer thunder rumbled, low over the coast, and Ronan hugged his cloak about him as Bryn prayed silently for the rain to hold off until they reached Ebor.

It began just as they handed the tired horses to one of the dogboys. "Where is Gareth?" Bryn asked the freckle faced lad.

"At home." The boy jerked a thumb over his shoulder, toward a timer house built on stone foundations that had been old when the Ninth Legion was stationed here.

Two hounds lounged at the door, under the eaves and out of the rain. A harpist sat on the threshold, restringing his instrument with fresh gut. The dogs growled as they approached but the bard knew their faces and passed them by.

The Ironhand sat in his chair by the wide hearth, two of his children playing at his feet, oblivious to the newcomers' bitter faces. But Gareth was taken aback by their expressions, and waved them to the bench by the fire. "What brings you back so fast? There's foul weather on the way, and I'd thought you would wait it out in Dubgall rather than race the storm."

They sat, and Bryn glanced sidelong at Ronan before he gave the chief his attention. Gareth waited speculatively, and Bryn could see the suspicion in his eyes. "They said you'd have the hide off me, Ironhand. But flog me if you must. Fear of a whipping was not enough to stop me,"

"Stop you doing what?" Gareth leaned back into the chair, which creaked under his weight. "I'll be the judge of when you feel the whip, and how hard."

"I went into Derventio last night," Bryn began, "under cover of full darkness."

"We went," Ronan interrupted. "I share his blame, my lord. If you punish him, then punish the both of us."

"Ronan!" Bryn remonstrated. "The crazy notion was mine, you tried to argue me out of it." He turned back to Gareth. "No one saw us go in or come out, but we saw them. Britons, held in shackles in the slave pens. The women are whoring in their halls." He paused, trying to read Gareth's face, but the chief was very adept at masking his thoughts. "They are our people, Ironhand. Fortune let them survive the battle and the burning as we did, Ronan and I, only to end their lives as slaves."

Gareth's mouth pressed into a hard line and he leaned forward, elbows on his knees. "I have told you before, ap Gruffydd, time and again, we are not ready to fight again. Not yet, not this season."

"Kyn says we could," Bryn protested, knowing he was on thin ice now.

"Kyn," Gareth said flatly, "is a fool in matters of the heart. And he is not the chief here, I am. If that does not please you, the gate stands open and you are at liberty to use it whenever you please. Till then, bend your stiff neck to my wishes, Bryn, as the others do."

Colour leapt hotly in Bryn's face and he lowered his head. The Ironhand accepted it as a gesture of contrition. In fact, Bryn was filled with a heat much closer to anger.

"Just so," Gareth said softly. "Do you think I don't understand your pain? What kind of man do you take me for?"

Softly, and with a faint smile, Ronan spoke for Bryn. "That was never questioned, Ironhand. We know you better than to believe you unfeeling. But Bryn has just seen a woman in Derventio. The woman who might once have been his wife. She is whoring in chains, and he is filled with anger."

The chief sighed, and his right fist locked about the hilt of the dirk he wore at his right side. He half drew the blade, but sheathed it again. "How many more will lie dead if we march again before we should — before we *can*? I can still feel my own wounds, Ronan. I can barely swing a sword without catching my breath in pain, and the surgeon told me, if I fall from a horse, it will be a full round of the seasons before I drag myself back to my feet. If we fight so soon, my wounds will be open again, and many among us are the same. Old wounds can kill you in new battles. Warriors don't grow old, Ronan. One day they follow foolish orders and die hoping to find some little honour in their pointless deaths."

For a long time they were silent, and then Bryn lifted his head, blinking in the fire's acrid draught as the wind spiralled in through the smoke hole. Drops of rain spattered into the glowing log embers. "So what's to become of our people? They have made work beasts out of out men, and whores of the women and the prettiest of the lads. What of them?"

"Their dishonour shames us all," Gareth agreed, "but they could easily be the death of us. I'll take dishonour over death, for the moment. I make you the same pledge that I gave Kynddelig, the last time we fought, the same promise I made you the night you arrived in Ebor. Next season we fight. Next season, we knock some Angle heads together, we take back Derventio, and we *sell* all the Angle prisoners we can capture, for labour in the mines in Cambria, where they'll work their lives through in the cold and dark, and wish they were dead a thousand times before their gods grant them that release. Dishonoured or not, Derventio's survivors have lived this long. They'll live out the winter, and their vengeance will be sweet."

It was as far as Gareth would go, and he was immovable. He was also right. Bryn knew this in his mind, while his heart wanted to fight until the last Angle had been driven out of Derventio. He licked his lips and looked sidelong at Ronan.

"And what of me — or us, then, Ironhand? We went against your orders and Kyn's. The fault was not Kynddelig's. We know there must be a reckoning."

"Aye, so there must." Gareth gave them a rueful look. "You know full well, I have an army of mercenaries camped inside these walls. If I give them even half an idea that they can disobey me and go unpunished, I'll lose my grip on them. I might as well pay them off and send them away, and Ebor will be so weakened, we will be easy prey, the next time Angle ships come up the river." He picked up a pitcher of ale and brimmed his cup. "It will be done at sundown. Come to the hall, come contrite and resigned. Leave behind your jewellery and finery and your weapons. Come with downcast eyes and quiet voices, and we'll have it out before a gathering of the warband. Either that, or you leave Eboracum today, and you don't come back. The choice is yours."

Bryn's throat constricted, but he bent his neck. "For myself, I'll stay and take justice as you choose to deal it, Ironhand. Ronan?"

"The same." Ronan sighed heavily, and with a hand on Bryn's arm drew him out of the house. They hurried through the sporadic rain to the great hall, which was crowded in this ill weather. A pig was turning slowly over the fire, and a serving girl filled their cups, fetched them bread and meat. Ronan watched Bryn eat and said quietly, "You knew what Gareth would say. All of Eboracum is his responsibility. If the warband is broken, the Angles would hear of it and they could be here in a day."

"I know." Bryn reached for Ronan's hand. "And Gareth is right. Next fighting season, he said. It seems so long away."

"Not so long." Ronan studied their clasped hands. "A year for us to be in love and have each other, before we risk everything. I don't want to die. Bryn. But I don't want to live without you. I look at Kyn, and every day I wonder how I would live if you were gone, as he lost Fergal."

"Oh, Ronan." Bryn put down his cup and pulled Ronan into his arms. "Lovesome fool that you are! I was furious with you when you insisted on going with me last night, and then I was very glad that you came. Bed with me this afternoon, please. We'll not want loving tonight, after a whipping, but come and lie down with me now, for I'm tired, and I need you close to me. With your arms around me, I might sleep."

"I would bed with you any time," Ronan said, flushed with emotion as he drew back. "We were so lucky, Bryn. I don't think I realised how lucky, till we saw the prisoners. That could have been us, so easily." He held his cup to Bryn's mouth, and Bryn drank.

* * *

Unarmed, clad simply, with lowered eyes, they presented themselves a few minutes after sunset, before an assembly of the chieftains, mercenary captains and warriors high in favour. The hall was packed, and as they entered Bryn's heart squeezed as he saw the cleared area between the hearths, and the bench set out in the full of the lamplight. On the rare occasions when a man was punished here, he prostrated himself on such a bench, there was no mistaking the evening's business. A rare assortment of birches and whips lay on the bench, and Bryn eyed them warily as Gareth called the assembly to order.

It was Kynddelig who stated the case, and even to Bryn's ears, he spoke fairly. These two had broken the chief's law, but with good reason. They had taken every precaution to ensure that they would cause no harm by their actions, and yet they *had* gone against Gareth's orders. They had also discovered prisoners in the Angle camp, men and women who would be known to many of Eboracum's warriors, and those slaves were the reason for Bryn's and Ronan's disregard for Gareth's orders.

"What is to be their penance?" Kyn finished mildly. "Their punishment will be decided by the whole corps of you. For defying the chieftain's orders, they will bear lashes, but how many, and how heavy, and dealt with what, is yours to decide."

It was a curious arrangement, but at once Bryn saw the sense of it. By allowing the warband to set its own punishments, judge the severity of crimes and mete out its own justice, Eboracum's fighting men could never claim that they were tyrannised. And the men would think twice before they broke the law, when they knew that they would be judged by their peers, and chastised by them.

Many of the faces Bryn saw were filled with compassion. There were murmurs, too, from men and women of the warband who suspected that their friends and kin were prisoners in Derventio. Perhaps they had wanted to go in and see for themselves. Perhaps some of them had, but had chosen to keep that secret, since they had found nothing.

The mercenaries argued it out amongst themselves. Not to Bryn's surprise, they asked for a great deal more money before they would fight in Derventio, and Gareth assured them, the fight was not about to happen. Several mercenaries from Lindum spoke up in defence of Ronan and Bryn, pointing out the courage the foray had taken. Others praised the initiative, the skill, and pointed out that the Angles knew nothing of it. What harm had been done?

But the matter of the broken law persisted, and at the last it was the mercenary captains who insisted on justice. Big, bald-headed, tattooed Kier slammed down his ale cup and jabbed a finger at Ronan and Bryn. His voice was hoarse, rasping, since he had been cut about the throat in a battle when he was even younger than they. "If you," he told them, "were you part of my company, I would lay fifty lashes of a horse whip across your backs for defying me. But I would also recognise your courage and make allowance. Thirty lashes of the horse whip. I would also recognise that you were driven by guilt and anxiousness, for your kin. Ten lashes of the horsewhip. I would also commend your skill, in that you were in and out like thieves, and the Angles none the wiser. Ten lashes of the heavy birch. I would also commend your courage in speaking out of what you saw, when the knew that you would answer for it. Ten lashes of the light birches. He shook his head now. "But less than that will not smart enough for the punishment to deter others from emulating you."

Murmurs of agreement whispered around the hall, and Bryn looked at Gareth and Kyn, hoping for a reprieve. There was none — how could there be? And Kyn beckoned them both to the bench. Ronan was pale, and Bryn guessed that his own face was bloodless as he took off his tunic and lay down on the bench. He looked up into Kyn's face as Kynddelig picked up the bundle of light birch canes that would be used.

"Breathe deep and look into the fire," Kyn whispered. "Imagine that you are far away and it will soon be over. Ten only, and the light birches won't open your skin. Kier was most fair, Gareth himself could have been no more lenient. Are you ready?"

"Who will deal it?" Bryn asked breathlessly.

"Eris, the warband's scourger." Kyn was moving back to let the man approach even then.

Bryn knew the scourger by sight. It was he who chastised the boys in training and the bonded people, and Bryn relaxed just a little, for Eris was very good. Once, a merchant had caught a young girl thieving in the market and demanded that she be flogged, the full one hundred lashes for stealing. She had only stolen a bauble, to sell for food, but the Roman merchant was so angry, so uncaring, he would have sold her to a slave dealer. The girl was tied to Eboracum's gatepost, and Eris strode out of the crowd to deliver the lashes. The merchant handed him a driving whip, and Eris took it with white, bared teeth. He could have killed the girl with it in four or five blows; instead, he dealt the whole one hundred so lightly that the fair, white back was only pale pink as a rose petal. The merchant was furious.

The same Eris picked up the bundle of light birches and tried their weight and flexibility in his hands. From the look on his face, he had kin or friends in Derventio too; but he was also a soldier, and had been since his own youth. He was forty years old now, and he was one of those closest to Gareth. Wide brown eyes looked down into Bryn's face and he said,

"You know why, boy?"

"I know why." Bryn licked his dry lips. "Are you waiting for me to absolve you?"

"No." Eris's face creased in a grin. "But it would be nice if you did."

"Let me see how you deal them," Bryn growled, "and maybe I'll absolve you after, if you've enough compassion to know *our* why, and don't see only your own."

"Oh, I can see it," Eris assured him. "But there's two hundred mercenaries with the bit between their teeth out there. Put yourself in Gareth's place."

"I have." Bryn settled himself and closed his eyes. "Now, you put yourself in ours for a moment, before you flog us."

"I have," Eris said in a deceptively mild tone. "And if I were in Derventio, if I were in chains there, I'd be proud of you."

But the ten lashes were still heavy enough to leave Bryn bathed in sweat, leave his back afire and his head spinning. It felt as if the skin had been flayed from him, but he knew this was only imagination. There was no blood, he would only come up in great red weals and then be black with bruises for a week, ten days. He was gasping, his eyes filled with involuntary tears, as Eris finished, and he was too dizzy to stand. Hands helped him as the hall reeled and bucked, and slowly righted itself. The heat of the fire was intolerable on his back and he turned to face it, wiped his face on the tunic Ronan handed to him. So this was how it felt to be flogged, albeit lightly. Bryn was surprised that most of what he felt was anger, dishonour, even shame. His face burned, but it was sting of embarrassment raising the heat in his cheeks, while he felt a white-hot fury as he watched Ronan go down onto the bench.

"Gently," he panted at Eris, "for the idea was mine, he tried to talk me back. He counselled sense and discretion when I was for rushing in like a fool."

"Is that right?" Eris's bushy brows rose.

Kynddelig was standing by Roan's bowed head. "Quite right. I had the whole story."

"Then I'll be thinking of that," Eris promised, looking thoughtfully at Ronan's back.

The skin was perfect as a child's, white and flawless, and Bryn felt a terrible surge of guilt as he remembered Ronan had never been beaten before. To suffer the first time here, as a freeman warrior before the whole company of his fellows, was harsh justice, and yet Ronan seemed merely resigned as Eris swung the birches. Six or seven canes crackled across his back and the weal was first white, then blood red and livid. Ronan jumped and gasped, and Bryn felt nothing of his own soreness, when it was all he could do not to snatch the birches out of Eris's hand and throw them into the fire.

The first four were dealt quite heavily, leaving Ronan's back scarlet and ridged, and then Eris began to pull the blows. The next three were lighter than those Bryn had received, and the last three, lighter again, though they landed amid already scorching hide and made Ronan gasp. It was over that fast, and Kynddelig reached down to help Ronan to his feet. Sweating, flushed, Ronan held his tunic against his chest and turned so that his back was not to the fire. He looked up at Eris and nodded; he looked at Kier and said, "Are you satisfied? It was enough?"

The big mercenary pulled at his beard. "For the first offence, aye." He glared at his captains. "But the next man who offends will pay a higher price for ignoring this warning, and the man after that will take the horse whip, and I'll have the hide right off him!"

Very carefully, Bryn put on his tunic. It felt as if he were being scoured by a handful of sand, but he could bear it, if he left his baldric very loose. Gareth was smiling ruefully at him, and when the chief handed him a cup of wine, Bryn took it.

"You'll not break with my orders again," Gareth guessed.

"No, my lord," Ronan assured him. "Not for all the gems in Rome. This is the first time I've felt a whip across my back, I've no desire to feel it again." He ducked his head. "But it was earned, we had a price to pay, I don't dispute that."

"But you've paid it, and it's forgotten now." Gareth beckoned them closer. "Come, sit. Eat with me. Let me tell you about the Druid teacher who is on his way up from Caerleon."

Forgotten? Was it? Bryn could barely move, his back felt as if the skin might be hanging in flayed strips, and he suspected that he would remember the whipping for days. But he knew what Gareth meant. There had been a price to be paid, and they had paid it. No grudges would be borne against them, and once Gareth had had his due, it was over. With great care he sat, sipped his wine and tried to eat, though the meat almost choked him. From the shadows, bondsmen looked at him and Ronan, large eyed. They must see warriors whipped on very rare occasion, and only when the crime begged for it.

Crimes of honour, Bryn thought. Crimes of guilt and anxiousness. Even now, he regretted nothing, save that a number of Britons, Aemilia Duratius among them, were in the Angle strong-hold, and suffering the gods only knew what. The little flogging he and Ronan had received was nothing.

He looked into Ronan's face and saw a surreal calm. Ronan was strong, stronger than Bryn himself had ever been, and Bryn took his strength from that. From somewhere Ronan found a smile, and when the Ironhand paused to confer with a lieutenant he leaned over and said quietly, "The time will come, Bryn. There *will* be a reckoning, but the time is not yet."

"I know." Bryn wriggled inside the tunic. "Oh, I know!"

"Sit still, let it cool down," Ronan counselled.

"Yours is not the voice of experience!"

"No, but I've seen others whipped — aye, and much harder than that! Just sit still and let the heat cool down. Later, cold water, dock leaves and a night's sleep. Tomorrow, it will be swollen and sore, but there's no blood. Eris is better than that. Remember the girl, the thief in the market?"

"I remember." Resigned, Bryn took a draught of ale and tried to follow Ronan's advice, but the cost of that foray into Derventio had been high, and no amount of rueful humour at his own expense took the heat from his back. Oddly, Gareth, Kynddelig, Kier and Eris all seemed to have forgotten about it already. The bench was taken away, men were throwing dice where it had stood, and the only reminder that any judgement had been made, any punishment meted out, was the sweat standing on Bryn's own brow, and the drops of moisture on Ronan's upper lip.

For the moment, the matter of Derventio was decided.

13

Fog crept silently out of the east before dawn one morning, very early in summer, while the east wind was almost still, and for days the pall hung like a burial shroud over Eboracum, from the Ambri to the jagged coast. No chant or prayer would move it, and with its dampness Eboracum was subdued. People shuffled listlessly from riverside to market, or else clung to their hearths.

The fisher people in particular had prayed for clear weather, and when the wind swung northerly, slicing down out of Pictland with an edge like a sword and at last driving off the mantle of wet fog, they gave thanks. But their gratitude to attentive gods was brief.

Before the day was out, the wind that cleared the fog had whipped itself into a gale and Eboracum battened down. For a time it seemed winter had returned. The last, late blossom and new foliage were torn from the trees, and roofs were ripped away. It did not occur to Ronan to think back, now, to the long-dead old folk of Whitestonecliff, who had prophesied a good year to come. It all seemed a lifetime in the past. Youth, time and love healed his wounds as they healed Bryn.

Twice since they had faced and accepted the warband's judgement, they had stood duty in Dubgall, but still they had never glimpsed Britons working in the fields across the common land, and still the Angles kept to their own side of the frontier. Skirmishes were fought when hunting parties met in the woods, but never the confrontation that Gareth was determined to avoid.

Hammers were still ringing across Eboracum as the daylight dwindled into a short, angry dusk. The northeast was blue-black with storms. The roof of the cavalry barracks had been repaired already, the gaps in its walls plugged with pitch. Boys were hauling in logs to supply the hearth as Kynddelig, Taran and Cora slammed the door and threw down their packs.

The work at Dubgall was wet and muddy — Ronan and Bryn had stood an uncomfortable duty there just a week before, and now they were in Ebor to welcome the others back. Life among Eboracum's warriors was pleasant, Ronan thought as he poured a cup of ale and sat on the floor by the hearth, at Bryn's feet. His lover's hands rested on his shoulders and he leaned his head back into Bryn's chest. The company was agreeable, and he knew of worse places to spend a year or maybe three.

Still, he felt the urge to wander. The wind beckoned him with promises of places undreamed of, and he was always eager for marketplace stories of Artos, and the Druid sorcerer who had taught him since his childhood, and the great warband that now marched from Caerleon and routed the Saxons in the south and west.

Bryn was watching Cora deftly unbraid her hair to brush it. She was a handsome woman, and Ronan knew Bryn liked to watch her. Did he compare Cora's charms with those of his lover? Ronan mocked himself. If Bryn did make the comparison, what of it? When the lights burned low at night, all Ronan needed to know was said in silence, with hands and lips and the glide of soft skin. In any case, Cora shared her bed with one of Gareth's elite cavalry. She lodged in a house by the gate rather than in the barracks, and she turned aside offers from other men as adroitly as she blocked their swords.

Two other women rode with the warband, but they were hardly what Ronan would have called seductive. Eilund and Maura were drinking and gambling mates, right arms to be depended on when there was trouble. Both were stout and thickly muscular, handsome in their own way, but not, Ronan decided, quite what he or Bryn had in mind to pass away a long, cold night.

Just then Bryn leaned down to press his lips to Ronan's ear, and Ronan laughed quietly. Perhaps Bryn had been thinking the same thoughts. He slipped off the bench and knelt by the hearth at Ronan's side, to hold his hands to the fire. The acrid draught of woodsmoke wrinkled his nose. Did his face become bleak as he thought of Aemilia? As he sighed Ronan looked drowsily at him.

"Leave it alone, Bryn." He spoke very softly, uneager to have Taran or the others start another heated debate on the subject of the fighting. "It's like a sore old wound. If you keep on poking it with a stick to see if it's healed, it never will be."

"I know." Bryn rested his chin on his fist, blinking at the heat of the fire. "But you of all people, closer to me than any man ever was, must know what's in my heart."

"I know too well," Ronan said bleakly. "She was very beautiful, and the Angles can not be blind to that. But see, Bryn, she is alive because of her beauty." Or, he added silently, because Aemilia Duratius had not the courage or strength to fight when the time came, the way Sian would have fought. Was it charm that consigned her to bondage, or was it cowardice? Ronan said nothing of that.

"You call existence in the Angle camp life?" Bryn lifted his head and looked searchingly at Ronan. "If it were you in that place, I would call in a half-life. Or, a half-death."

Ronan sighed. The gale tore at the thatch again, finding every crack in the wall and stirring the hearth smoke. The bull calf tethered in the corner sniffed sleepily at the draught, but his head soon lowered and his eyes were closed. A bondsman offered Ronan another cup of ale, but he shook his head.

"Perhaps we could raise a force of mercenaries," he suggested as Bryn accepted a cup. "Red has won three scurries for us. A few more, and we could afford to hire a band of men to fight for pay."

"And who would command them?" Kynddelig leaned down between them, quietly but firmly interjecting himself into their debate. "They would never follow your orders. You're too young, too green and raw. They would take your money happily enough, and then would run wild. I've seen it happen."

"So you command it," Ronan suggested.

"Me?" Kyn was surprised. "I don't command, Ronan, and won't. I could never give an order that sent a friend or a brother to his death."

"But you could follow one," Bryn observed,

"It's my trade," Kynddelig said mildly. "Not I, Bryn. Choose another. Or be sensible. Mercenaries are the best and worst of men. Some, you could trust with your life, your money or your virgin sister! Others, you could not even trust not to betray you and join your enemy the afternoon before the very battle you hired them to fight."

"And you've seen that happen also," Bryn guessed. "Then, what choice have we?"

"Only to wait until next season," Kyn told him. "Do as Gareth bids you. He has a wise head on his shoulders, perhaps wiser than you realise as yet." He nodded at Taran, who was working the injured arm to and fro. It was still weak, pale and withered.

But Taran was smiling as he rolled the dice, his favourite game. He had a flair with the old Roman dice. An area of the earthen floor had been swept clear, close to the wall. Money changed hands rapidly and Taran was slowly gathering the fortune that would one day pay his way out of the warrior's deadly trade. No one knew where he kept the money hidden. Ronan watched Taran's dextrous fingers appreciatively. When Taran challenged him to a game he accepted, rather than encourage Bryn to an evening's moodiness.

The night was wild and cold, and the sky was still blustery at dawn. Bryn lay buried under a weight of sheepskins as Ronan sat up in bed, listening to the howl of the wind — and something more. He cocked his head to the sound, unsure what it was.

"Come here, it's too early," Bryn grunted, and caught his arm, trying to tug him down again.

"No, listen," Ronan insisted, though he allowed himself to be pulled down. Bryn pressed his face to Ronan's breast, rubbing his stubbled cheek over one sensitive nipple. "Bryn, listen!"

"I am listening." But Bryn took Ronan's nipple between his teeth and teased it deliberately.

The wind dropped just a little for a moment, and all at once the sound resolved. It was voices. Men were shouting from the river, and despite the sudden pleasure arrowing into Ronan's groin, he was taut as a bent bow, listening. "Bryn, I'm sure something's wrong." He fended off the distracting hands and mouth. "I can't make out what they're shouting."

With a sigh, Bryn released him and closed his eyes, the better to listen. "Voices," he said after a moment's concentration. "And I hear the clatter of spears. They've turned out the guard. Now, why would they do that?" He frowned up at Ronan. "You're right, something *is* wrong."

Ronan was out of bed a moment later, hastily dressed, a heavy blue cloak about him. Bryn was on his heels, swearing furiously as they stepped out into the blustering wind and intermittent, stinging rain. They were still buckling on their swords when they saw the dog handlers, the mastiffs padding morosely on short chains, and the guardsmen whose war spears formed a jagged forest of fangs along the riverbank.

Despite the season, the wind cut like a knife and Bryn pulled the heavy wolfskin collar of his cloak higher about his ears. He and Ronan stood in the lee of a massive, time-gnarled oak, watching the dog men struggle with their animals. Only feet from where they stood, the rushing grey river waters were treacherous with half-submerged debris.

The mastiffs were surly, half wild, snapping even at their handlers. One slipped his collar, turned bare teeth on his fellows, and the dog men were still wrestling them apart when Gareth Ironhand himself appeared. The scarlet Roman cloak was spread wide across the flanks of a tall, dappled grey horse, and from that vantage Gareth could see along the river bank. His voice was hard as steel as he bawled, "What in Camulus' name is the commotion about? Kyn!"

"See for yourself," Kynddelig invited, pointing. Gareth had already seen.

Broad waisted, low in the water and wallowing like a pig in its favourite mud bath, the boat was a trading vessel. It was made for hugging the coast, or on very rare occasion when the sea was a mill pond and a gentle east wind blew, for heading out across the Narrow Sea, from the ports of Germania and Gallia. She was an Angle ship, and at the sight of her Bryn's eyes narrowed. Ronan gave him a wary, calculating look, but Bryn was intent on the vessel. And on its captive crew.

They had rowed her upstream, and the current ran strongly against them. Despite the chill, the oarsmen were ruddy faced and panting. The long oars splashed into the grey surface with an ordered rhythm until, at a command from the big, red-haired taskmaster who stood in the bow, the starboard blades trailed while the port oars were lifted up. The trading vessel turned smartly in her own length and drifted in toward the landing,

A squad of Gareth's river guards stood along the gunwale, and between two of the largest guardsmen was a young man. Tall, blond, broad-shouldered, long-limbed, handsome, with high cheekbones and a clean-shaven jaw. The Angle had apparently surrendered, for although he wore light chains on wrists and ankles he was unhurt, and he stood straight, proud, even defiant. As the boat was secured fore and aft alongside the landing, the river guards jumped off the rolling deck and saluted Gareth.

The Ironhand nudged his horse down among the men and women on the creaking timbers of the landing. He spared the oars-men a glance before turning his attention to their captain. For an Angle, he was very tall. And handsome, Ronan thought, getting a clearer look at him. The young man's features were straight and fine, and his hair was the colour of wheat at the harvest, long on his shoulders. He wore wolf hides, black skins and soft leathers, and Ronan perceived a look of breeding about him. Even Gareth, who disliked Angles as a race, could not overlook it.

"Is he a young chief, do you think, or the son of a chief?" Bryn whispered.

"Not on a trading vessel," Ronan guessed. "I think, a mer-chant price. A price of trade."

For some time Gareth and the Angle captain looked levelly at once another, rudely appraising, and then the Ironhand leaned down toward the young man. "Do you speak our language?"

The blond head inclined. "Aye, I do. I am Eadhun, till lately a freeman from Germania. My father is a merchant also, trading in the south, in the ports of Rome. The east wind blew me in from the sea, and I tried to take shelter in your river."

"As much as that, we know," Bryn growled. Ronan glanced sidelong at his bleak face, but Bryn only shook his head now, and listened.

"Where were you headed?" Aware that Eadhun had only so many words, Gareth spoke slowly, simply.

"To the port known to Romans as Iarum." Chain rattled be-tween Eadhun's wrists as he gestured north.

Ronan's innards tightened as fragments of memories returned to taunt him. He heard again the potter's voice: *Get out while you can! They marched over the moor from Iarum. . .* He blinked the memory away, trying to see an innocent stranger where Eadhun stood, rather than an enemy he must attack, must assault at once. It was not easy to see past Eadhun's yellow hair, blue eyes and Angle blood. The same senseless fury that froze Bryn's face pulled Ronan's into a bitter mask, and he felt the muscles set in place like hard old leather.

"And where are you bound from?" Gareth asked. "Where do

you anchor?" His tone was still pleasant, and he gave his river guards a warning glance to be still.

"From the Saxon shore to the south of your lands." Eadhun gestured with a nod, in the direction of the distant Saxon shore. "We carry ale and barley spirits, silks, fine leathers, furs, gems. And my cargo is forfeit, I don't doubt." He spoke less with remorse than wry amusement.

Gareth's flinty eyes narrowed on the stranger again. The loss of the cargo clearly meant nothing to him. Was he a rich man, whose people would pay handsomely for his return? "Aye, your cargo is forfeit," the Ironhand affirmed. "And your ship." The vessel was not badly damaged. Broken yards could be repaired, and she was valuable. Britons seldom built ships like this trader, and even more seldom the kind of vessel which could match warships from across the Narrow Sea.

"And my crew?" Eadhun asked in his thick accent. "Myself?"

"Come to Eboracum. Perhaps arrangements might be made," Gareth offered, "that would suit us both."

The dappled grey cavalry horse wheeled about and the river guards urged the weary Angle crew off the deck. They moved without protest, forming ranks as they followed the horse, and behind them. Kynddelig watched the dispirited captives, and laid a hand on Bryn's shoulder.

"If you want retribution for the friends and kin you lost in Derventio, here it is. Angles in our own chains now. Angles toiling for us. What say you of that?"

"For how long?" Bryn's dark eyes smouldered on Gareth's back, on the billow of that unmistakable scarlet centurion's cloak. "You heard Gareth. An 'arrangement', he said, to suit them both."

At Kyn's right hand Taran echoed, "An arrangement? You mean, ransom? It's possible. That yellow-haired bastard looks as if he'd be worth he weight in silver."

"So he buys his way to freedom," Bryn said bitterly, "and for him, his falling into the claws of his enemies is but a minor inconvenience for a season or two, while our people rot in the pens in Derventio!"

"Singing that song again won't change the words!" Kyn said sharply, "and you'd best not let Gareth hear you. Let him choose his own way. As long as I've known him, no one has ruled his mind for him. . .and as long as I've known him, he's never yet been wrong."

Bryn lapsed into a surly silence as he and Ronan followed the party of prisoners and guards up from the storm-battered landing and through the gates of Eboracum. The Angle oarsmen were hustled away, thrust into a granary, and hammers chimed on steel as they were chained. Eadhun himself was escorted to the great hall, where Gareth sat in his stout, carved chair and took a cup of hot wine.

The chain fettering the young Angle's wrists tinkled as he reached for the cup he was offered. He sat on the floor by the hearth, a little way from Ronan and Kyn. Ronan lifted a cup to his lips and frowned over the yellow-haired stranger. So this was the face of the enemy. It was deeply disturbing to be so close to one of *them*. One of the kind who had destroyed almost everyone he had ever loved. And Eadhun was a warrior. It showed in his stride, the way he held himself, the tilt of his head, and his empty scabbards. Broadsword and shortsword had been taken from him on the river.

Feeling the scrutiny, Eadhun turned his pale blue eyes toward Ronan. His face was speculative now. Ronan rolled the cup between his hands, searching for words while his heart was a confusion of anger, pain, questions. "Why?" he asked at last, and knew it was not enough.

"Why. . . ?" Eadhun echoed the question, far from understanding.

"Why do your people come here and kill us, steal our land?" Ronan's voice was soft, yet demanding of answers. Gareth was listening, though he did not look up.

For a long time Eadhun frowned into his cup, and at last he shook his head. "We must."

"Must?" Ronan echoed.

The Angle gestured into the east. "A tide is rising out of the bowels of the earth. It is not a tide of water, but of men. They come from strange lands we have no names for. They speak tongues we do not understand, they have strange faces, they swear by demon gods. They burn us, hunt us, put us to the sword, chain our children and rape our women. So we run. There is no honour in flight, but what can we do? What else is left to us?"

"You could stand and fight," Ronan said hoarsely. "By gods, you fight us soon enough, when you come here!"

"Because our backs are to the wall," Eadhun told him honestly. His voice had sharpened but he spoke sadly. "Beyond this island is only the black water. There is nowhere else to go, and no way back. We cannot fight the tribes out of the east. They are mad in battle and great in number, like ants on a broken nest. They swam like hornets. They feed like rats. They will devour Rome herself soon enough, already they are at her gates, beating for entry.

Stand and fight, Briton, and you stand and *die*. So we come here."

"To kill us, instead," Bryn hissed.

Eadhun's wide shoulders lifted in an expressive shrug. "For myself, I come to trade, to barter. I did not come to fight, I have no desire to kill anyone."

With a whisper of steel on leather, Bryn's knife slid out of his right boot. The lamps and torches glimmered on the polished blade as it turned in his hand. "Perhaps you will meet men here who would like to see what colour Angles bleed."

The pale blue eyes narrowed. "If you are going to slit me ear to ear, you had best do it quickly. My gods will welcome a man who went bravely to his death, even an unarmed man, chained at the feet of his captors."

In the tense silence each glared at the other, and at last it was Ronan who said, "This is no fit time or place for a vengeance killing, Bryn. Put away the knife. What good will spilling the blood of an innocent merchant do? Will it punish the guilty?"

The blade slid back into its sheath without a sound, and Bryn reached for the cup of ale he had set down. "Merchant or no, his blood is Angle."

"His blood," Gareth said pointedly, "is both innocent, so far as any man here knows, and valuable to us all. His throat is not yours to cut, ap Gruffydd. Tell me, Eadhun, what are you worth?"

Unexpectedly, Eadhun smiled. "To my dog? His life. To my lover, her heart, I hope. To my father, his fortune. Which do you want?"

The levity was spontaneous, and even Gareth smiled faintly. "Only a ransom. But a rich one, or you and your crew will remain captive here, and not as honoured guests. You expect as much from us, I don't doubt. We've no love of Angles, whatever your troubles with invaders out of the east. Our neighbour at Derventio was recently overrun, his town torched, his people butchered or chained as slaves. Yon thunder-faced lad is Bryn, his last surviving son and heir. Little wonder he has a yen to slit the first Angle gullet he finds."

Eadhun's pale eyes returned to Bryn. "For what it is may be worth, you have my sympathy. I lost most of my family to the barbarian raiders three years ago. My wife and two young sons were murdered before my eyes. It was as if my heart were cut out while I lived and breathed and felt every moment of it."

The words lanced painfully through both Ronan and Bryn. They shared a sidelong look, and Ronan saw a flush of colour in Bryn's fair cheeks. Eadhun was an Angle, but not a coward, nor a savage. So the rieving invaders were men also. Sobered, Ronan sipped his ale and listened as Gareth laid out the conditions of the ransom.

The Angle crew would be held prisoner, but Eadhun himself would have the freedom of Ebor from sunrise to sunset, so long as he was guarded. The Ironhand crooked one ringed finger, beckoning Ronan closer. Ronan put down his empty cup and moved to Gareth's side.

"The task of guarding him, I give to you, if you'll have it."

"Why me?" Ronan wondered aloud. "I've less love for Angles than any of your men, and you know that! I have even killed one of them!"

"I know." Gareth's face creased in a faint smile. "But if you've the fangs to guard this windfall of ours jealously, you've also a head on your shoulders that will govern your passions. We all have fangs, but. . ."

"But too many of us," Kyn concluded, "have hot heads." He leaned on the high back of Gareth's great chair and looked levelly at Ronan. "You shall have to keep him from harm, as much as keep him from doing harm. He could die in the night, and we may never know whose knife was responsible."

"On my honour," Eadhun said in that thick, foreign accent, "if you treat me and my men fairly, I will offer you no cause for grievance."

For a moment the Ironhand frowned at the yellow-haired stranger, and then nodded. "I believe you. You'll have fair treatment, but know this. Break faith with me, and the contract is over. Your men will labour their lives through in my fields and quarries, and your good looks will take you to the cavalry barracks for the amusement of my men, until you're too old to turn their heads and quicken their loins. You understand?"

"I understand." Eadhun lifted his chain-bound wrists. "So, will you strike my bonds?"

But although Gareth wore a pleasant face, he shook his head. "I will not. Not so soon. Let me know you better first, and come to place as high a value upon this honour of yours as you do."

Eadhun dropped his hands back into his lap. "And my men?"

"Treated fairly," Gareth growled. "Their terms are simple. They will be fed, watered and warm. They can work for their keep, but it will be honest work. If they steal, touch a woman of my town, or make a run for it, they'll have the birch in answer, with twenty cuts for the first offence. I'll double the number for each new offence until, by gods, they learn better manners. Tell them.

All I want from them is obedience, and they'll be fairly done by."

"Which is more," Bryn whispered, "than was handed out to the captives just north of our own frontier." His eyes flickered to Gareth, but the chief wore a resolved expression and Bryn knew better than to press it further.

"I will tell them," Eadhun said quietly, very much aware of Bryn.

"Then Ronan will make arrangements." Gareth got to his feet. "Secure him in the barracks after sundown, and keep your eyes on him by day. He will be safe enough until we have sent a message to his kin. Who are they, Eadhun, and where are they?"

"Send word to Karitia," Eadhun mused. "A free trader would carry a message. Romans pass that way, and stop also at your own ports. Many of your goods are traded to Angles and Saxons across the sea. We use your lead, tin, salt, hunting dogs."

"Then we are waiting for a Roman freetrader to anchor here," Ronan concluded. "Waiting for an east wind." He stood back from the hearth and inclined his head before Gareth. "Your leave, my lord. Let me see to the prisoners at once."

With a frown, Gareth let them go and they were outside when Ronan hissed, "Bryn, will you wipe that look off your face!"

"What look?" Bryn demanded, though he did not seem surprised.

"The look that's going to get us both whipped again! That surly look, as if you could wring a man's neck as soon as look at him." Ronan was striding away toward the granary, where four guardsmen and two mastiffs stood duty.

"Perhaps," Bryn said acidly, "I could!" And then he sighed. "The fire in my belly is to no good, not now. Douse it for me, Ronan. Only you have ever known how to set me at peace."

Ronan arched one brow at Eadhun. "You will spend a good deal of your time in our company after this, and will realise sooner or later, Bryn and I are lovers. Bedmates. You understand? I don't know what words you have. If men being bedmates offends you, perhaps the Ironhand would set someone else to guard you."

"Lovers?" Eadhun seemed taken aback. "Like Greek sword brothers?"

"Perhaps." Ronan waved to the guardsmen at the granary door. "You are not offended?"

"Should I be?" Eadhun asked indifferently. "My god is Wotan of the single eye, who hung upon the tree of Ygdrasil for nine days in search of enlightenment. My people are not lovers by nature, Briton. We rarely speak of such things."

"My name is Ronan." He paused upon the granary threshold, and looked back. "What enlightenment did your god discover?"

"Who knows?" Eadhun licked his lips as the sentries glared at him. "Perhaps that life is brief and fragile, and that we would live longer, and happier, if we allowed every man to call god by whatever name sounds right to his ear, to worship in his own way. . .and to love however he chooses."

"Wise," Bryn growled. "If your god is so powerful, why does he have one eye?"

"He traded the other for wisdom." Eadhun drew himself up to his full height.

Ronan pushed open the granary door and stepped inside. "Tell your men what rules Gareth laid down for them. It will do them no service if you lie. Gareth is not a cruel man, but to save killing in the end he will certainly give the scourger a morning's work. The scourger who will punish your men is from the cavalry barracks, and you may believe me, he has a heavy hand when it's warranted."

He was also fair, Ronan thought as Eadhun stepped into the granary. Eris did not relish the sight of a man writhing in blood and pain, but he could flay skin as easily as he could deal a hundred lashes and not even bruise.

The Angle tongue was strange, guttural. Twenty seamen listened for five minutes while Eadhun gave them every word Gareth had said. Chastened, dark-eyed and pale, they wagged their heads in agreement, and at last Eadhun turned back to Ronan and Bryn. His face was a bleak mask. "Like fighting men anywhere, they will chafe at their captivity and servitude. But I told them, a cavalry scourger will flog them without mercy if they break the vow of obedience I gave your chief. They will be docile. . .not like lambs, but like chained wolves who know better than to beg for a kicking."

"Good enough." Ronan stirred. "I'm hungry. I'll have the guards feed them, but if you want to break bread with us, Eadhun, you're welcome."

Bryn swore quietly as Eadhun accepted, and Ronan gave him a wry glance. Their house was still warm, their hearth still smouldering. He shut out the wind as Bryn put a kettle onto the hearth stones and hunted out bread, cheese, pork and onions. Eadhun sat quietly, wary, watchful, and Bryn's mouth compressed. He dropped his arms around Ronan from behind and deliberately kissed his neck.

"I said, douse the fire in my belly, Ronan, before it eats me up."

"How?" Ronan turned into his embrace. "Will kisses douse it? What will Eadhun say to that?"

"I don't know," Bryn said dismissively. "Nor do I care." He caught Ronan's face between his palms. "Perhaps he could look the other way."

"Perhaps." Ronan fixed Eadhun with a piercing look, but the Angle seemed amused. "Like Greek sword brothers, you said. Then you know about love between men. Look away, if you choose to."

"If you can set him at peace and keep my throat whole, do so by whatever means. I shall not complain," Eadhun said wryly.

"Then let me try." Ronan slipped his arms around Bryn and kissed his mouth hard. Bryn's hands cupped his buttocks to hold him, and for a long time they were almost oblivious to the young merchant. At last, when Bryn withdrew from the kiss to breathe, Ronan whispered. I can do no better than that."

"It will do." Bryn had relaxed little by little, and rested his head on Ronan's. Only then did they think to look at the prisoner, but Eadhun was eating deliberately, his teeth working on a slab of bread and cheese, his eyes on the fire, as if he were alone in the house.

"Bryn?" Ronan whispered.

"You are my conscience." Bryn pressed his face to Ronan's soft hair. "Without you, I don't trust myself."

Ronan drew back and stroked the shape of Bryn's mouth with his fingertips. "Perhaps. But I trust you. And who knows you better than I do?"

14

Barely enough space separated the banks of the little Usan river for the Angle trading galley to turn about. The manoeuvre was managed by men and horses on each bank, with heavy lines attached fore and aft. All oars were raised and the boat was manhandled about, pushed and pulled, until her high, beaked prow was to the east.

Eboracum had two other ships, one very old and leaky, the other smaller, though sounder, suited only to coastal raiding. Eadhun sighed over the loss of his vessel, but he was resigned. It could be replaced.

The wind was northerly for more than a week, and no traders came up the coast. Eadhun settled to wait. Like any seaman, he could read the sky. Each morning he stood in the marketplace while Ronan bartered for fresh eggs and bread, intent on the clouds, their patterns and movement. He knew when he could expect a ship, and when he could not. Fishermen returning to Eboracum spoke bleakly of the open sea. For the time being little was moving, and all vessels hugged the coast.

Between dawn and sunset Eadhun was free to wander within Eboracum's walls, but he chose not to, for the town was filled with men who wished him ill. Often, it seemed that only the presence of an armed guard with Gareth's authority prevented violence. Some men looked upon Eadhun with fear, others with hate. And some were hot-eyed with lust. Eadhun retreated to the cavalry barracks or the great hall, and avoided men he did not know.

But even Ronan, who was charged with keeping him from harm, was not friendly. If food and drink were served, Eadhun received a fair share. At night, when he was confined, his chains were long enough to allow him to rest easily, and he had enough sleeping skins to be warm. But he enjoyed no gestures of friendship.

When the bards began to sing Eadhun's face was a mask. He spoke the language well enough to smile at the humour, but no one smiled back, and when the bards sang war songs, of battles and vengeance huntings, of great loves and great fights, the lone Angle in the hall drew smouldering glares. Most men only tolerated him.

Ten days after the storms blew him into the river, Eadhun's wrists were raw. The irons had chafed his skin to blood. Ronan stood by the fire in the barracks, watching his charge and listening to the chatter between Bryn and Kynddelig, who were shelling eggs they had boiled in a helmet in the hearth. Eadhun looked up at Ronan, his pale blue eyes wide in the dimness, and Ronan saw their mute protest.

"I have done nothing to warrant these shackles," Eadhun said quietly. "Will you not strike them at last?"

Bending to scoop another egg out of the water and ouching as his fingers scorched, Bryn looked across the fire at Ronan. Ronan clenched both hands into his hair, tugging it by the roots as if he could pull the decision from his own mind. He was caught between honour and compassion, and it was a curious trap. Eadhun had been faultlessly honest, he had earned a measure of trust, but was it a ruse, before he wreaked havoc the instant his bonds were released, left blood and pain behind him, and made a run for freedom? If that happened, Gareth would be furious. The Ironhand was rarely roused to such ire, and Ronan had no desire to make an enemy of his only patron.

Seated on the edge of his skin-strewn cot, the Angle waited. His wrists were extended to display their rawness, and Ronan saw the brightness of new blood. Kynddelig tossed the fragments of egg shells into the hearth and brushed off his palms. "Well, Ronan? Gareth would stand by your decision."

"I know he would," Ronan said slowly. "And if I am wrong?" He gave the Angle a hard look. "You will not try to escape?"

White teeth bared in a wolfish smile. "Why should I be mad enough to throw myself onto the spears of your river guards? A ship will come, by and by. Soon, I hope. I pray for it every day. Wotan will send a Roman freetrader, and I will send a letter to Karitia. All I have to do is wait, and I live."

"And you will keep peace within these walls?" Ronan added.

"On my honour." Eadhun looked up searchingly at Bryn. "I will need a guard, for the opposite reason, I think. Men look at me with dangerous eyes, and I am unarmed." For a moment the pale gold face clouded with resentment, frustration, then Eadhun's head drooped. "You have stripped my honour clean away, will you take even my dignity? Can it mean nothing to you? Wotan! Beyond the Narrow Sea, they call you honourable men!"

"Honourable," Ronan echoed, "not stupid." He sighed heavily. "And not especially malicious, either." He beckoned the thin, dark youth who ran their errands. Just a little while ago, it would have been Ronan of Whitestonecliff who had run his master's errands. "Go quickly, John, and fetch the smith. Tell him to bring his tools."

The lad ran out, banging the door behind him, and Bryn dropped to a predatory crouch before Eadhun. "Break your word to him, Angle, and I will hunt you all the way to the sea. You'll not get off this island before I find you, and if my mate has been whipped bloody on your account, I'll bleed you like a pig and throw what's left to the fish."

"Bryn," Ronan whispered, not sure if he should remonstrate or not.

"I mean it. Every word," Bryn said harshly. "If he breaks faith with us, it'll cost us every denarius our lives are worth, and half our hides too."

The merchant's eyes were level, clear, and Ronan was impressed by their honesty. "I am a freetrader," Eadhun said, "though on occasion I will fight, to fend off pirates. I am not here to make more enemies. . .yet we were born enemies, you and I, because you were sired on this coast and I was not."

"Then tread lightly," Bryn advised, straightening. "Ronan may speak softly, but his swords are honed keener than mine. Betray him, and you answer to me."

Wearied beyond his years, Eadhun set his chin down on one fist. "All I want is to be at peace until I can get out with my hide intact. Run, fight, and I'll die here. You must think me five kinds of fool!"

"Forgive Bryn his fangs." Ronan rubbed his palms together. "I have the same teeth and claws, but my head is not so hot. Perhaps it would be if I had seen my own old friends in the slave pens in Derventio." *If I had seen Dafydd.* He closed his eyes, squeezed them shut, trying to thrust away the old hurt. "You were bound for the ports along the new Angle shore. Do you know the Angle chief at Derventio?"

"I never knew the name of Derventio," Eadhun mused. "But you have spoken of it so often — your north frontier. The chief's name is Malla. Malla the farmer, the warrior, the hunter. The Goths burned him out three years running, killed two of his sons, raped and maimed his young wife. He saw his baby daughter impaled on a spear and thrown, still alive, to the wolfhounds. Malla brought his people here this season when their scouts in the east saw yet more Goth campfires. They could not fight again. I watched their ships sail."

The silence in the barracks was like a funeral shroud. Colour rose in Bryn's face, and Ronan's head buzzed as if he had drunk far too much, too fast. He looked at Kyn, who was pale, and Kyn's throat twitched as he swallowed. Unable to be still, Ronan got to his feet and paced restlessly between the cot and the fire. "Malla the farmer suffered no less than the people of Whitestonecliff suffered," he said, a hoarse rasp. "Or the people of Derventio. Who are these men, these Goths?"

"Strange tribes from we know not where. Horsemen," Eadhun said, hushed. "Better cavalry even than you Britons. And there are so many of them, they will ride against a Roman cohort. They ride *through* a Roman cohort, cut them down as you scythe wheat, and feed the dogs on the dead meat. The come out of the dawn, so many of them, one day your hills are filled with them and it is time to run and run. Save that our coasts are west coasts, and where shall we run to?"

At last Ronan came to a halt by the hearth and beckoned Bryn closer. The door banged open, admitting a gust of wind, a patter of rain, John and the cavalry's big, smudge-faced blacksmith. Bryn, Taran and Cora gathered by the hearth as Ronan said softly to

Bryn, "How many Britons are in the pens in Derventio?"

"As we told Gareth weeks ago, twenty, perhaps thirty, but not forty," Bryn said. "And then, four that we saw are women."

"And how many men did we take from Eadhun's ship?" Ronan mused. "What price Angle honour, do you think? How much would they pay for the freedom of their countrymen?"

"What, sell the crew to our neighbours?" Taran echoed as he warmed his hands over the fire.

Ronan gestured at Eadhun. "You heard what he said of this man, Malla. Their people have suffered no less than ours. We share the same pain, we have all lost loved ones, and be truthful, Taran. No soul among us is without sin. Were we pressed against our own coasts by strange tribes like a flood out of the west, what would be do? What *could* we do?" He looked into Bryn's wide, dark eyes. "We would run east, and when no chief there would let us camp for more than a night before we were moved on, lest our flocks and herds take their graze, one day we would fight to win a home of our own. We would have to, just as they do."

"But, selling the crew to Malla," Cora echoed doubtfully.

Bryn shook his head. "That's not what he's talking about. He means a trade, don't you, Ronan? Malla the farmer will pay Eadhun's ransom, and the payment might be rendered in lives. Angles for Britons."

"I'd have said Britons for Angles, but the ransom remains the same." Ronan stirred. "Would Malla do it? Would Gareth?"

The iron about Eadhun's sinewy wrists fell loose as the smith pried out the long pins. The merchant stood, stretched his shoulders and worked his abused hands. He shrugged up the black sheepskin collar of his cloak and moved nearer the fire as the smith gathered his tools and left. He was like a big animal, Ronan thought, young and strong. Dangerous, with an independent spirit.

"What price Angle honour, indeed?" Bryn speculated. Eadhun looked sidelong at him. "Do your countrymen take their brothers' captivity lightly?"

"No more than Britons take the bondage of their kind." Eadhun cocked his head at Bryn. "But I do not think your chief will send you to war over it. Nor would Malla make war to save us from shackles here. After every battle there are captives. Every war has a victor and a vanquished, the master and the slave. It is the way of war."

"True." Ronan arched his brows at Eadhun. "And yet, I see more in your face. I see something shining in your eyes. . .you pray to your one-eyed, tree-hung god that when Malla learns who is in chains here, he will send the warband to take Eboracum."

"Perhaps." Eadhun shrugged expressively. "Who is to say that my kin in Karitia will not sail to join forces with Malla, once you have told them you have me? As yet, I am mourned in my home ports. They will believe me sunk, drowned in the storm. But, tell them the truth and perhaps it will be war, for the sake of slaves in Eboracum."

"My gods." Ronan rubbed his face. "The secret of these captives could get out, Bryn. A thousand ways, Malla could come to know of them — perhaps even the same way we came to know of the slaves in Derventio. Gareth does not want to fight before next spring, but he could easily find himself forced into it."

"Malla also does not wish to fight again this side of winter," Eadhun added. "He has built fences and stayed behind them. But if my kin send men to strengthen his warband, he can fight again sooner. I cannot say that he will, or will not, Ronan. For myself, I would sooner pay the sum Gareth named and walk away, rather than see blood spilt. If Malla marches on Eboracum, I will surely die in the fighting when Bryn or some man like him puts a sword in me. I like the look of the future no more than you do."

For some time Ronan and Bryn studied each other bleakly. Bryn rubbed his face hard enough to raise heat in his cheeks and said challengingly, "You're a merchant, Eadhun. Talk to me of trading. Lives for lives. Yours, and your crew, for the men and women Malla is holding. Would he make such a trade?"

A frown creased Eadhun's brow. "I cannot know. I would like to say yes, but to be certain is not so easy. Malla is a man of good blood and good word, but these are hard times that will grind honour underfoot. He paused and looked from Bryn to Ronan and back again. "At least Malla would listen to the proposition. I know him well enough to say that much in certainty."

Bryn smacked his fist into his palm. "That is hardly enough to persuade Gareth! But the alternative is to sit here waiting for a ransom, and when it comes it could be paid in sword steel!"

"Worse, spies could creep through the woods, as you crept into Derventio," Kynddelig added, "and if they should see Eadhun and recognise him. . . Angle, are your kinsmen rich?"

"Very," Eadhun said, and did not need to say more.

"Then, let Gareth decide." Ronan picked up a cup of wine. "We'll put this to him, Bryn. Kynddelig says Gareth is a wiser man than any who's commanded a warband yet. Trust him."

"I trust no one," Bryn said tersely as he snatched up his cloak and followed Ronan to the door. On the threshold he turned back

172

to Taran and Cora. "Watch the bastard. He's out of his irons for the first time. Don't take your eyes off him."

Lamps flickered in Gareth's house with the bright cheer of a home, some quality that would never be enjoyed in the barracks. The two hearths were alight, bread baking in the cooking hearth, the dogs asleep on the bearskins in the warm, smoky draught. Gareth's two daughters — twins, so very like their mother — were playing with skeins of wool while Gareth watched them, drowsy and subdued. His fingers stroked the long-coated black cat that slept on his knee.

The seneschal, Marcus, ushered Bryn and Ronan inside and fussed over the weighted deerskins at the door. It was dark outside already. Marcus returned to his work and Gareth beckoned his visitors to the fire. The daughters did not even look up.

"What brings you here? It's late, that Angle should be confined to the barracks."

"He is," Ronan said quickly, "and Taran and Cora are guarding him. I sent for the smith a little while ago, to strike his fetters, Gareth. His wrists are chafed through to blood, and I think we can trust him. He has been a shadow to me lately. He has seen that many men would enjoy letting his blood."

"Yes." Gareth's brows had arched, but he nodded assent. "Have you eaten?"

"With the warband." Bryn cleared his throat. "My lord, Ronan has a scheme which bears listening to. We all second it, and Eadhun can tell you Malla's position, near enough."

"Malla? Who is Malla?" Gareth frowned deeply.

It took only a few moments for Ronan to outline the whole scheme. Gareth heard him out and his expression only darkened. At last Ronan fell silent and sat back to wait for judgement. Gareth stroked his chin thoughtfully, looking into the fire as he mulled over every word, every argument. Servants and children went on as if they had not heard a word. The black cat turned around on Gareth's knee and he petted it absently.

"How well does Eadhun know this man, Malla? How well does Malla know him?" he asked at last.

"He knows the man well enough to know Malla does not wish to fight before next season," Bryn said shrewdly. "Which means he has talked over the chief's plans, intimately, and been trusted with this knowledge. I would say he knows Malla quite well — and from across the water, too. He told us how Malla lost his family. Eadhun must have traded along both coasts for years."

"So Malla would listen to Eadhun as well as to any man,"

Gareth mused. "Still, I don't like the sound of it. Too dangerous." He gave Ronan and Bryn a calculating look. "And yet, how shall we shut out spies who creep like thieves into Ebor, by night? If you entered Derventio and got out again unseen. . . Good gods, Angles may have been in Ebor already. Malla may know every secret we possess." He passed a hand before his eyes. "Someone will have to ride into Derventio and confront Malla with the offer."

"Me." Bryn was on his feet.

"Us," Ronan corrected. "We know the land better than any of your people, Gareth, and the camp. Much has changed since the old town burned. We are the only outsiders who have been in there."

"And do you know how thin are the chances of your riding out of there again?" Gareth put down the cat as it began to bite. He got to his feet and paced the house, stiffly at first until his old wounds eased. "Will Malla not call you liars and put a sword through you, or simply chain you with the others?"

For some moments they were silent, and then Bryn suggested, "Eadhun must send a message, something that could come only from him, and that Malla would recognise."

"Words are only words, and precious cheap," Gareth said dismissively. He knuckled his eyes as wind from the hole in the thatch wafted smoke into his face, and waved to Marcus to fetch his cloak. "Let me talk to the Angle. He will know better than we how far we can go." He fastened the cloak brooch at his left shoulder and settled the heavy scarlet fabric about himself. "I don't want to see you two dead, or in irons. Not after the gods have let you escape twice."

"But you know the alternative," Bryn said quietly. "Unless you want to fight again this season, as you swore you would not, you don't dare send a message to Karitia. The ransom is a handful of smoke. And we will never be sure that the night has not brought spies."

Gareth was out of the house before him. He marched into the barracks and stood, fists on hips, studying Eadhun until the younger man clearly began to wonder if he was to be punished. At last Gareth said tersely, "Malla will kill my men if I send them across the frontier without some message from you. What can you offer me that will keep them safe and fetch them back to freedom?"

"This, my lord." Eadhun stood, and his long fingers worked loose the heavy, inlaid silver medallion he wore at his throat. "Take this to Malla." He handed it carefully to Ronan. "It is very old and has been in my family since the time of my grandfather. Once, Malla tried to buy it. I told him no, for it will be passed to my son upon my death. He will recognise it now. Tell him. . .tell him, it belongs to him, if he will make the trade."

The piece was very heavy, a coiled serpent with gleaming blue gems in its eyes, the whole thing scarred with age though it was kept polished. Ronan turned it to the light and frowned sidelong at Gareth. "We can do it, Ironhand, with your order."

Silent for a long time, the chief studied Eadhun. "We place a great deal of trust in you, Captain. How true do you speak? What will become of you, if my lads are thrown back into Dubgall with their throats cut?"

"I imagine," Eadhun said bleakly, "you will cut out my tongue to curb its lies, and throw me to your soldiers for their sport, for so long as I can survive. Your men would make away with me, despite my good intentions."

"Good intentions," Gareth echoed. "Many a man has gone to his death on good intentions. But it's a man's right to choose his own cause to die for. You'll wager your necks, then, will you, Bryn, Ronan? Those are the stakes you're gambling for, before ever you get as far as arranging the trade."

Every man in Ebor knew that Bryn's heart had been set on this for a long time, but he wore a frown as he turned to Ronan, and Ronan was pleased to be asked. "You swore your allegiance to Gruffydd once. After they burned Derventio, you swore allegiance to Gareth. You owe Gruffydd nothing. You don't have to go."

"Save that the whole scheme was my idea," Ronan said drily. He turned the medallion to the light again. "You think I'll back out now? With this silver serpent, and with luck, we'll come to no harm." He gave Eadhun a piercing look, and then a faint, crooked smile. "Or, I pray we will not, for we'll not be the only ones to suffer, if Malla is a bastard." Eadhun looked away, for he knew the dangers just as well. Ronan turned back to Gareth and asked without preamble, "When shall we go, Ironhand?"

"Tomorrow, if the weather holds fair." Gareth gathered up his cloak and strode to the door. "I'll give you an escort to the frontier, but beyond that I won't risk Kynddelig or Cora or one more sword from this warband. If it goes awry, we'll be fighting soon enough. I'll need the best I have, alive and whole. Go at dawn. Take my advice, and put your affairs in order tonight." For a moment he frowned at the two younger men, an expression of exasperation and admiration, and then the barracks door slammed shut behind him.

"Ride at dawn," Ronan whispered, only now beginning to realise what they had begun. Dry-mouthed, he studied Eadhun's medallion and did not stir until Bryn took him by the shoulders.

"He's right," Bryn said quietly. "We must put our affairs in order, and we've not got much time." He nodded goodnight to Taran and the others, and shepherded Ronan home.

Ronan was still studying the medallion as Bryn lit the hearth and found them supper, and at last Bryn took it out of his hands.

"Tonight should be for us, Ronan. The night before a battle is always for lovers. Tomorrow will bring no battle, to be sure, but we may not see the day out. Tonight may well be our last, and I want you." Ronan looked up at him. His eyes glittered, and the tears spilled. Bryn held him.

They made love with curious gentleness, neither willing to be the aggressor. Instead, they moved slowly against one another, shifting restlessly from position to position. Bryn slid down to take Ronan's proud cock into his throat, and Ronan twisted about, pressed his face into Bryn's groin. They settled like that at last, and made it go on and on.

The last time? Ronan was haunted by the thought. His half-closed eyes looked down the length of Bryn's beautiful body, from the curve of his bony hip to the hard contours of his breast and shoulder. Bryn's mouth still held Ronan's cock, sucking him slowly while his fingers stroked the ripe, swollen balls. The shaft in Ronan's hand was familiar, warm, moist, like velvet over iron. Love throbbed through him, for a moment eclipsing lust. He closed his eyes and his hand splayed across Bryn's taut buttocks.

Afterward they lay awake for a long time. "What affairs shall we set to rights?" Ronan asked softly. "Perhaps we should ask Kyn to hold out money until we return. And if we don't, he and Taran should divide it evenly between them."

"Gareth should have the racehorse," Bryn decided. "We owe him a great deal. Red will repay him time and again on our behalf, and every time the horse wins, our names will be remembered and celebrated. I can think of no more we can do."

"Nor can I." Ronan sighed heavily. "Save that affairs should also be set to rights between us."

"Between us?" Bryn propped his head on his hand. "How so?"

"Much is left unsaid." Ronan smiled at him. "And it should be said, even if only once." Bryn's brows rose, and he waited. "I love you," Ronan told him. "If I could wed you as a man can have a girl, I would. I will surely die without you, since where would be the cause to live?" He put a finger to Bryn's mouth to silence him as he

176

tried to interrupt. "It is a time for settling accounts, Bryn. Say only that you care for me."

"I love you." Bryn pulled him closer. "No matter what befalls us tomorrow, no one can take that from us." He wriggled down into the sheepskins and held Ronan against him.

15

The only route by day into Malla's lands was to ride up past Dubgall and right into the teeth of the new chief's sentries. Bryn had seen them often enough, patrolling the common land. Big, burly spear carriers, every one a blooded warrior in his own right.

The night had been restless and Bryn was tired as he mounted up. Ronan was silent, as if resigned to whatever took place. Kynddelig and two score men from the cavalry were their escort, but their fangs had been drawn. What could they do? Bryn and Ronan must enter the Angle lands alone, or the ground would be red by noon.

The sky was sullen. A northeast wind drove palls of grey cloud before it, and the sun was not yet up when Gareth appeared to farewell them. He was wrapped in that scarlet cloak, his dogs at his heels, an anxious look on his face. Taran and Cora had taken responsibility for Eadhun, but the young merchant had done nothing to make them suspicious.

Eadhun stood at the door of the cavalry barracks, as uncaring of the weather as any seaman. He reached up to offer Ronan his wrist. Ronan hesitated, and then took it. "It's odd, Angle. I am your enemy, or should be, yet I can't be at odds with you."

"I have never been your enemy," Eadhun argued in his thick, guttural accent. "It was not I who marched on your village and killed your clan. I am a trader. I shall buy my way into Valhalla, not fight my way there. Hie you well, Ronan of Whitestonecliff. Wotan go with you. Give Malla my silver piece, and tell him this. Mind that you remember the very same words!" Ronan listened intently. "Tell Malla that Aethella still loves him."

"Who?" Ronan gathered the reins.

"A woman in Karitia. Repeat her name!"

"Aethella," Ronan said, trying it on his tongue.

Satisfied, Eadhun stepped back as the big warhorse began to prance. "She told Malla that he would very likely die here, but if he did not, he should send word to her, and when it was safe perhaps she would join him. I was to carry the message for her."

"That will convince Malla," Gareth mused, "even better than the medallion. It should win you safe conduct where elaborate lies and a warband behind you would only fetch blood." He stood with Taran and Eadhun and raised his hand in farewell. "We will watch for your return. Go carefully."

The horses wheeled swiftly about and were out through the gates of Eboracum as a wind, high up, swirled a clear area in the mist of cloud. It would be a long ride to Dubgall, into the teeth of that wind, and Bryn thought he smelt stormy weather to come.

He looked back at Eboracum as they turned onto the north trail. The stone Roman city, once the home of the doomed Ninth Legion, brooded under the sullen sky, and yet it had come to mean home. Bryn shrugged deeper into his cloak as Kyn and Ronan began to hurry the pace.

They were halfway along the wagon-rutted road when the sky darkened as if some god was furious, but the rain held off as the wind fell. They pressed on, and in the afternoon saw the heather-thatched roofs of Dubgall. Boys ran out to take the horses, bring them ale and food, but Bryn could not eat. He and Ronan accepted a hearth and mulled ale, sat close together and watched the sky.

At the door of the building where the warriors camped, Kynddelig gazed out toward the ruin of Derventio. "You will be on their land in another half mile. Better to wait here and go on in the morning, I think. You don't want to arrive late and spend the night in a slave pen." He looked down at the younger men. "You need daylight on your side, and that sky is promising storms."

The moor was a desolate landscape, too bleak for those not born to it. Strangers often found it ugly or even frightening. The Romans had hated it, fought against it as if the very land were their enemy. Perhaps it was, for sometimes the land won. As they drowsed over the fire that night the ballad singer told the story of the Ninth Legion, the Hispana. The moor and the mist swallowed all of them. Sent north to Pictland, which the Romans claimed and called Caledonia although they never really tamed it, the Hispana marched out to quell an uprising. They never returned.

Summer thunder rumbled, eerie, hollow and haunted, and despite the season it was cold. Chilled by the ballad singer's story, preoccupied with its ghosts, Bryn settled to rest with Ronan in his arms. He did not expect to sleep and was surprised when Kyn shook him awake before dawn.

The sky was pale, watery blue and the wind had calmed, but the moor was sodden. Kynddelig whistled for two horses to be brought up, and Ronan's mouth compressed as he saw the nags.

"You're giving us the poorest animals of the lot, Kyn. You think we're not coming back, don't you?"

"No," Kyn said mildly. "I think Malla will accept Eadhun's message about the woman. But I also believe that he will seize your horses and throw you out on foot. Horses are worth their weight in copper or tin, and the Angles have few of them. These old lads are spent, no use for riding to war. But they're *lads!*" He slapped the rump of the brown-coated veteran closest to him. "They have the balls to breed up better stock, mated to Angle mares. No good for farm labour, but they have their uses! These two won't be spitted over a fire tonight, and they won't be worked till they drop in harness. They'll stand at stud, shoulder-deep in clover. Aye, well, they've earned the retirement. And as for you two. . ." He looked up at Ronan, as he swung up onto the squeaking leather of a battered old saddle. "You're armed."

Both Ronan and Bryn wore broadswords and knives. "We might fight out way out, if we're jumped by a scouting party well short of the stockade," Bryn said tersely. "We have to survive long enough to get to Malla, speak to him. We may not live that long if we go in unarmed."

"And you think Malla the farmer will listen to a word you say, after you've killed his young men?" Kyn shook his head emphatically. "More likely, he'll cut off your foolish heads."

"You want us to leave our weapons?" Ronan's fist closed about the hilt of his sword.

"Leave the obvious ones," Kyn advised. "Take the knives, they give you the chance you need, especially you, Ronan. I never saw a more deadly hand with a knife. Here, give the swords to me."

"Under protest," Bryn told him, but handed the weapons down to Kyn.

"We'll watch and listen," Kyn said quietly, "but you know you're on your own."

"We know." Bryn took Kynddelig's hand in a firm clasp for a moment. "It will take some time to make Malla understand. We may have difficulty with the language. Don't fret for us before afternoon, Kyn."

"But if you don't see us by tomorrow noon," Ronan added in the same mild tone, "go back to Eboracum and tell Gareth to treaty with his neighbours in the south. He will be fighting before Samhaine, ready for it or not." He touched his heels to the horse and moved off, out into the common land of the frontier.

Behind them, children and dogs played unconcernedly in the moorland puddles and in the woods, but the news had raced through

Dubgall, and men and women stood by the walls to watch them ride by. More than once, a man or woman touched Bryn's hand, or Ronan's, and invoked a god to bless them.

The old horses laboured over the sodden surface and soon tired. It was difficult to tell where Gareth's land ended and Malla's began, but sure enough the Angle scouts were already out. Bryn drew Ronan's attention to them. "We've been seen. There, in the trees. Five men, bronze helmets, sheepskins."

"I see them," Ronan grunted. "Spears, dark faces. Five warriors, Bryn. These are nor farmers. See those spears?"

They were war spears, their gleaming blades upthrust like massive fangs. "Mercenaries out of the Saxon shore," Bryn guessed. "I heard this at Catreath, when I was there with my father, the time we bought Red. Saxon mercenaries are hiring their skills even to Angles, though the Saxon chiefs trust Angles and Danes no more than we do." He reined back a little to slow their pace.

The men were small in stature, thick with muscle, wind-tanned, like old leather. Slowly, carefully, Bryn and Ronan swung toward them. They let the reins lie loosely and held up their empty hands, an obvious gesture. Though their scabbards were empty, they had eight assorted knives about them. The Saxon mercenaries would have seen the hilt of every blade, but no fighting man would expect an envoy to ride out completely unarmed.

The five powerful men came out from the blue shadows beneath the sycamore. If they spoke the British tongue, they made no offer to use it. They made no sound, neither threat nor greeting. Bryn brought his horse to a halt and cleared his throat. Their death warrants could be issued on a single word. Beside him, Ronan held his breath.

"We come from Eboracum." Bryn spoke slowly and distinctly. "We have business, and bring a message to Malla, from the merchant captain, Eadhun of Karitia."

Most of what he had said must have been unintelligible, but the Saxons clearly recognised the name of Gareth, who was well known in the south after several campaigns. They heard Malla's name, too, and possibly they knew Eadhun's — the merchant swore he had traded from Pictland to the Saxon shore, since he was a boy apprenticed to his uncle.

The mercenaries growled in the guttural Saxon tongue, speaking guardedly amongst themselves. Ronan and Bryn could only wait, and an icy sweat prickled Bryn's ribs and face. Silently, he crossed his fingers. If Malla did not speak the Britons' language and had no one to interpret for him, negotiations were hopeless. It would not even be possible to give him the message from the woman he wished to wed.

Now, it was all a gamble and the gods themselves were rolling the dice. Bryn had consigned his life into their hands as he and Ronan rode out of Dubgall, and yet now the moment had arrived his belly crawled uncomfortably.

The Saxons were a strange breed. They looked and sounded so little like Britons that Bryn felt his hackles rise, though no threat had been issued yet. They even *smelt* different, in a way that made him shiver. The mercenaries had the whip hand, but they made no move to use it. Bryn listened closely to them, trying to pick up names, and he had heard Malla's several times before these men seemed to reach a decision.

Pale blue eyes glared up at the intruders. A spear blade thrust at them and then jerked in the direction of the stockade. Ronan nudged his horse forward a pace, but as it moved three of the Saxons barred his way.

"Dismount," Bryn whispered. "They don't trust men on horseback, remember. Cavalry is the thing these people fear most on the battlefield."

"This isn't a battlefield," Ronan muttered, but very slowly he and Bryn slid to the ground. Two of the Saxons grabbed the bridle straps and at once tugged the horses out of reach. Bryn and Ronan moved closer together, and Bryn thought that he had never felt more vulnerable and naked.

These men did not ride, or they would have mounted up. Instead, they led the cavalry nags away while the prisoners were urged at spearpoint toward the gate in the high timber stockade. They were resolutely infantry, Bryn thought with a sniff of disdain. He had once scorned infantrymen. Then, he had been so sure that he was born to command a warband of elite cavalry, and the knowledge was his conceit.

Those days were gone forever. He was a soldier now. He fought for pay in the warband of a chief to whom he had sworn allegiance, and if there was noble blood in his veins, it was worthless as water. All this was cruelly reinforced as the Saxons brought him and Ronan through the gate and into the camp. It was the first time they had seen it by daylight. They had seen little by night, and now they were both shocked.

Derventio seemed to have been erased. They were unable to recognise anything. The fires must have cut the old town right down to its stone foundations, Bryn thought, for not a structure standing today survived from the old days. Only the old Roman foundations survived, and they were so strong, so deep, they would be impervious to time. In a hundred years, and a thousand, a spade in the ground would still find them.

The Angle camp was rough-hewn, raw and new. Bryn's throat was dry as a great shouting and commotion greeted their arrival, and all at once he and Ronan were surrounded by Angles. But these men were farmers, armed with tools and implements, and their faces betrayed as much fear and anxiety as anger. Ronan's hands were seized and slapped onto his head. One by one his knives were confiscated, and then Bryn was similarly stripped of his weapons. Hands on their heads, they walked the last of the way ringed about by Angles, completely unarmed, and Bryn thought that death seemed to stare unblinkingly from every face about him.

They were not surprised when their hands were jerked down behind them, bound so tightly that in moments Bryn had lost all feeling and knew his fingers must be blue. A chieftain searched them to the skin as the women and children crept closer to peer at the enemies, for Ronan and Bryn were the first Britons they had ever seen. It was like being an animal exhibited in a menagerie, or a slave on the auction block, and Bryn's skin crawled.

It was difficult to get his bearings, but he smelt the river, away to his right, and he knew the way back out. The bulk of the stockade was to their left, and inside the stout fence was what Eadhun called the *tun* of Malla's people. Before them was the long, low hall where they had snatched a glimpse through warped timbers and seen the captive women.

Spears prodded at their backs to move them on, and Bryn cast about for a man he might recognise as a chief. Three steps led up to the double doors of the great hall, and at the top three men waited. Surely, the figure in the middle could only be Malla.

His hair and beard were still dark, though silver coiled through his braids. He was as broad shouldered as any of the younger men, big bellied, but not soft. Muscle thickened his arms and thighs, and he wore a heavy bearskin cloak, fastened at the throat by a chain Bryn was sure was gold. Fists clenched on his hips, he watched with a thunderous face as the intruders were thrust to the foot of the steps. Bryn looked up into flint-hard eyes and swallowed. Did the man speak their language?

A spear-haft in the middle of his back shoved Bryn to his knees, and Ronan went down beside him a moment later. The ground was muddy, wet and cold, but Malla was speaking, and Bryn held his breath to listen. At the chief's right hand stood an older man in a coarse, brown robe, thin as a reed, with gaunt features and white,

blind eyes. A slave? Bryn wondered, and yet the man was not col-
lared, nor marked in any way.

As Malla fell silent the blind one spoke up. "By Tor," he said,
clearly repeating every word the chief had said, translating without
addition or omission, "you had better have reason aplenty for this,
or your heads will be on Malla's gate in an hour."

Taking a deep breath, Ronan lifted his head. The blade of a
spear touched his chest, right over his heart, and Bryn's throat
squeezed. He looked up at Malla, let the chief see the fear naked in
his face. How Ronan steadied his voice, Bryn could not guess. "Well
met, my lord," Ronan said slowly, speaking both to the chief and
the old blind scholar. "I am Ronan of Whitestonecliff, in the serv-
ice of Gareth Ironhand. With me is Bryn ap Gruffydd, who is the
son of a chief. We bring messages."

Every word was relayed without any twitch of expression from
the scholar, and Malla spoke again in that deep, rumbling voice,
like gravel. "Well met." His face denied the greeting. "What busi-
ness has the Ironhand for me?

"Trade," Ronan said slowly. "A trade of hostages, arranged by
the merchant, Eadhun, who sails out of the port of Karitia. You
know him well, so he claims. He was bound for Iarum to deal with
you, when his ship was blown into our waters by the storms."

The chief's eyes narrowed as the scholar translated, and his
face seemed to be made of quarried rock. He growled like a bear,
and the blind man's light voice said moments later, "You hold
Eadhun in Eboracum?"

"And the crew of his vessel," Bryn offered, "and his cargo."
He licked at dry lips. "It is Eadhun's wish that a trade be arranged
between Malla and Gareth. The merchant and his men, exchanged
for the people of Derventio who are held here in slave irons."

As the scholar translated this last, muttering broke out among
the crowding onlookers. Malla glared down at Ronan, and for the
first time he said in an accent so thick, a knife could have cut it,
"Malla holds no Britons here among his slaves."

So he did speak the language, albeit haltingly. Bryn shivered,
and very carefully Ronan framed their answer. Call this man a liar,
and they would die here, on their knees in the mud. "With respect,
my lord Malla, the slaves have been seen. Some have been recog-
nised. Gareth is in no doubt."

The Angle's heavy brows twitched together. "Smart boy," he
grunted. "Call Malla the liar and live to tell the tale. But Malla can
call you the liar, just as easy. Who says Gareth got Eadhun? Maybe
Gareth got Eadhun like dead body, and the head on Eboracum

gate!"

"If it would please you to be sure," Ronan said very softly, "I have proof, my lord. Will you loose my hands?"

"No." Malla glared thoughtfully at him. "You got tongue. Speak."

Ronan breathed deeply two, three times, and Bryn felt the knot in his own belly, sickening him. Fear was a ferocious enemy. "Then," Ronan went on, "take the pouch I wear at my throat, beneath my collar. He lifted his chin. "Your proof is in it." He knelt like a statue, waiting.

Now, Malla conferred with his scholar, since some of these words were difficult. The strange, blind eyes looked down at Ronan, and Malla said through his lips, "The pouch contains bad magic."

"It does not," Bryn assured him. "It contains Eadhun's property. Something known to Malla."

"Treachery, deception," the scholar accused.

"Proof. Good faith from Eadhun," Ronan insisted. "Please, take it. If I lie, cut my throat as soon as you see that I have lied."

At Malla's left hand stood a man not much older than Bryn or Ronan. He was tall, with wide shoulders, big hands, a mane of coarse fair hair and the arrogant manner of one who was born to command men. A glance at him, and Bryn recognised Malla's son. Moreover, he saw a little of himself in the young man, for he had once behaved with this same arrogance, carried his head that way, looked at the world with the same disdain, since he knew that it belonged to him. Malla's hand lay on the young man's arm, and the two spoke in undertones for a moment before the chief fixed Ronan with a flinty look.

"Here is Malla's son. Malla's heir and first-born, Wulfhere." He stabbed a finger at Ronan. "If the pouch got bad magic, Wulfhere will open your throat. Understand?"

"I understand," Ronan said tautly. "There is nothing to fear, my lord."

There was a swagger in Wulfhere's walk, and Bryn wondered if he had swaggered that way himself, when he had been a chief's heir. Wulfhere came down the steps, pale blue eyes flaying the very flesh off Ronan's bones. One big, brown hand closed about the pouch and the rawhide thong snapped against the back of Ronan's neck, making him yelp. The pigskin bag was handed up to Malla, who took it as if it were dung.

"Poison?" he asked in his own voice as Wulfhere returned to his side.

"Open it, and you will find only a silver medallion," Ronan

said levelly. "You will know it at once. Eadhun said, you wished to own it."

For some moments Malla studied the Britons without the twitch of a muscle, and Bryn's heart began to race. He felt the press of a spear in his kidney. One thrust of the blade and it was over. Malla the farmer held their lives in the palm of his hand.

He pulled open the pouch, held the silver serpent to the sun, and swore lividly. Bryn heard the names of Wotan and Tor from both Malla and Wulfhere, and Malla's eyes were blazing as he roared, "This, taken off dead body of Eadhun!"

"No," Bryn said quickly. "Given into our hands yesterday. "Eadhun said you may have the piece. Keep and own it, if you will cooperate with his plan. He also gave us a message that you have been waiting for."

Malla leaned toward the scholar and the blind one whispered into his ear. "Message?" he asked then. "What message you got for Malla?"

"One that Eadhun had intended to convey himself," Bryn said slowly. Malla glared down at him, and Bryn glanced at Ronan. If the chief believed them at all, now was the moment. "He says to tell you, the lady Aethella, whom you left in Karitia, still loves you."

The scholar translated and the crowd hushed. Bryn's heart skipped as he waited for Malla to draw the broadsword that rode sheathed at his left hip, its hilt thrusting at the bearskin cloak, or for Wolfhere to draw the twin daggers from his belt. Death seemed an instant away.

And then Malla's seamed, leathery face split into a grin and he barked with laughter. "By Wotan, Wulfhere, they got Eadhun. Safe? Eadhun live, well? Ironhand treat fair?"

"He has Gareth's hospitality." Ronan was breathing again. "He has some little freedom in Eboracum, and his crew is fed. But they are Angles in an enemy camp, and they would sooner be free."

"Aye, truth in that. Much truth." Malla cocked his head at them and stroked his beard as he examined them as if they were horses, or slaves, at market. "Come to my hearth. Tell of Eadhun. How many his men you got in Eboracum?"

The spear blades swung back to let them rise, and Ronan and Bryn mounted the steps slowly, carefully. Wulfhere was the last to step aside, and drew himself up to his full height. He was taller than Bryn, broader, and he breathed deliberately into Bryn's face. His breath smelt of ale and onions, and Bryn smelt his body too, some musk from his skin, and the odour of sheepskin and leather.

For a moment Bryn feared that Wulfhere would not step aside to let them pass. He and Ronan waited with downcast eyes, barely breathing, but at last the Angle swung away into the hall and spearpoints jabbed into Bryn's shoulders to urge him forward again.

He clenched and unclenched his fingers to ease their numbness, for the binding cords had cut off his circulation minutes before. "Ronan?" he whispered.

"I'm all right," Ronan murmured, and then spoke up. "We have all of Eadhun's crew, my lord. None were killed. Twenty seamen who did not fight, but surrendered their vessel and cargo. It is Gareth's understanding that you have twice that many here in Derventio."

"In what?" Malla looked up over the silver serpent, shared a glance with Wulfhere, and his bushy brows knitted. "What is Derventio?"

Bryn took a breath. "That was the name of this town before you captured it."

"This has been no Roman camp in year and year, boy." Malla gestured at the cluster of huts and fences. "Mallatun. The *tun* of Malla's people. My people. You see no Roman here."

"My lord." Ronan stepped between them. "Forgive us. We knew this place before your people came."

The Angle grunted and thrust Eadhun's medallion into the breast of his tunic. A seneschal held open the door skins and they stepped inside, and Bryn caught his breath on the smoky air. In the sudden dimness he was almost blind and a dozen strange smells assaulted his nose. Malla hooked his thumbs into his belt and turned to confront them, looking Bryn up and down with an expression of distrust. "What of ap Gruffydd? You are a chief's son?"

"I was." Bryn licked his lips and glanced sidelong at Wulfhere, who did not seem to speak a word of the language. He was drinking, intent on his ale, oblivious to conversation he did not understand, but his eyes never left the strangers, as if he found them somehow irresistible. "Derventio was my home, my lord Malla," Bryn went on. "It is gone now. I see none of it left in Mallatun. I am just a freeman warrior like Ronan."

Malla lowered his stout frame into a great carved chair by the hearth. At his feet a serving boy held a cup of ale, but for the moment the chief was too engrossed in his prisoners to notice. He beckoned the blind scholar to his side again, and for several minutes spoke in growling undertones with him, and with Wulfhere. At last it was the blind man who said,

"Gareth believes that Malla has twice as many Britons as he

186

has Angles. How does he know this?"

The question was probing; an honest answer could be their death warrant. Bryn and Ronan looked warily at one another, and Bryn cleared his throat. "My lord, spies came into your camp by night."

The scholar translated and Malla's eyes flashed anger. Wulfhere swallowed the last of his ale, threw down the cup, and his fists clenched. The chief leaned toward Bryn and Ronan, but his words came from the blind man's lips. "This is impossible. Now my lord Malla knows you lie. Shall he have the truth out of you at the end of a whip? Mind your tongues, for you could lose them."

"It is the truth, Malla," Ronan murmured. His eyes moved restlessly about the hall, seeking any route of escape, but the only way in or out was the main door. The crowd had come inside with them, and no fewer than forty men stood between them and that door. They were trapped, and only soft, clever words would get them out of here. "My lord," Ronan began again, "we have no cause to lie. Our lives are in your hands, you could kill us at a word. We are young, and have no wish to die."

Again the scholar translated, and Malla listened, stroking his beard, even while Wulfhere growled in protest. Malla's face was thoughtful now. "Spies? How?"

"Across the field where you graze your pigs," Bryn told him, "at night. Your guardsmen were drunk and asleep." He saw Malla's mouth compress as the scholar whispered all this into his ear. Punishment would be undertaken later, but it seemed that the chief had his suspicions, since he was not surprised. "Shadow to shadow, my lord," Bryn went on. "The stables, the slave pens. Then, a gap between the timbers in that wall. Women were seen here. Four women. One of them was recognised."

For some time Malla was silent, but his mouth worked and his hands rubbed the polished wooden arms of the chair. Wulfhere looked sullen, dangerous, and Ronan and Bryn lowered their eyes. Now, they could only wait. Murmurs sped about the hall — was Malla listening to his people, was he listening to Wulfhere? At last he leaned forward again, one elbow on his knee. "Cuthred!"

A man stepped out of the gathering. Malla spoke to him rapidly in the harsh Angle tongue. and a knife was drawn. Bryn's heart leapt into his throat, but the knife merely whittled at the tip of a writing quill. So Cuthred was the chief's scribe. Bryn's heart slowed as he watched the brown-faced little man work with the ink and scraped vellum, right there on the floor at Malla's feet.

The air was heavy with the smell of stewing meat and vegetables, bread and ale. Bondsmen brought out food, but the captives were not untied. Malla was not ready to extend his hospitality, perhaps in the fear that it would be construed as an offer of friendship. Wulfhere's face was dark as a thundercloud, and it was clear what fate he desired to bring about for the intruders in this camp.

But Malla spoke slowly, pacing his words, waiting as the scribe wrote everything at a laborious pace, in careful Roman capitals. Bryn rolled his shoulders as his muscles began to cramp and looked sidelong into Ronan's face. He saw a flicker of hope there, and nodded. If Malla's words were being written down, then some form of them — the agreement itself — must be delivered to Gareth, and who better to deliver them than the envoys who had brought in Gareth's message?

At last Malla turned his attention back to his prisoners. "Tell truth. Why Gareth send you? Why not other men?"

"Because we two were trained as warriors here, my lord," Bryn told him. "We alone escaped from Derventio with our lives that night."

"You mean, ran like dogs, left your brothers to die?" Malla demanded sourly, with a sidelong glance at his son. Wulfhere's lips curled back from his teeth.

"No, my lord." Bryn lifted his chin. "We were not in the town. We saw the smoke and quickly returned, but it was over already. We made all haste to Eboracum to warn Gareth."

"So you escape. The gods smile on you," Malla rumbled grudgingly, and beckoned the blind man closer. The scholar continued for him, "You would have been proud of your sword brothers. They fought like men. And they died like men, when we cut them down like ripe wheat. After the battle, some refused to be chattels here, and chose death. They died under the whip, at the hand of my lord Wulfhere, the death of a slave, since they were warriors no more. But they died well, also, without a sound. Your gods embrace them."

Pain twisted Bryn's insides, and he looked away from Malla's face. "Ronan and I escaped to fight some other day, my lord."

"To fight me?" Malla gave a short bark of laughter and nudged Wuldhere with one big elbow. Wulfhere's eyes flayed Bryn and Ronan to the bone.

Ronan said, quietly and levelly, "If you march on Eboracum, my lord, and if we are still alive and in Gareth's service, of course we will fight you."

"Well said," Malla allowed. "Aye, the old town burn to cinder. One hour, all gone. If you come late to the fight, better run like sheep than die like wolf. Honour, you can win back later."

"So what message shall we take to Gareth and Eadhun?" Ronan kept his eyes down, but the question probed.

The blind scholar translated, "You assume you will be leaving." The words were dark, bleak, and for some time Malla was silent, considering the whole scheme.

The scribe whittled his quill again, and Malla beckoned Wulfhere back to his side. He had that battle-hardened look, Bryn thought, as if he had seen hard times, much bloodshed. As if he had learned to hate, and to be vengeful. Whose terrible vengeance did he win, when he flogged to death the prisoners who refused to be shackled after the battle? Bryn gave Wulfhere an ice-cold, grudging respect, and in that moment was very much aware that Bryn ap Gruffydd was not yet blooded, though no man in this hall save Ronan knew it.

The Angles and their Saxon mercenaries studied the prisoners with blood in their eyes, but life and death were Malla's to decide. He spoke in whispers with Wulfhere for some time, and at last, when he turned back to Bryn and Ronan, Bryn feared the worst.

"My son wish to collar you with the rest and sport with you later," he growled. "But maybe you got luck. You go. You tell this to Eadhun and Gareth," Malla said gravely. "It is fair exchange if Eadhun bring to Malla half his cargo. That cargo is mine. Paid. Give Malla half. Other half, Gareth may keep, good trade for gift of life. . . Eadhun and his crew. If Gareth agree. . ."

The scholar spoke for him now, when the words escaped Malla. "If Gareth wishes to trade, these are the conditions. Eadhun and his crew, and half the cargo. Betray us, raise a sword against us, and the deal is cancelled. Your sword-brothers will die in irons."

"And what shall we receive?" Bryn asked.

"Your people." Malla leaned back in the enormous chair. "Eight and thirty men, alive, in the pens. Six women. Malla give all."

"Then, you may count the bargain struck," Ronan said quietly.

Wulfhere grumbled, deep and bass, and Malla leaned forward on his knee. "You speak with Gareth's voice?" He sounded dubious. "You are a boy,"

"A blooded warrior," Ronan corrected.

"Blooded," Malla growled, "in Angle blood."

"In a fair fight." Ronan lifted his chin. "The man was trying to kill me, and would have. I was quicker by a whisker. My whole family died that night. Do you know a village in the woods on the fringe of the moor, under a cliff of white stone?"

"I know it." Malla cocked his curiously head at Ronan. He turned to Wulfhere and made some remark that sent his son's brows up.

"The village of Whitestonecliff." Ronan's voice was hoarse. "I was born there. I almost died there. I live, because an Angle warrior died."

The old man sighed and shook his head, and the scholar said, "It is the way of war, boy. In Gallia and Germania, nothing is different. All is blood and pain. If you speak with Gareth's voice, then the Ironhand trusts you to strike his bargains."

"He sent us here, my lord," Bryn said pointedly. "We will tell him Malla's decision, word for word."

"See you tell right." Malla stabbed a finger at the copy his scribe had produced. "Malla got whole deal, here. See? Writ-down, no mistake. Gareth betray. . ." He jerked a thumb at his son. "Wulfhere play the blood-game. Understand?" He reached for the cup of ale that had been waiting for him and drank it to the bottom. "Five day. At noon, we camp on the frontier. What called?"

"Dubgall," Bryn whispered. His heart fluttered like a bird. *We're going to get out!* His throat was too dry to swallow.

"At Dubgall, noon, five days," the scholar translated for Wulfhere. "Tell this to Gareth. One chance, you are granted. A sword, an axe, raised against us, and you will hear the screams as your swordbrothers die. The blood of treachery will be on your own hands."

Malla was beckoning the Saxon mercenaries and as the scholar fell silent he growled, "The Saxons take you out. Do not return."

Spear points grazed Bryn's breast and back as he was hustled out of the hall a pace before Ronan. He had no idea how Gareth would respond to the demand for half the cargo, but Eboracum was rich, and half a cargo seemed to be a small price to pay for the lives of the captives. Gareth would keep Eadhun's vessel and, Bryn was sure, this was what he really wanted.

The crowd of onlookers went with them to the gate in the stockade, but only the Saxons ventured beyond. Even Wulfhere stayed on the north side of the timber, dark faced and with fire in his eyes. The very look of him made Bryn shiver, and he wondered again what had been done to Wulfhere, what had been taken from him, to leave such hate and such thirst for blood. The blood-game, as Malla called it.

Then they were out and moving. On the fringe of the paddock where pigs and chickens rooted for food, a knife slit the cords, freeing their wrists. Pain flared in Bryn's hands as they were pushed out into the no-man's-land. The Saxons barred the way back, and as a spear nudged Bryn's shoulders once more he moved out into the wide, open common ground.

He could barely believe that they were out and alive. Relief was dizzying, and the sky actually spun. A pace ahead of him, Ronan stumbled through the sodden grass and swore lividly as he worked his bloodless hands. "Kynddelig was right. They took the horses, damn them."

"Who cares about horses?" Bryn was rubbing his own hands. "We're out, Ronan! I thought we would never breathe free air again." As they passed out of sight of the stockade he slung an arm about Ronan's waist. "Kyn won't fret for us until noon." It was minutes before he began to breathe properly and heart slowed. His body was stiff and trembling with reaction, and when Ronan pressed against his side, Bryn was glad to have him there. "Never go back, he said."

"Never," Ronan agreed. "Why would I want to return there?"

"That place is not Derventio. Mallatun, is it? Haunted," Bryn said darkly. "Did you feel it? There were ghosts everywhere. The Angles are welcome to it."

"Ghosts." Ronan looked back over his shoulder at the timber stockade, half-seen through the trees now, and he shivered as if he too felt the presence of the dead.

Some swore that the city of Eboracum was still haunted by the ghosts of the Ninth Hispana even a century after the legion was destroyed. Now, would Derventio — Mallatun — be haunted by the ghosts of the men and women who died there?

"Come on." Bryn tugged Ronan forward. "Kyn will be waiting,"

In fact Kynddelig was watching for them. He was sitting up on the wall, where Bryn had so often sat in the evenings when he and Ronan had stood duty here, and he had seen them as they appeared across the common land. Dubgall's farmers clustered with the garrison, eager for news. Kyn embraced them, sent for wine, but the bonded lad would not go for it until he had heard the story.

They told it breathlessly by turns as they walked back to the barracks, and at last Ronan looked to Kyn for judgement.

"I told Malla he could have half the cargo. It was that or nothing, Kyn. What else could I say? Gareth has the ship. I don't know what the cargo is worth, but Malla has forty-four men and women in his slave pens. How much is a life worth?"

"How much indeed?" Kyn embraced him again and clasped

Bryn's wrist. "Put it to Gareth. I have never known him to be cruel or ungenerous."

"Which is why I stuck the bargain." Ronan rubbed his face hard. "I spoke for Gareth Ironhand as if we are his trustees, gods help us."

"You are his trustees," Kynddelig said drily. "Come and eat, now. We can be in Eboracum by nightfall if we take the fastest horses and don't tarry on the road." He cast a rueful glance across the common land. "I see they took the nags."

"As you knew they would." Bryn ducked into the garrison hut and saw his sword, and Ronan's, waiting on the table. Both were resheathed as Kynddelig sent for food and ale. "Five days, Kyn, right here, on the frontier at Dubgall."

"Tell Gareth this evening." Kynddelig lifted his cup in salute. "He will be thinking you are dead, you know. I thought I had seen the last of you. What manner of man is Malla?"

Bryn's brows rose, and he looked at Ronan, who was eating ravenously. Fear always made Ronan hungry, Bryn knew that well enough. "Malla is getting old, and he's ugly as a frog. . .but he's strong as a bull, and no man's fool. And I think he's fair," Bryn said carefully. "An honourable man, as Angles go. From what we saw, he has few real warriors, and I think that many of them were killed that night, when Derventio was taken. Saxon mercenaries are guarding the frontier for him now."

"You find many Saxon hirelings in the warbands along the coast," Kyn mused. "Gareth won't like the sound of that. It's one thing to fight your neighbours, who can only afford to spill so much blood before they must cry for peace or run away. Another thing to fight an army of mercenaries where the ranks are filled afresh every season." He sighed and tossed down the last of his ale. "Still, it is for Gareth to fret on that score. If Malla can hire mercenaries, so can he. And Gareth does, as you know!"

Painfully hungry as his taut-strung nerves relaxed, Bryn fell on the food. He and Ronan sat close together, listening as Kynddelig called orders to the garrison. The news would spread like wildfire to the hamlets between Dubgall and Eboracum.

When his belly would hold no more, Bryn threw the scraps of pork and bread to the dogs, sat back against the slatted wall and closed his eyes. Kyn was already calling for fast horses, but Bryn was tired after two sleepless nights. Ronan leaned heavily against him, but Bryn roused him with a little shake.

His lips brushed Ronan's mouth as he pushed up to his feet. "Time to ride. We can sleep later. We bed at home tonight." Ronan's tongue flicked out, hungry now for some little gesture of affection, which Bryn was delighted to give.

And then they were on the road, headed south, on the fastest horses Kyn could find.

16

They had expected Gareth to be waiting for them, but were surprised by his affection as they rode into Eboracum late that evening. Gareth embraced them both, took them to the hearth in the hall and let them tell all they knew in their own words, their own time. Most of the warband seemed to gather to listen. Drowsy by the fire, Ronan let Bryn speak of Malla and Wulfhere and the Angle camp, but when it came to the details of the trade he silenced Bryn with a hand on his arm.

"I spoke with your voice, Gareth, and had to make a bargain with the Angle warlord, on your behalf. There was nothing else for it. I will take responsibility for what I did, not Bryn. I know the price of this particular sin, if I did wrong! But Eadhun and his crew are not the sum of it. . .my lord Malla wants half the cargo also. And if he sees a sword raised against him at the exchange, every last man and woman he is holding will die."

"Half the cargo?" Gareth's brows arched. He leaned on the arm of his chair, chin propped in his hand, and in the firelight his deep eyes glittered with amusement. "And I suppose you promised him this."

Ronan felt his cheeks warm and lowered his head. "I'm sorry, Gareth, I did. I had to. Malla would accept no less, and would have refused the trade otherwise. I thought, that is, Bryn and I have thought, we will give you our horse in exchange, if he will cover the cost of the forfeit cargo. The roan racehorse is a stallion, and will sire you colts for many years. We were offered a fine price for him, just weeks ago." He looked at his lover, and Bryn nodded. They had agreed on this on the ride from Dubgall. "He is yours, Gareth. What else could I say to Malla?" Ronan asked quietly.

"I would have agreed to Malla's terms." Gareth laughed quietly and teased, "Bryn, your mate blushes, pretty as a girlchild. Advise him not to, else he is not safe. This warband is full of rakes! Ronan has his admirers, you know."

"Has he?" Bryn took Ronan's hand as Ronan's colour only deepened. "Gareth, he knows he took liberties. He expects to pay the price, and so do I. Let us give you the horse."

"Not the animal, but his services," Gareth amended. "I've a dozen mares who might be mated this coming season, and give me fast colts worth a dozen times the Angle's damned cargo. Let Malla have what he wants. Loan me the horse."

"Done." Bryn relaxed against Ronan's shoulder. "In five days, at noon, it will be complete. But there is dire news to end with, Ironhand." Gareth waited, and Bryn took a breath. "The Angle has hired a good number of Saxon mercenaries. He may hire more, and when he marches on us — as Eadhun says he will, as soon as he's ready — it will be with a force of fresh men who are paid to make war, men who love the battlefield, not war-weary farmers."

Of a sudden Gareth seemed to age. He looked mortally tired, and Ronan saw a shadow about him as he closed his eyes. "It is no more than I expected. It is the same in the southcountry, Bryn. It was Britons who invited the Saxon into this land, did you know that? Aye! Mercenaries, Hengist and Horsa, fetched in to do battle for a chief who had grown too soft-bellied, too *Roman*, to fight his own wars. How do you imaged our people were conquered in the beginning? Did we fight Rome and lose? We did not! No, Caesar sent a force of auxiliaries against us. We fought Gauls levied from our brother tribes across the Narrow Sea, and it was they who defeated us. Since they were our cousins they knew every move we would make, and every mistake. Traitors," he added bitterly. "Traitors to their kind, since the battle of Avalon." He knuckled his eyes and called for a cup of wine.

"But we also use mercenaries, hirelings, Gareth," Kynddelig said thoughtfully. "Lindum is filled with them, since the fighting has been so intense along the south coasts. I know Lindum quite well. Let me ride there with a call to arms — and soon, with your marching orders."

Gareth finished the wine, handed the cup to a girl and clapped his hands. "Yes, I think you had better, Kyn." He gave Kynddelig his hand in thanks. "Leave at first light, offer fair pay for a job done, a battle fought. . .and then tell them that if the gods see fit to smile on us, there will be no battle at all, this side of winter. Oh, enough of this sobriety! Where are the bards? Music! A man would think this was a wake, not a celebration of freedom and a homecoming for two brave lads!"

But Ronan and Bryn wanted no more than their own bed, an hour's pleasure and a night's sleep. With a quiet word of apology, Bryn urged Ronan to his feet. Behind them the ballad singer struck up a ribald verse. At the door, Taran and Cora still shadowed Eadhun, who had been brought to the hall to hear the news.

He had a cup of wine, and raised it in salute before Bryn and Ronan. "I owe you a debt of gratitude. It took great courage to ride into Malla's camp. I would not have gone, in your place."

"You might have," Ronan said tiredly. "Your hands are sword-callused. I've seen your scars. You've fought beside men you called sword-brothers. If your friends were in the slave pens, you would have gone,"

The Angle's wide shoulders lifted in an expressive shrug. "Who can tell? Perhaps we shall meet again, some day. Next time, gods willing, it may be as friends."

"I doubt it," Bryn said bluntly. "Tell me, Eadhun, have you fought beside Malla's son?"

The good humour faded swiftly from Eadhun's face. "I have. I fought alongside Wulfhere at Karitia, when ships came south out of the fog and out of nowhere the raiders were upon us. Wulfhere . . .knows little of pity."

"Why?" Ronan hugged himself against the night wind as they left the hall. "I could have sworn it was lust in his eyes, Bryn, when he looked at me, though I don't know what kind of lust it was. A thirst for blood? If Malla had refused us, I have the most terrible notion, I would not have lived to see the dawn."

"You may not have." Eadhun's eyes were low. "Wulfhere has been especially punished, as if the gods have picked out him alone to pay the price for his people's sins."

"Punished?" Bryn wondered.

The Angle gestured eastward, over his shoulder, toward the troubled lands across the sea. "Four years ago the night brought savages, and Wulfhere fought in the hills with the men while the women and the old men took the children and hid in the woods. There were caves, they thought they were safe. In the morning, when no one returned to the village, warriors went to the caves to fetch them home." Eadhun's eyes closed. "Most of them were dead. Some were gone. Wulfhere's children were slaughtered, his wife was stolen. Six months, he searched for her, but she was gone. He swore then that he would never wed again, never lay hands on an honourable woman of his own kind, a woman fit to take to wife."

"I can feel for that," Ronan said guardedly.

"He turned to men for solace and comfort," Eadhun continued. "Like yourselves, like the men of Gareth's warband. He gave his heart there, too. . .and it was cut out of his chest in a battle last season, on your own coast. His lover was a Saxon, big and blue-eyed, who played as rough as Wulfhere likes to play, since Hildegard was stolen. There is no gentleness in him, and his bedsport is better suited to men. His lover was taken prisoner not very far south of this land, and beheaded. His head was spiked on the gate, and rotted there, food for crows and ravens. Wulfhere arrived while time and flesh enough remained for him to recognise the face of his beloved." Eadhun looked away. "Now, the only game he cares for is blood."

"Gods forgive him, gods forgive us all," Ronan whispered. "Then it *was* lust I saw in his face when he looked at me. Blood-lust and the hunger to mate, both."

"To mate, and bleed, and kill." Eadhun lifted both hands to his face. "Wulfhere was once a kind man. Never gentle. Understand. . .always rough and rude. Always with the heavy hand — he is his father's scourger, and very good with the whip. I have seen him kill a man with four lashes, or deal two hundred and leave only bruises. Lately, it is always bleed, always kill." He looked darkly at Ronan and Bryn. "Never come under his hand. You understand? Never, never come under the hand of Wulfhere Mallasson."

"Oh, we understand," Bryn said bleakly. "But what about them?" With a nod he indicated the men and women in the slave pens at Derventio. At Mallatun. "Will they have come under his hand?"

"Some of them." Eadhun licked his lips, a quick, nervous gesture. "Some will have died. Some will carry the scars the rest of their days. Malla holds him on the leash when he can, but also he knows that this particular hound was not born mad, he has been goaded to madness. And this hound is his son, his heir."

"So, now and then, when the occasion warrants, the hound runs loose," Ronan finished.

"Yes." Eadhun pulled straight his back. "When there is a need for discipline, often Malla leaves this to Wulfhere, as if his prayer is that enough blood will wash the madness from Wulfhere's heart and leave behind a man who can weep for those he has lost."

A shiver took Ronan unawares. Could a man's soul be washed clean in the blood of innocents, prisoners and war prizes? And Ronan thought of himself, fallen under Wulfhere's hand — the prisoner, caught trying to escape. Would Malla have given him to Wulfhere for correction? Heat flooded him and he stepped away into the dark. "Good night," he bade Eadhun, in a tight voice. "Bryn?"

Darkness swallowed them and Ronan's head whirled with the day's images and Eadhun's stories of another's agony. Still, Ronan could not forgive the murder at Whitestonecliff and Derventio, and he knew he would never forget. Was that in itself a kind of madness? If some bloody end overtook Bryn, would Ronan become like Wulfhere? Ronan was too weary to fathom it.

He fumbled with flint and steel, and when Bryn took him to bed he was passive beneath the gentle hands, accepting of anything Bryn wanted. He lay pressed into the sleeping skins while Bryn oiled him carefully and pierced him to the heart, like a lance thrust into him. For an instant Ronan saw the scarlet of blood, and yawning darkness, and he cried out, his hands clenching into fists. Bryn stopped at once, and Ronan shivered as if someone had walked on his grave.

"Am I hurting you? Ronan? Love, what is it?" Bryn stroked Ronan's smooth flanks and buttocks. "Tell me if I'm hurting you."

"No," Ronan said, shaken. He gasped in a breath and shivered again. "Just . . .as if someone walked on the place were I lie in the ground. Or *your* grave," he added hoarsely.

Carefully, Bryn withdrew from him and lifted Ronan into his arms. "You're shaking. What is it? Ronan, what did you see? Are you fey? I didn't know."

"If I am, I never knew of it either! It's nothing. Really." But Ronan's fingers clawed into Bryn's arms and he went on in a rasping voice. "Oh, I saw blood and darkness." He pressed closer, as if he could get into Bryn's skin and share it with him. "Make love to me, Bryn. For the gods' sake, make love to me."

"Shh, I will." Bryn turned him over, covered him with his own weight and heat and entered him again without preamble. Ronan took him deeply and moaned woundedly. Bryn moved strongly, nothing would stop him now, and he sank his teeth into the tender flesh of Ronan's neck. He rode Ronan as if he were a horse, as if he lay flat across the horse's withers and they flew across grassland, wild and free, and under him Ronan whimpered and cried out as the possession consumed him.

At last they were almost too exhausted to move, but Ronan was still subdued, trembling, and Bryn's face was troubled as he bathed them. Ronan saw the frown there and summoned strength enough for a caress. Was he right, *was* it premonition? Had someone walked on his grave, or Bryn's? And then Bryn rolled them in the sheepskins and held Ronan hard against him.

But one thought refused to be banished, and Bryn whispered it into the darkness, against Ronan's hair. "I am. . .I'm not blooded," he murmured. "I am Gruffydd's heir, the last of him that lives in this world, Ronan, and I'm not blooded. Camulus! How many men die in their first battle? Have I lived for nothing?"

"Hush, you're making no sense," Ronan admonished, and hunted for Bryn's soft mouth in the gloom. The kiss at least silenced him for long enough that Bryn was ready to sleep when they broke apart.

* * *

The morning befor the exchange, preparations were underway early. Much of Eadhun's cargo had been broken up, sold or offered for sale. Gareth had given orders for it to be recovered, and Eadhun himself handled the manifests, a bound set of vellum tally sheets, on which were listed every last item, every splinter of wood and splash of ale that had been aboard. Only an Angle could make any sense of that writing, and among his crew, only Eadhun could read. He read the manifests aloud as labourers pieced together what part of the cargo could be located.

The crew of the galley still languished in chains, but they were unhurt, idle, growing soft and fat in confinement, like bears preparing to hibernate. They heard the news from Eadhun and they cheered. He promised them a new ship in Karitia, a voyage to Africa, where they would take on dried fruits, wine and silk for the rich Saxon Shore. All this, Eadhun told Gareth as the sailors marched about the city wall for exercise.

"Rich pickings," Bryn growled as he surveyed Ronan's shuttered face wish a sigh.

"What ails you?" Gareth demanded, whistling for his dogs. Three enormous deerhounds loped toward him and he called them to heel. "You sound sour as last week's milk. Is it that you lost so much, you cannot tolerate the thought of an Angle growing rich?"

"Growing fat, like a maggot feeding on the dead carcass of this country," Bryn said with a stony reserve. "You have yet to be sacked and plundered, Gareth. I pray you will never know the feeling."

"Time is the greatest healer of all," Gareth told him softly. "My mother told me that, and she was wise. The blade of memory dulls little by little, until at last it fails to cut. Soon, you will be able to think of your home and family without pain."

Bryn looked away as his eyes prickled. "I hope you're right, Gareth. Kyn has gone to Lindum — I saw him leave. He's to fetch back mercenaries? Those Saxon mercenaries in Malla's camp trouble me still. Were I in your place, I would not feel secure until I had the same strength as that Angle."

"Ride after Kynddelig if you wish," Gareth invited. "Do you wish to stay away from Dubgall altogether, and the frontier? I know how hard it must be for you to be so close. I shan't send you back, after this, if you prefer."

"No. Yes. I. . ." Bryn took a breath. "Perhaps you're right. Ronan felt the ghosts of Derventio, and so did I. They haunt us, and likely always will." He rubbed his face hard. "Forgive me, I've been at odds with myself for some time. Will the whole warband escort the Angles to Dubgall?"

"The prisoners will ride there by wagon," Gareth told him. "And I want half our garrison behind them. "I don't trust my lords Malla and Wulfhere any more than they trust us. You imagine the Saxon mercenaries will not be there, armed to the teeth?"

"They're be there," Bryn said bitterly. "Then, you expect a fight?"

"Don't you?" Gareth threw back the scarlet centurion's cloak and drew his shortsword. The blade turned to the sun, cast a blinding glare of gold light, as he inspected its edge. "So long as we have our people safely back, the rest is in the lap of the gods. Those Saxons may not have fought in this part of the country yet. They may be eager to test out mettle, Bryn, and they would have their own reasons for doing it. I have heard of strong, restless chiefs in the south. So we will make ready to fight, even if it comes to nothing. I've a feeling in my bones that's either a chill — or foreboding!"

He strode off toward the river, the dogs on his heels, and Ronan came closer. He leaned on the sun-warmed wood beside the granary, closed his eyes and turned his face to the sky. Bryn settled beside him and he said, "I think you'll soon be blooded, Bryn. It is what has always concerned you, isn't it?"

Taken aback, Bryn was about to deny it. "And if it has?"

"Then you'd do well to be concerned!" Ronan rested his head on the timbers. "You will fight well, and you'll have me for your shadow. All these weeks, you and I have played rough with a warband that never knew us as boys. They saw us as men when we came through that gate, Bryn, and they cut us no slack! What, do you doubt yourself, your skills?"

"No." Bryn moved closer, one hand on Ronan's shoulder. "I fear only one thing. Being without you." Ronan opened his mouth to protest and Bryn kissed him thoroughly. "No, Ronan, enough. If you are killed, or I am, that also is in the lap of the gods. Now, we've work to do, especially if we have Gareth's orders to prepare for this as if it were a march to war."

Ten wagons had been pressed into service. The wheelwrights were checking them as Eadhun went over his tally sheets for the final time. A full half of the cargo had not been recovered, but

Gareth had replaced the missing goods with tools, tanned hides, lamp oil, medicinals.

"Malla will be satisfied," Eadhun guessed. "He will have to inspect each wagon minutely to know what is missing, and by then you will be back in Eboracum."

He and Gareth were watching the last of the wains lashed down, while the sailors were given their evening exercise. With morning they would be moved out, and they were restless, eager to be free now that they could sniff freedom on the wind. After weeks of resigned, passive captivity, of a sudden their bonds had begun to chafe. Now, more than ever before, there was danger.

Sitting on the threshold of the barracks, Ronan and Bryn performed the task every warrior would perform that night. The whetstones rasped to and fro across the blades of shortsword, broadswords, knives and dirks, until each was like a razor. The steel was oiled, cleaned with ragging, and sheathed. They had already attended to their harness and horses. Nothing else remained to be done.

The last knife sheathed with a soft sound of steel and leather and Bryn stuffed the rags and oil back into their bag. Ronan was still working on his last blade, his hands moving mechanically while his mind wandered. Bryn sat back against the door port to watch him. Ronan's hands fascinated him, for they could fetch him to rapture, coax a wayward horse to obedience, soothe a child, or so easily kill. Bryn shivered and studied his own hands. They were hard, callused; they also could give pleasure, woo obedience from an animal. And soon, he was sure, they would spill blood. They must.

Half the cavalry garrison was ready to ride, but they would hold back, a quarter mile down the road and out of sight of both Dubgall and the frontier. Gareth was not trusting, but he was determined not to deliberately trigger trouble, like starting a grass fire. Bryn and Ronan had already received orders to ride at the head of the column of wagons. Theirs were the only faces the Angle warlords would know. Eadhun would ride with them, but his crew would remain in their wains, bound by the wrists, until the last moment.

"Gareth is anxious," Ronan observed, stirring Bryn from his thoughts. "See the cords in his neck, and the clench of his hands? He's tight as harp strings. Did you know that he plans to ride with the cavalry tomorrow? I don't know that he's ready. That wound is still nagging."

"He had the cavalry physician open it again and let out some fluid," Bryn mused. "Still, he knows better than any man what's right for him." Bryn stretched out his legs and turned his face to the evening sun. "And he has no need to fight. He can as easily stand well back and watch. It's Malla he wants to see."

"I don't fear Malla," Ronan said thoughtfully.

"You should," Bryn cautioned. "Power lies in his hands."

"But not evil or madness," Ronan added.

Bryn turned his head on the sun-warmed wood and looked, slit-eyed, at his partner. "You fear Wulfhere?"

"Don't you?" Ronan demanded. "It wasn't you that Wulfhere looked at as if he wanted to flay the flesh off your bones and eat it!"

Bryn's heart squeezed. "I saw the way he looked at you," he said quietly. "If it had been any other man, and south of the frontier, I would have called him out for that. I would have cut the price of it out of his hide."

"I can defend my own honour," Ronan said stubbornly.

"Not in that camp, you can't." Bryn waved to the lad who was to look after Red in their absence. "In that camp, you are *meat*, Ronan. Remember what Eadhun said. Never, never come under Wulfhere's hand."

Ronan looked away, "And yet he is Gareth's neighbour, until the fighting next season. And then, who knows?"

"Which is why Gareth wants to see Malla with his own eyes ...and Wulfhere," Bryn agreed. "And the Saxons. The next time he sees them, they may be marching through the gates of Eboracum!"

"Only," Ronan said tartly, "if we have given our lives to defend this pile of Roman brickwork, and are lying dead, for the amusement of flies!" He sheathed the last blade and pushed his whetstones back into their leather bag. "Come and eat."

"You're fretted," Bryn observed. Ronan looked sharply at him and Bryn hunted for a smile. "You always eat when you're fretted. I know you, remember."

"On the eve before battle I've cause to fret! And I'm hungry." Ronan put his pack and weapons with Taran's and Cora's, just inside the barracks' door. They're turning a pig over the fire in the hall, with rosemary and onions. I can smell it."

The ballad singers told of battles long in the past, heroic deeds, great loves and lusts. Bryn was diverted, but all evening Ronan sat looking into the fire as if he had not heard a word, and when they bedded that night he wanted only to stare into the darkness, moody, taciturn, and for once, unreachable.

With a sigh, Bryn let him sleep. He rolled over, put his back to the hearth and his face to the wall, and tried to shut the morrow out of his mind.

* * *

Dawn was clear, bright, and a warm south wind promised fair weather. Drays backed into harness and the wagons rolled out while the sun was still low over the woodland. The cavalry formed a serpentine column, trailing the heavy vehicles, just out of sight and earshot.

If he looked back over his shoulder, Ronan could catch sight of them, but from the woods and slopes ahead the column would not be seen. Gareth rode his tall black gelding, the scarlet Roman cloak furled over his shoulders. At his left had were Taran and Cora, his old friends and, in Kynddelig's absence, his most loyal guard. Kyn should have left Lindum already. With luck, he would be in Dubgall with a force of mercenaries before the exchange of prisoners took place.

And at Gareth's right hand were Ronan himself, Bryn and Eadhun. The Angle was mounted on a white pony, clinging to the saddle as if he had never ridden before. His right boot was chained to the stirrup, since he was still a prisoner, and the reins were in Ronan's right hand. But Eadhun seemed too nervous of the pony to make a break for freedom. It was mid-morning before he was sufficiently accustomed to riding to be able to spare the breath and attention to talk at the same time.

"You should drop back, Gareth," Ronan advised as they saw the thatch at Dubgall. "I don't know if the Angles have archers, but I'd not like to see them put an arrow in you."

"He's right," Cora agreed. "Taran and I will drop back with you, while Ronan and Bryn take the Angle on ahead." She twisted in the saddle to look back down the road. "They're too close! Damn, I can see them clearly, and if I can, so will Malla." She spun the pony on its haunches, heading back fast.

Bryn shaded his eyes to look out past Dubgall. It was just short of noon now, and sunlight glittered on some mirror-polished surface. A moment later Ronan was pointing and Bryn said softly, "I see it."

"War spears." Ronan gave Gareth a glance. "They're waiting for us."

"I see them." Gareth drew rein, and behind them the column of wagons came to a halt. "So this is farewell, Eadhun. In an hour you will be among friends, and I don't think we shall meet again."

From somewhere the Angle produced a smile. "Then give me your wrist, for I was never your enemy, my lord. Only your guest for a time. I will tell Malla that you treated my crew fairly and showed me what hospitality you could."

"You're a strange one." Gareth took Eadhun's wrist in a warrior's clasp. "Steer well north of the Ambri in future. Especially when the east wind blows."

"Fare you well, Ironhand." Eadhun withdrew from the clasp and tossed the yellow hair out of his face. "Mind you treat that ship of mine kindly."

Ronan still held Eadhun's reins and was waiting for Gareth's signal to go on. The Ironhand wheeled his horse about, riding back to the cavalry contingent in Cora's wake, and only Ronan and Bryn remained at the head of the column.

The drivers from Eboracum were weary and skittish as they urged the drays on. Long whips cracked, the wains creaked and rumbled through the dappled sunlight; in the wagon beds, Angle seamen muttered and growled amongst themselves. What they said, Ronan would never know, but Eadhun barked at them to be silent and they fell into a sullen quiet.

The wains were rolling into Dubgall then, and right through the camp, but the whole place seemed deserted and Ronan's flesh crawled. "Where are the people?" he whispered. "No one is here at all."

"They'll be in the woods, watching," Bryn guessed. "Like Gareth, they fear treachery — and they know their turn comes next, if the Angles march south by so much as a mile."

"The Malla I know will be as good as his word," Eadhun promised.

"Until he has you, your crew and cargo in his possession." Bryn's eyes narrowed as he looked out across the common land. Thirty, Ronan. Count them. Thirty war spears."

Thirty Saxon mercenaries, and behind them, Malla's own men, farmers and shepherds, to be sure, but every one of them armed, and nursing a heart that longed to be avenged. Where was Wulfhere? Ronan looked for him, but the distance was still too great, and just then Bryn was talking.

"How long before Kynddelig could be expected to arrive here?"

"I don't know," Ronan said quietly. "He could be a mile away, or less. And how many swords will have answered the call to arms?" He gave Bryn a sidelong look. "Kyn will be here as soon as the gods allow." He counted the Saxon spears again and loosened his grip on Eadhun's reins. "Go ahead of us. Tell Malla your men and cargo are in the wagons behind us, but we want our people released before we make Malla the gift of you."

"I shall tell him that you don't trust him," Eadhun said rue-fully, and as Bryn unchained his ankle from the stirrup iron he slid gratefully to the ground. "I shall also tell him that you have a cavalry band on the road. You have seen the Saxons." His teeth worried at his lip and his brow creased deeply. "You may be right to distrust Malla."

Ronan's heart squeezed, and Bryn shot the Angle a flint hard look. "I thought you knew him."

"I do know him." Eadhun straightened his tunic and pulled his fingers through the tangle of his hair in a vain attempt to straighten it, perhaps to make himself more presentable before he showed his face before a warlord of his people. "I know Malla as a friend. You know him as an enemy. The same man will wear two different faces, one for me, one for you. And as for Wulfhere. . ." Now he shrugged, shook his head. "Wulfhere is no man's friend and the sworn enemy of every god." His blue eyes were very pale in the sun as he looked up at them. "Take care, Bryn ap Gruffydd, Ronan of Whitestonecliff. I wish you no harm, but my loyalty is to my people and their welfare comes first to my mind." He offered his hand, but Bryn would not take it. Eadhun sighed and offered the clasp instead to Ronan. "Hie you well. I will tell Malla also to beware. He is not the only man here capable of deceit."

With that, the Angle merchant was gone. Bryn and Ronan shifted closer together to watch him run stiffly out across the common land. He waved, shouting in that strange language, and voices answered, deep, bass and rasping. Shapes detached from the ranks of the Saxon mercenaries and Ronan took a breath. Malla and Wulfhere were all too obviously father and son. They had the same big shoulders, the same tendency to girth, and the way of walking that Ronan would recognise anywhere.

In Malla's right hand was a polished axe. Wulfhere carried a war spear longer than he was tall, its collar dressed in scarlet and black feathers, and behind him were a company of the chieftains. Old men, young men, some still limping after the battle for Derventio, others in whose faces the blood thirst was terrible to behold. Swallowing his heart, Ronan turned in the saddle to look for Gareth, Taran and Cora.

They were coming up slowly along the line of wagons. The cavalry had fallen well back, but the Ironhand and his closest guards were well covered. Archers were up in the trees now — Ronan saw them, saw half-drawn bows, and began to breathe again. Gareth was intent upon his enemy. As intent, Ronan realised, as Malla was on Gareth. Wulfhere's teeth were bare, as if he longed just to wreak havoc, and more than once Malla snarled at him as if he were a hound. Wulfhere's rope was at full stretch, and Ronan's belly turned as the Angle's blue eyes sought him out, settled on him, and seemed to burn the flesh from him.

Gareth and Malla studied one another over the distance, and Malla did not even glance at Eadhun until he was close enough to bend his neck in greeting before the chief. "Listen to him, Malla," Ronan hissed as Eadhun began to speak rapidly, with many gestures toward Dubgall. "Listen, and believe him!"

"We outnumber them," Bryn mused.

"Only the Saxons," Ronan murmured, "and only the ones you can see. If he turns his own men out to fight alongside them, we are too few."

"We are cavalry." Bryn tightened his reins as his horse began to grow restless. "They fear cavalry more than anything."

"Which did not stop them fighting at Eboracum last time," Ronan argued, "and they punished Gareth's men almost to the point of an Angle victory before they were turned back to the river." He stood in the stirrups. "Where are our prisoners? I don't see them, Bryn. Come on, Eadhun! Make the stubborn old badger keep his half of the bargain!"

"There." Bryn drew Ronan's attention to the trees beyond which the mercenaries stood guard on the common land. "There they are, you see them? Roped together in the shadows."

"I see them." Ronan's tongue flickered over parchment dry lips.

At Malla's side, Eadhun began to wave. Ronan turned in the saddle and cupped his hand to his mouth. "Gareth! Eadhun has spoken for us! Will we send them a wagon out?

"One wagon!" Gareth shouted. "And ride with it, Ronan. Tell Malla he'll not get the rest, not one stick more of the cargo, before we have his prisoners."

"He may not believe me," Ronan warned.

Gareth budged his horse closer. "Then tell Malla to fetch his prisoners out into the open, where they can be properly bartered. Four men for each wagon, if he'll do it no other way. And tell him to get those Saxons back. These wains are driven by Eboracum's freemen, not by soldiers. If harm comes to them, by Camulus, it'll be paid for in blood!"

"I'll try to tell him," Ronan said doubtfully. He beckoned the driver of the lead wagon, in which five of Eadhun's crew were seated on bundles of cargo. "Pull it forward! We're going out. We'll ride with you." Ronan drew his sword.

The horses laboured to haul the wagon over the muddy, rutted common land. The driver swore at every turn of the wheels, and glared up at Bryn as he shook out the long reins. "I want my nags back! I'm going to cut them out of harness as soon as they stop. They stole cavalry horses last time, but they're not getting my animals."

"Aye, that's fair enough." Ronan rode at one side of the wagon, Bryn at the other. "I'll put my horse between you and the Saxons while you cut the traces. I don't want those mercenaries catching any glimpse of a knife."

"You trust them so little?" Bryn had not taken his eyes from the bronze helmeted soldiers in minutes.

"I don't know them," Ronan muttered. "A man earns my trust, I don't give it freely."

"As I earned it?" Bryn whispered, so softly that only Ronan could hear him. He kept his horse close, his eyes on the Saxons, until they had come far enough. Malla and Wulfhere were holding position, not fifty paces away. "Wait here, driver," Bryn told the man. "Ronan, go on ahead, speak to Malla. He listened to you last time. And you," he told the driver, "get your precious horses out of here as fast as you can."

The man was already scrambling down. He had only to draw a long-bladed skinning knife, and the traces fell loosely. The dreys answered his call, and with a bridle in each hand he was heading away toward the column at an arm-flapping run.

Wulfhere growled like a pit-trapped bear. Malla just watched the driver go, and his voice was a bass rumble as he addressed Ronan. "What is he doing, boy?"

"Taking his horses, my lord." Ronan reined back a scant dozen paces from the Angle chief. "You took our cavalry animals last time. You could take these horses too, and the gift of them was never part of he bargain." He looked back over his shoulder. Bryn had the five sailors out of the wagon, and Eadhun was calling to them. "My lord Malla, Gareth wants you to move back your Saxons before we begin, and fetch the prisoners out into the open."

"Gareth wants, Gareth wants," Malla mocked, and spat into the grass. "Give me the men and cargo. Then you get your people."

Beside him, half a pace behind the older man, Wulfhere was overtly brooding on Ronan, and Ronan's belly turned over. "With respect, my lord," he said cautiously, "the Ironhand wishes to see your mercenaries stood down. He offers to exchange each wagon for a number of men. The first wagon is already here."

"The Saxons remain where they are," Malla barked, and turned to his son to pass on Gareth's request. Wulfhere's eyes first widened and then narrowed to dark slits, and he stroked his jaw thoughtfully as Malla turned back to address Ronan. "Your cavalry is in the trees just there. We know. You could overrun us in a moment. Butcher us. My Saxons will not stand down."

"Then fetch out the prisoners, my lord. Bring them into the open," Ronan said reasonably while his belly churned and an iron band seemed to tighten about his chest. Wulfhere's hands were clenched about his weapons, caressing them, and Ronan found the deliberate movements troublingly erotic.

"Fetch the prisoners, so you can steal them?" Malla snorted.

"So that we can see that we are receiving our side of the bargain." Ronan paused as the first of Eadhun's sailors passed him by. Shouts and cheers greeted them, and when the noise had died down a little Ronan called, "Eadhun, tell your chief that Gareth will give him no more until we receive some part of the bargain."

The merchant's face was grim, and he returned to Ronan's side just as Bryn moved up behind him, like his shadow. Had Bryn seen Wulfhere's face, his hands, how his eyes stripped every thread off Ronan's body? Eadhun had seen, and he spoke in undertones, well below the level that Malla and his son could hear.

"Take care, Ronan. Wulfhere has seen you."

"I know. He saw me last time we were on Angle land," Ronan whispered. "He won't make a move, surely, not while we have Angle prisoners."

"Prisoners?" Eadhun echoed bitterly. "No longer are they prisoners, honourable warprizes. They are hostages, and have been since we reached this field. Do you smell blood?"

"Not yet." Ronan took a deep, calming breath. "It has not yet come to that."

"I know some of the Saxons," Eadhun said tersely. "They shipped with a chief called Cerdic Halfhand, and when he was defeated at last in battle against the great warlord from the west, Artos, and his sorcerer, Cerdic and his mercenaries fled the killing field and hired their swords to any chief who would pay them." He caught Ronan's bridle. "Don't trust them. I have seen —"

"Come back here!" Malla roared. "Eadhun!"

"Be wary," Eadhun hissed, "I can do little to help, save be your tongue as you deal with Malla. The language is difficult, I know." But with that he returned to the chief's side, and to Ronan's unease Wulfhere moved up behind the captain, laid a hand on his back as if to take possession of him. Eadhun's whole body stiffened and he lifted his head, but his eyes closed.

A pace behind Ronan, Bryn swore. "Camulus, what is the matter with the man? Malla is no fool. He knows he won't get the cargo unless he gives us something. Is he so terrified of mounted swordsmen that he will force our hand, pitch us headlong into battle? If he's as terrified of cavalry as that, he would give us what we want without argument!"

Ronan's teeth worried at his lip. "You heard Eadhun. He knows some of these mercenaries, and the chief they fought for on the Saxon shore. Artos and the Druid sorcerer routed them — we had the news from a trader, do you remember?"

"I took little account of such tales," Bryn muttered. "I had better things to do."

"A boy you used to bed with, on the hill, I know." Ronan's tone did not sting. "I hung on every story, and I know the name of Cerdic Halfhand. Artos cut his army to pieces, if the ballad singers told it correctly, and the Druid wreaked a terrible magic over the battlefield. Cerdic was seen fighting further north, last winter."

"Yes." Bryn passed both hands over his face. "My father spoke of him. In the south, Cerdic Halfhand was a destroyer, grown rich on pillage —" He stopped short and sucked in a quick breath. "My gods, Ronan, these Saxons are not mercenaries. They're frontier scouts!"

"What?" Ronan looked sharply at him. "What are you talking about?"

"Frontier scouts for the Halfhand," Bryn said breathlessly. "Look at them! See how they command this field, while Malla should be giving the orders here."

Again, Ronan shaded his eyes and studied the bronze-helmeted Saxons, and this time he saw the mute signals that sped among their ranks. And between them and Wulfhere. "Sweet mercy," he whispered. "Has Wulfhere brought them in, to overthrow his father?"

"The old man has had him leashed too tightly, for too long?" Bryn twisted in the saddle to look back toward Gareth.

"You see them exchanging hand signals behind Malla's back?" Ronan murmured.

"I saw." Bryn shortened his reins. "Frontier scouts for the Halfhand?"

"Come to see what rich pickings lie along out coasts," Ronan agreed tersely, "so that we shall be attacked next, and perhaps they will use Angle camps to strike from. . .and then butcher the Angles when they have used up their hospitality. Camulus, does Malla know what scum he has brought into his camp?"

"Or did Wulfhere hire them?" Bryn shifted uneasily in the saddle. "See how he handles Eadhun."

"And see how Eadhun squirms under his touch," Ronan added. "If Eadhun knows the Saxons, Malla should recognise them, and even if Malla was duped, Eadhun should have told him the truth of it by now!"

All this time, Malla and Eadhun had been talking in growled tones, as if they were arguing, almost fighting, making their peace and beginning again, round after round of dispute and verbal battle, until at last the old man was gesturing angrily, and Eadhun was white to the lips with anger or fear, or both.

"Oh, Eadhun has told him." Ronan was intent on Wulfhere, who still kept one hand on Eadhun's back and the other clenched about a warspear that, to Ronan's eyes, had taken on the aspect of a great, brutal phallus. Eadhun was rigid under Wulfhere's touch, and the chief's son was furious. His anger was never far from the surface, and it had begun to simmer the moment Eadhun began to reason with Malla.

"One wrong word, and Eadhun could be dead," Bryn warned.

"I know. So does he." Ronan licked his lips. "And — Bryn!"

The Saxons were moving, shuffling slowly forward, coming up behind and around Malla and his chieftains. They were almost hemmed in now, and Eadhun stood in their very midst, still speaking in desperate undertones to Malla. Behind him were the young men who shared Malla's look — his colouring, his stature. Were they cousins, perhaps even much younger sons? Their faces were hard as leather masks, taut as stretched gut.

And their scabbards were empty.

"Bryn, they're unarmed," Ronan said sharply. "The chieftains are unarmed, no swords in their scabbards!"

"Oh, my gods." Bryn shortened his reins once more and his horse side-stepped. "Hostages? I don't understand any of this, and I smell blood, Ronan. This field reeks of it. Ah, gods, this is for Gareth to decide, not us. Speak to Malla. He listens to you!"

Speak to Malla? Ronan had opened his mouth to protest when Bryn waved back toward the woods that sheltered Dubgall, and issued a piercing whistle. The signal cut like shards of broken pottery, and any man in the cavalry knew it. 'Come to me.' Ronan spared him a glance, saw him point right at Gareth and then beckon again with urgent, jerky hands.

And then Malla's voice bawled over the field, "What are you doing, Briton?"

Taking a calming breath, Ronan drew his face straight before he turned back to the Angles and the watchful, gloating Saxons. Show them fear, and the day was forfeit. "We are fetching Gareth or his messenger, so that you can speak directly with him, organise terms. My companion is the son of a chief, my lord. You can trust him. Tell him what is your will, and he will give every word to Gareth just as it was spoken." He hardened his face and his voice. "But know this. The Ironhand will not give you one more hostage until every prisoner you have has been surrendered. These are Gareth's terms, we know them by heart." His eyes flicked to Eadhun. "Tell him in his own language, my friend."

Friend? The word made Eadhun's brows rise, and then Wulfhere did something that made the young captain catch his breath before he addressed Malla.

"Terms, terms," Malla growled.

"Bring out your prisoners." Bryn dared snarl — he was losing his temper, Ronan knew that sound, that look on his face.

The drum of hooves announced Cora and Taran, and Ronan kept talking. He would say anything, just to keep peace, to buy time. "Our drivers are concerned for their horses, will you trade for them also? You may have the wagons, and I think the drivers may trade for their animals." He kept still in the saddle by an effort of will, when he longed to turn and shout at Cora and Taran to ride back to Gareth and tell them that Wulfhere had brought in Saxon frontier scouts, and that Malla's chieftains were unarmed.

Bryn was already telling them. He had brought his horse around so that his back was to Malla and the Saxons, and Ronan caught one word in four as he spoke quickly, quietly. Cora swore lividly and Taran groaned, deep and animal, a wounded sound.

"Have you seen Kynddelig?" Ronan whispered, not taking his eyes off the Saxons, save to fret for Eadhun.

"An advance rider came up the road behind us. Kyn has a force of twenty mercenaries from Lindum, they'll be here in an hour," Taran told him.

"We could be blood and bone in an hour," Bryn said bitterly. "Taran, tell Gareth to expect treachery. We think Wulfhere has betrayed his father. He was signalling to the Saxons behind Malla's back —"

"He still is," Cora whispered. "Hold fast as long as you can Ronan, Bryn. Stay with them, Taran. I'll ride back to Gareth and have the archers stand to."

Now, Ronan dared turn in the saddle to watch her go. At the tail of the column of wagons, Gareth came forward to meet Cora and sat quite still while she delivered every word of the message with a toss of her head and gestures over her shoulder. Ronan saw the chief's shoulders draw back, saw Gareth's right arm come up.

In the fist was his sword, and Bryn muttered a very old, very bloody curse. It was Taran who said very quietly, "Gareth has met Cerdic Halfhand. I remember now, he told the story one winter's night."

"Met him in battle?" Ronan wondered.

But Taran's dark head shook. "In the slave market in Karitia, across the Narrow Sea. Karitia is a free port, you know? Open to all, even Romans and Greeks. Gareth had lost some of his people when a ship went down, and he found them in the market there. He and Cerdic bid against each other for the men, and almost came to blows. Ah, damn, this is bad. This is the worst. Cerdic will be safe by his home hearths, but look at those men! You see the black and scarlet feathers, like hackles, threaded into the helmet collars?"

"I see them. What of them?" Bryn was restless.

"Those are Cerdic Halfhand's colours," Taran said bitterly.

And Ronan drew his attention to the warspear, the haft of which Wulfhere was still caressing with maddening sensuality. "Then Wulfhere is carrying Cerdic's colours too."

"Damn," Taran whispered. "You're right, Ronan. I hadn't seen it. We should have known this would never work! It will be blood, before the hour is out."

"And Kynddelig might be here — before the hour is out," Ronan added.

"He had better be." Taran brought his horse around to look back, eyes shaded, after Cora and Gareth. "If the Saxons can press Malla's men into service, we're outnumbered."

Bryn gave him a sour look. "See how they're formed up around the chieftains? See the empty scabbards on those chieftain's hips?"

"Hostages." Taran licked his lips. "Then Malla's men will fight, for the honour of their chieftains. Odd, don't you think? That Malla, himself a pillager, a conqueror, should be played false, betrayed by his own hirelings."

"By his own son." Ronan stirred anxiously. "Eadhun said that Malla keeps Wulfhere chained, like a mad dog that is, nonetheless, his son and heir. The dog has slipped the leash, I think."

But Taran was intent on the company concealed under the trees, and reached out to lay a hand on Ronan's arm. "Hush now, and turn slowly. Gareth just gave the signal to move the cavalry up into the trees."

Like a puppet, Ronan turned in the saddle, slowly, so as not to draw attention to the line of his eyes. Taran was right. Gareth's sword was still over his head and making a circling motion. On the battlefield verbal commands were useless, and signals given by pipes or horns or drums were too easily faked by enemies, pipers and drummers too easily cut down. In the midst of the fray, the chief's colours would be raised, and beneath that banner signals were given visually. It was Gareth's way, learned from his father.

The trees skirted the common land, and the archers had been hidden in the branches since the Saxon mercenaries had been seen. If the cavalry was coming up, Ronan knew that every bow would be primed to fire. "What will Gareth order?" he asked quietly, looking to Taran for answers, since Taran had fought alongside the Ironhand for years.

"There is only one order he can give," Taran said darkly. "The prisoners are our priority. The *hostages*. If we don't get them, steal them out of the Angle hands, they can be used as a shield or a weapon against us. We might have a minute, Ronan, to get them. The warband will make one run — there is no place on this field for heroes! — one run in, for the hostages. If the Saxons get in the way, we will cut them down. But if we're swift enough we can be in and out, and safe. We're mounted. Infantry can only intercept us, not catch us."

"Good. That's strong." Ronan pulled a breath to the bottom of his lungs. "And us, Taran? Where do you want us to fight?"

"Gareth would tell you to choose your own place," Taran guessed. "Derventio was your home, those are your friends in chains, close enough for you to see their faces." His horse side-stepped, ears twitching, and he soothed the animal with soft words. "She can hear her herd mates in the trees. Soon, Ronan, Bryn. Very soon."

The Saxons knew, too. A pulse hammered in Ronan's temple as he watched the mercenaries, saw heads turning, a blade half-drawn, a spear shifted so that it angled toward Malla's kinsmen, the young chieftains. Wulfhere's teeth were bare, and the sinews in Eadhun's neck stood out like the ropes rigging a ship. Ronan's palms prickled with sweat on the reins, and he cleared his throat. "Eadhun, my friend, are you well?"

The Angle seemed to be panting as if he had run a race. His eyes went to Ronan but he did not move, even to nod. Right behind him, Wulfhere Mallasson growled like a hunting bear and spat something in his own language that could have invective or insults. Ronan's heart began to beat like a deum.

"Where is Kyn?" Bryn whispered. "He should be here by now!"

"He could be here," Taran speculated. "His men from Lindum

could have been sent into the woods with our own." Yet his eyes were bright with healthy fear. "When our warband makes its run, we must move, Bryn. We must get out of the Saxons' reach, or we will be the first cut down. We'll try to skirt Wulfhere's mercenaries, go around them."

Eyes shaded with his hand, Ronan measured distances. "No chance of that. There's half a mile to cover, and the Saxons are only a short run from the trees." He let down his hand and turned to fix his companion with level eyes. "Bryn?"

"I'm. . .all right." Bryn knew what he was asking, and gave him a nod. This was to be a rare blooding, not at all the usual ritual where a boy became a man. "We'll show them our backs when it begins, or circle around, join Gareth, fight with them. Yes?"

"Yes." Ronan's left hand cupped the hilt of his sword. "If Gareth fights, so do we both. Gareth was injured, so was Kyn, we've no right to set them to fight for the survivors of Derventio and then run to save our own skins."

A bark from Malla interrupted. His face might have been carved from granite, but he was showing the whites of his eyes like a horse about to bolt as the Saxons came in another pace and the sun shimmered on a drawn blade here, a spear tip there. "Malla will not change his terms," he bellowed. "Send the wagons, send now, and maybe your people live."

At the old man's side, Wulfhere stirred and Eadhun's breath caught in his throat. His cheeks were bright, his face twisted. Most of his crew was still held hostage, he himself was hemmed in and, if Ronan was any judge, in pain. Wulfhere was pressed half against him, moulded to him, and when he moved Eadhun swayed. Wulfhere leaned closer, whispered into Eadhun's ear, and the merchant's face was ashen.

"My lord," Ronan called to Malla, "Gareth would ask you to reconsider, or at least —" he broke off, thinking that he had heard some commotion from the trees, but it was only the geese. He swallowed hard. "Or at least to make some sign of good faith." He took a risk now, and gave Bryn a glance as he said, "Send us Eadhun, let him rejoin his crew. We can back off and begin again. Make him understand, Eadhun, if you can."

But Eadhun could barely hear, let alone translate coherently. Wulfhere seemed almost to be holding him up, and as he swayed now, Ronan saw that his left hip was red with blood.

Malla seemed on the point of answering when the shouting and alarm broke out in the Angle ranks. Swords and spears gleamed, men began to run this way and that, and Bryn, Ronan and Taran sprang apart. From the woodland south of the common land came two score riders, headed at a flat gallop toward the trees where the prisoners were tethered. The game was up.

Confusion scattered the Angles in every direction, but the Saxons swung together like professional soldiers. Warspears bristled, dozens of light hunting javelins appeared from the grass at their feet, and before Ronan could draw a breath the air was filled with steel.

"Move! Ronan, move!" Bryn was shouting as he tugged his horse's head about. "I saw archers in their back ranks!"

True enough, the rain of arrows had already begun, and it was as deadly to Angles as to Britons. In their own defence, Malla's people raised big, bronze shields high overhead, and as Wulfhere dived for his shield, which lay some small distance beyond him, he let go the merchant who had become his enemy.

Eadhun pitched forward on his face, and he might have been dead. He was thick with blood that had oozed over his buttocks and legs from a wound, or wounds in his back, but Ronan saw his hands reach around, feeble and ineffectual.

In that moment seeing only the agony of a man he had come to know well, an enemy he had learned to respect, Ronan swung his horse about, not toward the oncoming rush of Gareth's cavalry, but into the windmilling confusion of the Angle front rank.

Most of them were down on their knees, sheltering from their own archers, but the first hail of arrows had already gone by and the second was slow coming, since the archers themselves, safely in the back ranks, had taken cover. Tangled skeins of shafts arched overhead from the trees toward Dubgall; a few fell short, among the Angle ranks, but most were aimed at the archers, sending them to the ground and pinning them there.

Into this chaos, Ronan dived toward the ravel of sprawled limbs and blood that Eadhun had become. He heard Bryn shouting his name, bawling for him to leave the merchant to his gods, but Ronan saw only the blood, the young body fallen to the churned ground, and his mind, his heart, were filled with the nightmare of Whitestonecliff.

He slithered from the saddle, putting the horse between himself and the archers' fire, and kept the reins looped about his arm as he stooped and seized Eadhun bodily. The Angle screamed, shrill as a girl, as he was lifted, but Ronan shut out the sound. He would never know where the strength came from, but he lifted him, slung him face down over the saddle, and was up behind him a moment later.

The air was still thick with arrows as Ronan shouted at the horse, urged him with demanding heels. And then Bryn was there, never far from Ronan's side — his shadow, as he had promised. They made the run back together, and on the fringe of the common ground, within sight of the rooftops of Dubgall, they slithered into Gareth's advance camp.

Eadhun's blood was slick and sticky on Ronan's palms as he let the Angle fall from the saddle into waiting hands. Two old women gathered him up, not quite as tenderly as they might have, and Ronan's voice was sharp. "Be gentle with him. He was Gareth's true friend and ally. The warning of betrayal came from him, and your friends, your kin from Derventio may yet be free today because of this one!"

Glassy eyes looked up at Ronan, and then Eadhun slumped, unconscious. The old women took him between them, and all Ronan saw was the mess of blood that began in the middle of Eadhun's back, where Wulfhere had held him hostage with one easy hand. Ronan had no idea what Eadhun had suffered, but he could do no more for him, and he set the merchant out of his mind.

The horse wheeled about and came up, shoulder to shoulder, with Bryn's big black animal. Bryn's face was rueful. "Are you quite finished?" he asked as he worked his sword wrist to and fro to loosen it.

As he spoke they heard the first chime of steel from the battlefield, and of a sudden Ronan's veins were filled with icewater. It had begun. Flat over his horse's powerful neck, Bryn wheeled across the common ground, never more than a length ahead of Ronan. They had seen Taran and Cora flanking Gareth at the fore of the warband from Eboracum, but of Kynddelig there was as yet no sign. Gareth was guarded on every side by his most elite cavalry, and for that Ronan gave thanks, for the Ironhand was still nursing that troublesome old injury, and he could be prey today.

The cavalry was cutting the straightest, fastest route across the no man's land, and Ronan and Bryn caught them up, swung in on their left flank. Bryn was on Ronan's own left, and as they neared the forest of Saxon warspears, at last he drew his sword.

His hands were already filthy with Angle blood, and he thought how odd it was that it should be the blood of a friend. And then a javelin cut so close by his head that he felt the air rush on his cheek, and he felt something inside turn and tear. For this, he had let Cuddy the swordmaster take him apart, bone by bone, and remade him. For this, he had risked everything.

Yet it seemed the greatest risk of all was still to be taken, for Bryn was in the open, caught between the cavalry on his right and the dragon's teeth of the Saxon spears, and Ronan's heart was in his mouth. *As we fight in practice,* he told himself. *As we do it with the warband, under the walls of Eboracum.* He swung about to cover for Bryn as the Saxon mercenaries came in, and from the corner of his eye saw blood on the grass, heard the first screams of pain, fear, anger. Then, Ronan of Whitestonecliff was fighting just to survive.

How many young warriors survived their first battle? How many were burned, unsung, at the end of the day? Perhaps the greatest warriors were those who survived long enough to learn some magic. Ronan did not know. He lost all grasp of time as he and Bryn found themselves ringed about by Saxons on one hand and Angles on the other, and he saw no further than the blades threatening him directly, and those stabbing toward Bryn,

All too soon he realised that trying to watch Bryn was going to get them both killed. Cursing, he trusted his lover's life to gods he had never been sure he believed in, and of necessity left Bryn to look out for himself.

He killed twice, he was certain. His sword slipped into the very gut of a man, and Ronan knew the feel of death. Another cut opened the great vein in the throat of a Saxon, a man who fell to his knees, clutching his gullet as his life poured away. A hundred times blades came so close to stealing his own life that Ronan did not know how he survived, unless it was by speed and luck.

Where was Bryn? He spun his horse, his eyes everywhere until he saw Bryn, fighting now along with Cora, close on her heels. She was shouting, Ronan struggled to make out her words, and when he heard the name of Kynddelig he might have cheered. Bryn was half out of the saddle as his horse side-stepped and slipped, and Gareth was a pace beyond, coming about, sword uplifted to signal toward the woodland.

Kynddelig was there? Ronan stood in the stirrups, eyes narrowed, looking into the fast westering sun, and for the first time saw a blue and gold pennant streaming from the haft of a spear.

They came on at a canter, more than twenty heavy horses, and Ronan saw the sun on helmets and upthrust steel. Kynddelig was at the fore of them, and so intent on the Angles that he had no time even to salute Gareth. It would be Fergal in his heart now, Ronan knew. The lover Kyn had lost and would mourn forever. Some small measure of his vengeance would be won today.

The Eboracum cavalry and the mercenaries from Lindum met in a great, threshing mass, and in the midst of it Gareth lifted his sword to call order. Shouts would never have been heard, a battle standard or a piper would have been a ripe target, but the signals were quickly given, the sword withdrawn.

Now the cavalry split into two parts, and Ronan and Bryn were swept along with the body that included Gareth and Kyn, and Cora and Taran wheeled the rest about and dived in to divide the Saxons from the Angles. Where was Malla's group? The last Ronan had seen of them, they had been under their shields, taking shelter from the hail of arrows, but the place where it had all begun was empty now. He cast about, trying to pick Malla's bull-like form out of the melee, but it was Wulfhere he saw and knew.

The man could run like a deer. He was bolting toward the hostages who were still trussed like animals for the butcher, flanked at left and right by two Saxons who struggled to keep pace with him. Ronan's heart leapt into his chest and he bellowed Bryn's name. Bryn turned toward him, and Ronan pointed, calling Gareth now.

If they let Wulfhere get among the hostages, those men and women were dead. They had only been fetched out here as bait. Ronan knew that now. Derventio's survivors were the bait that had lured Gareth out to fight this season, when he wanted only to stay safe behind the Roman walls of Eboracum, heal and grow strong to fight next season. Did Cerdic Halfhand know Gareth so well that he knew exactly what lure would fetch him out? Ronan almost blamed himself and Bryn, for it was through his own urging that Gareth had become embroiled in this, and all at once Ronan could see how far it could go.

If they lost here, Eboracum was wide open. Cerdic Halfhand could be twenty miles away, waiting for a runner to fetch him the news of Gareth's death, or of the demise of the Ebor warband. Or Cerdic could be just a mile away, camped on the next hill, and watching. By the grimness of Gareth's face, he had seen this too, and he touched his spurs to his horse's sides, swinging wider about the Saxon warspears and taking his cavalry with him.

Wulfhere Mallasson was wild-eyed as he made the final sprint. Ronan was sure that he saw madness in the man's face, and yet Wulfhere moved with the certainly of one who would have earned himself the name of Ironhand, had he fought among Britons. He had thrown aside the warspear, or lost it in the fray. Both his hands were filled with hunting knives now, and as he dived into the midst of the hostages Gareth bawled for an archer to pick him off.

A few archers risked careful shots, but pale, frightened faces gazed up from the shadows beneath the trees. These were

Derventio's survivors, and among them, Wulfhere was more secure than anywhere on the field of battle. Ronan might have sneered, for a moment guessing that the man would hide behind his prisoners, but every fibre in him screamed its own warning.

Wulfhere shot through the mass of them, and as he flung himself into the cover of the trees he whirled, and wild eyes challenged the cavalry to follow. A javelin darted out almost like a shaft of light, and one of Wulfhere's guards plunged into the grass, the blade sunk to the haft in his thigh. The second Saxon turned at bay like a stag hunted to the end of its strength, winded and exhausted. He put up little challenge, and the name of Fergal was on Kynddelig's lips like a battle cry as the man went down.

But Gareth brought the cavalry to a slithering halt, short of the trees, and when Bryn made to follow Wulfhere, to ride him down, the chief called him back. Bryn's eyes glittered with an unholy light as he shouted, hoarse and rasping,

"He's getting away! He's running like a craven bastard — you can't let that one get away, Gareth! He brought Cerdic Halfhand's Saxons into this fight!"

"I know that." Gareth gave Bryn a glare. "But I'll not send cavalry into the woods, you young fool. Have you ever seen a horse with its legs cut out from under it? Cavalry has no place in forest, or have you lost your mind?"

The undeniable truth sobered Bryn a little. Ronan watched him back down, take a breath, blink his eyes clear. But Bryn kicked out of the stirrups a moment later, and fixed Gareth with a look as sharp as nails, and Ronan knew what he was going to say.

"Then send hunters after him. Let Wulfhere be hunted down for the animal he is."

Gareth's face was like a thundercloud. "You wish to hunt him?"

"I do." Bryn was tight mouthed. "Derventio was my home. Malla and his sons destroyed everything I ever possessed, and at the last, today, they are *still* using the survivors of Derventio to trap you, Gareth. To trap you into a fight you counselled against. It shames me, that my people should be used against you."

He was right, and Ronan slid to the ground. His sword, he sheathed without bothering to clean it, and instead he drew the brace of hunting knives with which he had fed his family in a time so long ago, it had begun to seem like an enchanted dream. "Let me hunt him down," he asked of Gareth. "You know that I'm the best hunter in Eboracum, and you know why. I told you where I'm from and what I was. I kept no secrets. Those are the skills that will bring down Wulfhere — he who is a traitor even to his own father."

"Ronan, no!" Bryn growled. "You won't go after him."

One brow crooked at Bryn, and Ronan shook his head slowly. "I'm not yours to command, Bryn ap Gruffydd. I am Gareth's to order as he chooses, and I am my own man. I owe these Angles as much as you do, for their sins against people I loved. And I'm as shamed as you are, that the people we thought we were fighting to protect have been used to trap us."

"But, Ronan," Bryn began.

"Gareth?" Ronan looked up into the Ironhand's dark face. "I'll go alone, if needs be. One on one. And I'll bring you Wulfhere. . . or his head."

"Not alone," Gareth said, hoarse and dry after so many bellowed commands. "You go with Bryn. And Cora." He beckoned the woman closer, and she sheathed her swords at once, kicked out of her stirrups and hit the ground with a thud of boots. "Cora hunted beside me when we were both children," Gareth said bitterly. "There's none better. She'll be the eyes in the backs of your heads."

"But we know these woods better than any of you," Bryn added sharply.

"Which is why I'm risking you." Gareth gathered his reins. "Bring back the Angle, if you can. I want to see him stand in irons before a court of his fellows and ours, and answer for his crimes, I want to display him before Cerdic Halfhand, perhaps even in Karitia, as a trophy of war, and tell Cerdic that if I see Saxons on my borders again, it will be blood. And then I want that bastard's head on a spike over my gate, until the ravens have pecked clean his skull!"

Ronan shivered, deep as his marrow. He had never seen Gareth so outraged. Then, he had never seen Gareth in a white-hot fury of betrayal. He had been used — even Malla had been used. If Wulfhere lived, he would be an outlaw on both sides of the frontier, and even the Halfhand would bear little affection for him, since so many Saxons had died here today.

17

With a white-toothed grin, Cora drew her knives and it was she who led the way into the trees, in the direction Wulfhere had vanished. Before she had gone a dozen paces Ronan called her back. "You're headed the wrong way. He'll go this way. Trust me, I know these woods, I grew up here. We'll pick up his trail by the river."

He was right. Bryn knew these woods just as well, and the only place Wulfhere could run was the river. If he trapped himself in the Angle camp, soon enough Kynddelig's mercenaries might be in there. If he ran north he would be in open country, nowhere to hide. South took him into Gareth's lands, where every man's hand was against him.

A pulse beat drummed in Bryn's head, he felt dizzy, drunk, as he plunged into the dim green woods with Ronan at his side. He was blooded. His sword had tasted the life of two Angles, and he had wounded two others, he was sure. One, he had cut down just before Gareth would have taken a sword in his back. Another died in the instant before Ronan would have been in the dirt under his horse's hooves.

Blooded! Was it the measure of a man, or the symbol of his masculinity? Bryn did no know, nor did he care to question too deeply, when Cora was a pace ahead of him and her tunic and leggings were spattered in scarlet. But Bryn felt that he had fulfilled his father's requirements of him, and for today it was enough.

If Malla had been betrayed, just as Gareth had been betrayed, the Angles themselves would demand justice from Wulfhere. Bryn's deepest desire was to kill him — for the way he looked at Ronan, if nothing else. But Gareth wanted that wild shaggy head spiked on Eboracum's gate after Wulfhere had been exhibited like a pit bear in the slave markets across the Narrow Sea, and Bryn would be satisfied to see that, also.

The sun was a little lower, striking between the boughs of the woodland canopy, and they were still a good distance from the river when Ronan slowed their pace. Cora hunkered down in the blind side of a fallen log and Bryn crouched with Ronan.

"Careful, now," Ronan murmured, "or we shall be seen in these patches of sun." He turned a dirty, smudged face to Bryn, but he was bright eyed with anger. "I'd as soon not kill him."

Cora gave a quiet snort. "I would tie him between four horses and have him torn limb from limb! But rather give him to Gareth and have justice done, not revenge."

"Wulfhere took someone from you?" Bryn wondered.

She spared him a glance and looked away. "I had friends in Derventio. I had real kin, the last of my blood kin, in the south. They fought Cerdic Halfhand when they could run no further, and those who were not killed were sold like cattle. And I have become fond, a little, of Eadhun, since he has been in the barracks.

I don't know what Wulfhere did to him, but I would have his eyes for that."

"Shh," Ronan hushed. "Let me listen!"

A thread of ice slithered through Bryn's belly and if he had been a cat his ears would have swivelled. But no, it was only a pig rooting for feed among trees, and with the battlefield behind them they could hear the river too, not so far ahead as they had thought. Ronan turned back with a finger pressed to his lips to caution quiet, and then moved on.

The hillside sloped down, always down, toward the water, and as the trees thinned the ground became muddy. It was just a question of deciding which tracks were Wulfhere's, and Ronan and Cora seemed to have decided that already, perhaps soon after they entered the woods and were certain of the exact spot where the man had stood. Not for the first time, Bryn envied such skills. In his boyhood he could have learned them, but there had been better things to do, and his father had often counselled that these were peasant skills, hardly suited to the sons of chiefs.

But it was peasant skills that sent them after Wulfhere, and Gruffydd would have been admiring. Ronan moved slowly, cautiously, but the Angle had turned south along the riverbank and kept running. Where in the gods' names was he going? Bryn was breathing hard and cursing the man, when his tracks led to the old timber bridge that had survived the fire, and once again Ronan crouched in the cover of the last bushes.

"He went over," Cora said bleakly.

"He had to." Ronan gestured south with one of his knives. "Another mile, and he could expect to run right into our own hunters and farmers. We knew he had to cross, but where is he heading? That's the better question."

"He may be just running," Bryn mused. "After this, his own people will turn on him, even his father. The Halfhand will blame him for the defeat, and he'll find no friend in Gareth's camp. There's death every way he turns."

"Aye," Cora agreed angrily, "and the traitor flees while the men he betrayed will be on the pyres in the morning!" She rose carefully and dropped a hand on Ronan's shoulders. "If we let him get too far ahead we'll be hunting him all week."

The bridge was old, the timbers worn, worm-eaten and sunwarped. They ran across swiftly, grateful that it had been built where the river was narrowest for miles, and once again they were in the sun-dappled shadows where even the air seemed green. Ronan batted at a cloud of midges, casting about this way and that as he hunted for the trail, but he had it as swiftly as a hound could have nosed it out.

They still moved cautiously but Bryn was aware of an acid sense of scorn. How quickly he had learned to despise Wulfhere. An hour before, he would have called the man out in single combat, to answer for the insults of the looks he gave Ronan. He would have offered Wulfhere his throat and challenged him to cut it. Now, he so despised the deceiver that he would rather fetch him back in irons to be publicly stoned — and cast the first rock himself.

Little moved in these woods; the hunting had been too intensive since the fires stripped Derventio's crop fields. A few birds scavenged but the forest was strangely empty of life, and so silent, the lowing of cows could be heard from the byres on the other side of the river. The trees muted the sounds of wind and water, and every rustle of Bryn's own feet was intrusive. Three of them moving through the underbrush were making an unfortunate noise, and he had begun to fret when Ronan held up his hand to halt them once more, and at the same time dived into the concealment of a cluster of moss-green boulders.

"Listen!" The lines of his face were drawn taut, every muscle tensed to fight or fly. His hearing was better than Bryn's, and Bryn knew to trust him implicitly.

They came up hard against the boulders, slithered around the curved rock until they were safe, and as his breathing eased Bryn sifted the muted woodland sounds. A moment later he heard it, and his heart skipped.

Voices. Angry, arguing, guttural and strange. Cora dragged her sleeve across her face and looked sidelong at Bryn. She made no sound, but she mouthed unmistakably, "Saxons!"

Saxons — the Halfhand's men, so close to Derventio? Bryn forced a breath to the bottom of his lungs and moved carefully by Ronan. Together they slithered on around the curvature of the boulders, and around the massive trunk of the oak beyond. A hillock rose before them and then dropped steeply away into a little ravine where a stream would race in wet weather. There, they dropped belly-down in the deep, rank humus and dared to peer over the edge.

For a few moments Bryn waited for his eyes to adjust to the dimness, for it was dark as a cavern in the bottom of the ravine, dark enough for the Saxons to have lit four pitch torches to augment the light of a campfire. As Bryn's eyes dilated he saw them clearly, and livid oaths died on his lips. He counted twenty men, and Wulfhere Mallasson, apparently trading insults with flailing arms and angry eyes. Behind them were three pack horses and five slaves, all young men or boys, big, strong enough to carry the work, young enough to survive the harshness of the life.

Or, most of them were big, strong. One was not. One was wrapped in a white cloak, his hands roped together before him, and he was sitting cross-ways on a pony hitched to the pack horses. His hood was back, his face was turned away as he listened to the Saxons, but then the pony shifted its weight, and as the boy sought his balance he turned back from the Saxons, and Bryn saw his face.

Ronan saw it also, and Bryn heard his breath catch in his throat. Cora had shuffled up beside them, knees and elbows digging into the stinking humus. Her voice was no louder than the hiss of the wind in the fallen leaves as she whispered, "You know him?"

"His name. . ." Ronan seemed to swallow his heart. "His name is Dafydd. He's crippled, he can't walk well. Camulus, Bryn, he's alive! What do they want with him?"

"He was one of Derventio's jewels," Bryn murmured. "Crippled or not, he was a beauty, and after the battle, who could tell the difference between princes and kitchen boys?"

"They'll not have him," Ronan said soundlessly. "Wulfhere won't have him."

Yet Wulfhere had clearly already traded him — and the load carried by those pack horses, and more than likely the young men doing service as stable slaves, too. This would have been part of the deal, the hire-price of Saxon mercenaries who never lifted a sword without gold in their palms. Bryn's eyes narrowed on Dafydd's face, trying to see if he was hurt, but the boy showed no obvious bruises. He was thin, pale, but he had always been delicately made, and that milky skin was part of the enchantment of him. Bryn had never slept with him, never tasted the deliciousness of seeing him naked, but Ronan had been the boy's lover for weeks, and he was trembling with anger and outrage.

"If this company crosses the river above Derventio and falls on Gareth's cavalry from behind," Cora whispered, "we could be dog meat. We might win the day and yet be gutted like fish." She rolled over, flat in the dirt, and gave Bryn and Ronan a hard, grey eyed glare. "I'll go back and warn Gareth. I can be back across that bridge so fast —"

"I'll go." Ronan's breathing was harsh. "I can run faster, Cora. I'm faster than Bryn, no matter what he tells you. I'll go." He clenched both fists and pressed them into his face, his eyes. "There's nothing three of us can do against *that*. We should have known Wulfhere was not just fleeing from the battle when it turned against him. Ah, gods, Bryn, will you take my swords, hold them for me, and don't take your eyes off that boy."

"I will." Bryn's heart was in his throat, choking him, but he took the swords as Ronan unbuckled the harness. Without them, he would be faster and quieter, and he would cut a line back through the woods, arrow-straight. Bryn set the swords aside, and as Ronan turned toward him, caught him in an embrace that crushed the breath from him. A brief, bite-like kiss tasted of blood and earth, and Ronan's fingers clenched into Bryn's shoulders for one desperate second before he slithered out of Bryn's arms and was gone.

He moved like a snake through the grass, keeping out of sight until he was back in the lee of the oak and the boulders, and only they did Bryn dare to breathe again. Cora shuffled closer, warm and hard along Bryn's right side, and now they settled just to wait. Down below, Wulfhere was shouting, anger becoming rage, a knife's edge in his voice as he confronted a Saxon chieftain a little older than himself, a little more thickset, with a beard that hid half his face and a braid of dark blond hair as thick as Bryn's wrist.

From their tone, the Saxons were abusive. Gestures were made, words flung at Wulfhere that might have been insults or threats. Wulfhere backed off, forced his temper down and began again, and though Bryn could not understand a word he could see and hear the tides of a verbal battle taking place in the ravine. Wulfhere was trying to convince his Saxon associate that if he would field his men, right *now*, the day was winnable.

And he was right. Bryn's blood cooled as he surveyed the mercenaries. How much had Wulfhere promised the Halfhand, to hire so many? Did he not know that once Cerdic had seized what had been Malla's land for so short a time, he would never let it go. Or had Wulfhere reckoned with this, did he plan to kill the Saxon usurpers in their beds?

If this was the world of chiefs and power and kingship, Bryn wanted no part of it. He was happier with simple things, a house with a roof that sheltered him from rain and wind, a warm hearth with a meal left to cook, a soft bed, and a lover's eager body waiting for him. These were Bryn's treasures, and when he looked back to the days of his youth, he asked himself what kind of fool had he been.

The Saxons were less confident than Wulfhere, and they laughed in his face. It seemed that Gareth's reputation, and Eboracum's, were to be reckoned with. For a time Bryn held his breath, praying that these mercenaries would just pull out, turn eastward for the sea, and be gone. But Wulfhere was persuasive, and as Bryn watched the Saxons grudgingly began to listen. Wulfhere gestured at the horses, the packs they carried, and at the boys who worked in irons. At the one boy who did not work at all, but sat watching this scene with a mask-like face, as if he were merely resigned.

They were coming around, and Bryn muttered the kind of curses for which Gruffydd would have boxed his ears not so long ago. "They're going to take the field," he whispered as Cora began to stir restlessly. "They'll ride up to —"

"Bryn." Her fingers cut like talons into his arm. "Oh, Bryn, tell me my eyes are deceiving."

He followed the line of those eyes, and as the pair of scouts stepped into the ravine he also recognised the load they carried between them. Ronan was unconscious, and Bryn saw the trickle of blood on the back of his neck. He could have been brought down by a stone from a catapult, or perhaps he had fought with his fists, since he had left his swords for the sake of speed. The means did not matter to Bryn. All he cared to know was that Ronan was deeply unconscious as he was dumped unceremoniously in the fire-light, and the Saxon scouts conveyed news that set the whole camp aflame.

If this one had been caught, were there others who had made it through? If the Britons knew where this camp was, there was no decision left. These Saxons ran, or they fought. One or the other. Bryn's hearth slammed at his ribs as he watched Wulfhere and the chieftains. Mallasson shoved Ronan over onto his back, bent over him, peered into his face, and the sound he made was like a wild boar in season. Bryn's belly turned and he swallowed hard before he could find his voice.

"Will they flee? Cora, I'm asking you. You had kin who fought these people, you know them better than I ever will! Will they flee, or will they fight?"

His eyes were wide, feverish, and her teeth worried her lower lip until Bryn saw scarlet. "They will fight," she said at last. "They are here for pillage, for rich pickings along coasts that can't stand against them. Gareth has given them a fight they won't soon forget — the trap did not spring properly. They'll be hurt by this defeat, but more, they'll be angry. When they're angry, they'll want to punish."

Bryn was watching Wulfhere, watching Ronan, while his head spun dizzily and sweat prickled his ribs. "Gareth must be warned. If he doesn't rally Kyn's mercenaries, we'll pay a dreadful price, Cora."

Her eyes dilated, like jet in the green forest light. "I'll go."

"Like him?" Bryn looked back at Ronan.

"He ran into the perimeter scouts." Cora took a breath and eased her baldric. "They're still in the ravine, Bryn. I won't run into men who aren't there. Ronan got rid of them for me."

"Better that he had killed them," Bryn said bitterly.

"He killed two," Cora assured him, grim faced as she also unbuckled the baldric and passed it to him. Her hand clasped his shoulder. "Perimeter scouts hunt by fours. Ronan dropped two of them with those knives of his. If he'd owned four knives. . ." She sucked in a breath, exhaled it through clenched teeth. "I'll be back across that bridge so fast, Bryn, they'll ride into a hornets' nest. And as he said, don't you take your eyes off them!"

With a terrible sense of isolation and impotence, Bryn watched her go. She slithered around the tree, the boulders, and then he was alone with a dread that froze him from within, as if he were suspended in icewater. In the ravine below Saxon voices were shouting, a whip cracked, a man cried out in pain or fear. Soldiers milled as the slaves hurried to fetch harness and weapons. Were they moving out, would they make a run for the coast? Or was Cora right, would they turn on Gareth like winter-mad wolves?

Still Ronan did not stir, and Bryn could scarcely breathe as soldiers stamped iron-toed boots too close to him, and Wulfhere's bellows were answered at last with a length of rope. Ronan was limp as he was bound, hand and foot, but at least he was safe as he was dumped on the other side of the fire, just out of the torchlight, with the pack horses and the pony on which Dafydd was trying to balance.

Plumed helmets were magnificent, but Bryn knew Cerdic Halfhand's colours. The hackles on these helmets were scarlet and black, and in the twilight of the ravine they had an evil aspect. One of the Saxons was a priest or a sorcerer. He squatted by the fire, and Bryn watched, fascinated, as he tossed a set of elk's antler runes. The man's skull was shaven, his face covered with the swirls and coils of ancient magic. Even Wulfhere waited to know what he read in the runes, and Bryn leaned closer.

The shaven skull nodded and the man rose to his feet. He towered over Wulfhere, and even he, a priest or magician, was clad in leathers and chain mail for the battlefield. So they would fight? Bryn's heart skipped. If they intended to fight, then this camp would be left intact at least until the tide of battle had been gauged.

The slaves were bound by the wrists, a looped rope about each neck, so that if one moved independently he would only strangle the others. They were hitched to the same stake that held the pack horses, a lash cracked a warning over their heads and they flinched as men did when they well knew the caress of the merciless leather. And then —

A sword raised, axes swung, and Wulfhere Mallasson fell into step with the mercenaries he had invited into this land, like fetching in the plague. Bryn's muscles bunched as he watched the company come together, and yet again thanked every god he could recall that Saxons were not cavalry. There were no better foot-soldiers on either side of the Narrow Sea, but like Angles, they were not at their best on horseback, and they knew it.

Cora was so fleet of foot, the wind itself could not catch her. She was almost as quick as Ronan, and Bryn was trying to gauge time, judge distance. She must be at the bridge again by the time the mercenaries marched out. She must be starting over the sun-warped timbers when they began to follow in her wake. She would be back through the woods in minutes, surely, and when Gareth knew he was about to be set upon, the tide of battle would be turned, the way even the ocean recoiled before the breakwater.

These were Bryn's prayers as he looked down into the ravine. His eyes covered Ronan bone by bone, head to foot, but he could see little. Ronan was trussed like a pig, not even moving, and Bryn had just begun to fret. With Wulfhere gone, returning to the battle, Ronan was more or less safe for the moment. He should be moving, surely he should be returning to his senses, even if they had clubbed him!

With the soldiers' exit, Dafydd had slid down off the pony and limped to Ronan's side. The boy was not shackled — where was the need to chain a cripple's feet? He sat in the dirt beside Ronan, his bound hands covering him, every joint and limb. The five slaves hunched in the warmth from the fire, nursing fresh welts and old anger, and Bryn spared them a glance before he turned his attention to the four guards who had been left behind.

Two were the perimeter scouts who had fetched in Ronan, the others were older men, lifetime soldiers still serving their lord in the best way they knew. Good sentries were rare, as Malla had learned. These were the best. Without orders, they had arranged themselves at the four edges of the camp, heavily armed, vigilant, warspears thrust into the gloom of the ravine beyond the ring of the torchlight.

Bryn's hands closed about Ronan's and Cora's weapons and, silent as a Samhaine ghost, he moved back into the murk of the forest.

* * *

The wetness on his neck was blood, but it had already become sticky and itchy when Ronan felt the boot in his hip, the shove that turned him over onto his back. He did not clench shut his eyelids, but relaxed his face, let his head loll as he smelt Wulfhere's breath and knew the man was leaning low over him, peering into his face. Hands covered him, felt out the shape of his chest, delved between his legs, and still Ronan did not move so much as an eyelid.

The Saxons were still shouting, and it seemed that Ronan had won Wulfhere's war or words for him. Of a sudden these men did not dare sit and wait, for if one frontier scout had been caught stealing away from this camp, what of the others who had made it away? Ronan was the only one, but Wulfhere and his mercenaries did not know that.

Odd, the way the threat of sudden death could make a man stand up and fight. Ronan could not grasp a word that was said over him, but he knew the sound of those voices. There was *fight* in them now. He knew that knife's edge when he heard it, and he relaxed a fraction even as Wulfhere began to manhandle him again. Ropes bit into his wrists, his hands and feet were bloodless before he was picked up bodily, carried a short distance and dumped down again where it was colder and more damp.

Now he dared crack open his eyelids, and he watched the soldiers come together through a dizzy haze. His vision was still misted, his head still throbbing, but the crack on the skull was not as bad as it could have been. He would swear it was a spear's haft that hit him, but the blow was only glancing, and almost spent. He had never seen or heard the men who came after him, but a gambling man would have said the situation was more than fair. Two Saxons lay dead in the woods to the north of the ravine, with Ronan's best hunting knives buried hilt-deep in their chests.

Lying motionless on the ground, pretending that he was nearer corpse than invalid, he could see little. The fire was between him and the Saxons, but he watched one man squat down and cast a hand of runes, and he saw Wulfhere's grin as the gods gave their approbation. Swords and axes gleamed like molten gold in the firelight as the mercenaries came together, and Ronan dared take a deep breath as they moved out fast.

They were barely away when other hands began to skim over him, but these hands, he welcomed. Even now he held still, listening until the last faint sounds of the soldiers became indistinguishable from the woodland. Only then did he whisper, very softly,

"Dafydd, hush now, else they'll hear us! I thought you were dead."

The hands stilled on him in surprise, or shock, and then the boy leaned closer. "Ronan, are you all right? I thought they had killed you. The cut on your head isn't bleeding now."

"It was a light blow," Ronan whispered. "Enough to put me down. . .enough to keep me safe, or Wulfhere would have made sport with me. There's no amusement in sporting with an unconscious man." He opened his eyes wide, and very carefully moved his head. "Dafydd, are you well? I thought you must have died in the fires that night."

The boy's face was thinner than he remembered, his eyes larger, his skin more translucent. He seemed less of this world than the next, and yet he found a faint smile for Ronan. "I lived. Sometimes it was not easy, but I lived. Others were less lucky."

"Your mother? Sian?" Ronan could hardly ask.

"Dead." Dafydd lifted his chin proudly. "She fought beside Gruffydd and Cuddy, and she died like a warrior. I was caught on the riverbank, trying to get to the boats." He closed his eyes as nightmare memories of that night possessed him, and then seemed to force himself back to the present.

"Are we safe?" Ronan was searching for sentries now, but he could see only two.

"As safe as slaves ever are." Dafydd eased himself down. "They have left four men to guard us. Please, Ronan, don't move. It will be their pleasure to kill you."

"Shh," Ronan whispered. "I'm a warrior, Dafydd, blooded and proven. Perhaps they will try to kill me, but the men I can see have more grey hairs than a badger! Can you find a knife? Get me out of these ropes, if you can." As he spoke he was looking into the face of another young man. Younger than himself by a year or two, Ronan thought, ripe for the picking, when slave takers stormed his village. Boys were more adaptable than men, their bodies more resilient, their hearts more accepting of hardship and discipline. A boy would bend to the will of his master and survive; a man would fight for his honour, and die.

This young man had seen Ronan move, and was peering into his face as Ronan whispered to Dafydd. And he was a year older than the others, he would have been on the very brink of manhood when he was taken, and would have felt the stirrings of a man's honour, before all that was cut away from him. His eyes were wide, his fair hair, clear skin and fine features giving him a handsome aspect that made Ronan suspect Wulfhere's involvement. Mallasson was cruel, and a predator, but his taste was impeccable. The five cavalry slaves were bound so tightly, their hands were blue, and confined with the animals, but this one at least was aware that a wolf was in the sheep pen.

Ronan's leathers set him apart as a warrior. The slave must have seen it at once. "A knife, Dafydd," Ronan repeated. "Get me out of these ropes, or I can do nothing for you."

"I can't," Dafydd protested woundedly.

"You can! There must be a knife around the hearth," Ronan growled, "they were cooking, I can see the meat scraps!"

"My lord will punish me," Dafydd whimpered.

A note in his voice made Ronan's belly knot. "Wulfhere owned you?" Dafydd hugged himself and rocked, and would not speak. "Wulfhere will not be back," Ronan swore. "Dafydd, listen to me. Listen! Wulfhere has led his mercenaries to battle on the frontier, but the cavalry from Eboracum is there. Do you hear me? Gareth Ironhand is on the field, and better cavalry than Wulfhere Mallasson can ever have seen before!"

The boy's eyes blinked, pain and fear diminished a little. "The Ironhand is here?"

"And Eboracum's finest." Ronan forced a smile to his lips. "Bryn ap Gruffydd and I have been in Ebor this whole time. We ride for Gareth now. Dafydd, the one you call your lord will not be back to punish you. You will watch him die, very soon. Give me a knife."

Walking was difficult for Dafydd. He did not rise to his feet, and Ronan watched him move on hands and knees toward the fire, where the cooking stones were still hot and the ground was littered with meat scraps. A dirk lay among the discarded rind, buried by its point in the earth, its hilt slick with fat. Dafydd's bound hands reached for it, took hold of it, and Ronan's eyes never left the guardsmen he could see. Two men, each of them big shouldered and thick with muscle, wearing the bronze helmets with the scarlet and black hackles that could look so magnificent on the field of battle, so evil off it.

They were faced outward into the woods, guarding the camp from without, not from within, and they did not see as Dafydd retrieved the dirk. Ronan watched him tuck it into the frayed sleeve of his tunic before he made his way back. Seeing Dafydd on his hands and knees, dirty and seemingly unaware of any humiliation, made the gall rise in Ronan's belly. The smell of fear about Dafydd when he was tasked to risk his master's ire made Ronan's hands long to clench about Wulfhere's throat and squeeze.

But then Dafydd was beside him, his hands trembling on the dirk as he worked it under the ropes binding Ronan's feet. The blade was like a razor and the fibres cut easily. Ronan's legs and spine eased as he was freed, and while he watched the sentries unblinkingly, he held his hands to Dafydd. "Boy, are you well?"

Dafydd did not answer, but the ropes fell apart, and without even pausing to rub his chafed wrists Ronan took him by the shoulders. "Dafydd, are you hurt? What have they done to you?"

Vast, bruised eyes looked up at him, and still Dafydd would not speak. Nor did he have to. Ronan clasped him tightly for as long as he dared, and then pressed him down to rest in the warm draught from the hearth, and picked up the knife. But Dafydd would not let him cut the bindings from his wrists, as if he prayed that he would not be implicated in Ronan's escape. . .as if he expected the bid for freedom to be repaid in blood. Ronan's lips compressed, and he did not press Dafydd. Not yet. Time enough to reawaken the living spirit in the boy when they were out of here, when time had healed.

For the moment, five youths little younger than himself were gazing intently at him by the pack horses, and as Ronan had expected the handsome, fair-haired boy was the first to hold out his hands to be cut loose. There was about him something of the warrior. Had he been in training when the Angles came? Was his father a cavalryman? After the long confinement and the gods only knew what ill treatment, he was eager to be loose and strike out. Ronan turned the dirk and very, very carefully crept closer to the slaves.

The fire was between him and the nearest sentry. He kept low to the ground, using the flames to one side and horses to the other to mask his presence until the dirk had slit the ropes and a master's worst fear was realised — the labour slaves were loose. He saw the blood in their eyes as they pulled the noose-like halters from their necks; he saw the fresh welts on their arms and shoulders, and he thought he smelt the rage rising from their pores, more bitterly acrid than any honest sweat.

He pressed a finger to his lips and bobbed up between the horses to search for the sentries. There they were, four burly men who had set themselves at the cardinal points and stood like statues, intent on the woodland. Ronan ducked down again and beckoned the fair-haired youth. The boy had his breath now, and his wits. He spoke with the accent of the moorland and his eyes glittered, in this moment not quite sane.

"Who are you? I know you! I saw you in Derventio, before!"

"I am Ronan of Whitestonecliff," Ronan told him soundlessly.
"You have a name?"

"Selgi." The young man was filthy and he smelt of horses and
leather. "How do you come to be here?"

"There's no time," Ronan whispered. "Can you fight?"

"No," Selgi said honestly, "but I can kill." And as Ronan
watched he opened the pack on the nearest horse, and from it lifted
not a weapon but a tool. The hammer was very like the implement
a smith would use to beat steel into swords. Oh yes, it would kill.
Selgi turned with the poise and sinuous strength of a hunter, and
glared at the back of one sentry in particular. "He is mine. Pick
your own, but that one, with the scar under his eye. . .he belongs
to me."

Ronan shivered. He thought he had never seen such hate in
one so young. Even after the raze of Derventio and Whitestonecliff,
he and Bryn had not been so consumed by the thirst for blood. But
they had been out and free, and they believed their kin had died
cleanly. Ronan frowned at Dafydd then, and as he saw the boy
lying hunched by the hearth he felt the fire rise in his belly, just as
it was burning Selgi from the inside out.

He nodded, dropped a hand on the youth's shoulder and fixed
the others with a probing look. "Fight if you will. Run if you will.
I can take one before they realise we are loose." He gestured with
the dirk. "Then, maybe I also will run!"

"It is for the gods to decide," Selgi said darkly. "They sent
you. They put the steel in my hand." He lifted his chin. "This is
for my brothers, who died under the whip. For my sisters, who
died in whore service. For my father, who died in the battle."

Murmurs of agreement from the other young men fetched
Ronan another shiver, and he watched them delve into the pack of
tools, each one selecting a piece of steel that may not have been
intended as a weapon but would surely serve as one. "Quickly then,"
he urged. "Keep down, don't let them see you until they must.
When they're coming at you, they're at their most vulnerable, for
they expect you to panic, turn and flee, and when they're coming
on they can fall onto your weapons with their own speed. Scatter
and run like rabbits, and they'll kill you. Meet them head to head
. . . and maybe they will be so surprised at the courage of slaves, the
gods will blind their eyes."

He was answered with a feral grimace from Selgi that might
have been a grin, and then Ronan was moving, silent and swift as a
ghost dancer. The dirk was not well-balanced for throwing, but it

would do. All the skill of a lifetime sent it whirling, arrow-straight, and Ronan gave a grunt of satisfaction as it buried, hilt-deep, between the shoulders of the sentry he had chosen for his own — the man who would see him most clearly if only he bothered to turn and survey the camp.

A stagger, a sound like a wounded bull, hands clawing uselessly at his back, and the man pitched onto his face. The sound was enough. Three other sentries were spinning around, warspears jagged inward, into the camp, and Ronan's heart was in his mouth. Beside him, Selgi was so quick, he was a blur in the corner of Ronan's eye as he drew back his arm and threw the hammer, like the boy's game of throwing at a target.

His target was the face of the man he had learned to hate, and Ronan watched with terrible fascination as the smith's tool found its mark. Steel became one with blood and bone, and the man was flung backward before he could make a move into the camp. Ronan glimpsed the scar on his face before the sentry's face was gone, and he had no doubt that the man's neck was snapped by the impact. He was dead before he fell, and Selgi did not pause to gloat.

The pack horses were loaded with tools. Hammers, chisels, axes and adzes. Five young men whose welted backs had begun to bleed afresh as they moved were well armed. Ronan was still diving toward the guardsman Selgi had dropped, to take his weapons, when an axe spun through the air and sank its blade into the belly of an oncoming sentry. It bit through chainmail as if it were butter, and the Saxon stopped in his tracks as if he had run into a wall. The warspear fell from his hands, he tore at the haft of the axe, but before he could drag it loose he was on his knees and toppling sideways.

"They sent us to log the forest," Selgi said through clenched teeth. "They had to teach Cadarn how to swing an axe, and when his hands were through to blood they rubbed him with salt until he screamed like the banshee. He has not had an axe out of his hands, these months."

"And you were bonded to the blacksmith," Ronan guessed.

"Aye." Selgi had gone back to the pack for another tool, a chisel as long as his forearm. "I sweated and I burned in the forge, and when I begged for rest in my fatigue they laid a whip across my back until I could not stand. And *that* one —" he was inarticulate for a moment as he looked at the man he had killed. "That one scourged me, for it is his pleasure to ply the whip."

"And he has died for it, let his gods judge him for his sins," Ronan said distractedly as he watched the last of the three sentries set upon by four youths maddened by fury and all armed with tools thrust into their hands by their Angle masters. The Saxon probed with a warspear longer than he was tall, but against four he was outmatched. The youths were young enough to be his sons, faster and keener, and in this moment of madness they did not seem to care if they lived or died.

One of them did perish, when the warspear plunged into his chest, but the very act of plunder left the Saxon without defence, and a hammer buried in the back of his skull. Ronan looked away, not wanting to watch as the body was mutilated in the final rage of vengeance before madness was purged.

Selgi had already regained his senses. It was he who stooped to Dafydd, cut his bonds and lifted him in arms grown thick with muscle while he laboured at the forge. Welts across his back were bleeding through his shirt but he did not seem to notice them as he cradled Dafydd against himself and rocked him. Ronan swallowed his heart, and laid a hand on the boy's head. "He was my lover, once, a lifetime ago," he whispered

"I know." Selgi's eyes were squeezed shut. "I remember you now. You were the one who came to train the horse, and Gruffydd sent you to be taught the warrior skills. Sometimes I would watch you. I thought you were dead in the night of the fires."

"I wasn't in Derventio," Ronan said thickly, reliving that scene in memory, as he did every time he closed his eyes at night. The flames, the reek of burning, the maelstrom of pain and fear, gripped him so tightly by the throat that the voice speaking out of the dimness was as shocking as a lance thrust.

"Bryn ap Gruffydd escaped Derventio also, by the grace of a young man's bed."

It was the last sound Ronan had expected to hear, and he spun. Bryn was standing behind the horses, carrying Ronan's weapons in one hand and Cora's in the other, and wearing a rueful expression on his face. "You were a little quick for me," he accused. "I saw Dafydd cut you loose, I was covering you from the trees." Bryn tossed Ronan's weapons to him. "If one of those sentries had even *thought* of cocking an ear to a sound he had heard —" he drew a forefinger across his throat, and then fixed Ronan with a look of mock accusation. "Then you moved so fast, all of you, it was over before I'd picked myself up out of the dirt."

"I knew you wouldn't be far away." Ronan had buckled on the baldric and now opened his arms to greet Bryn with an embrace that tested his ribs. "Cora?"

"Gave me her swords to keep and took off like a hare when

we saw you brought into camp." Bryn's brow creased in a frown. "They almost knocked your head off."

But Ronan fended him off. "A glancing blow, I made it look much worse. I wanted to keep Wulfhere's hands off me, if I could." He indicated Dafydd with a nod as he spoke, and Bryn's frown deepened. Dafydd was tight in Selgi's arms, had tucked his face into the young smith's strong shoulder, and would be as tough to move as a limpet. Something in Ronan grieved, that Dafydd had found someone else; something in him rejoiced, for even then Bryn's hand was on his arm and the voice he loved was saying urgently,

"The Saxons went by like a pack of hunting wolves. Cora would have been across the bridge and through in time to bring Gareth a warning, but they'll still be badly outnumbered on the field. A warning is not an ambush to even the odds,"

Ronan's heart squeezed. "We should return to the battle."

"We should." Bryn wiped the back of his hand across his forehead, leaving a smudge of earth. "It's not over yet. And I have a longing to put a sword into Wulfhere. I saw his hands on you, Ronan, and I swear, if I could have clenched my fingers into his throat —"

"Then avenge him." Ronan gestured at Dafydd. "The gods have been blind this time. Selgi?" The young man looked up. His eyes were sane now, simply filled with pain, his own and Dafydd's. "Is he injured?"

"No. He was examined when Wulfhere sold him, along with the loads on these horses and the five of us. We were part of the battle price for which the Saxons fought. Cerdic Halfhand's youngest son commands them — you saw him meet Wulfhere, like stags butting heads in the spring."

"Cerdic's youngest son?" Bryn echoed. "Damn, but Gareth will be interested to know that! If he lives long enough to be put onto irons. And maybe Cerdic will be interested." He lifted a brow at Ronan.

"Ransom?" Ronan wondered.

"Of a kind." Bryn licked his lips. "The Halfhand's son may live a long and healthy life in Eboracum. . .so long as Saxons are never seen here again. So long as Cerdic pulls back his warband and never raids, and never sends his mercenaries to fight with Angles on our shores. For, the next time Saxons are seen here, Cerdic's son will be the first to die. Yes?"

"Yes." Ronan felt a tingle the length of his spine. "It could be Eboracum's security."

"If only Gareth knew who is on the field," Bryn added.

"Eadhun would likely recognise him."

"Eadhun may be dead," Ronan said quietly. "I don't know what Wulfhere did to him. He seemed to be standing behind him, and laid a hand on his back, and I thought later that he was holding him, lest Eadhun bolt. Until I saw the blood on him, and he fell." He turned a bitter face to Selgi. "You know Wulfhere better than I ever wish to."

"I know him." Selgi was rocking Dafydd, gentle as a father with his child. "Your friend with the Angle name may live, or may not. And if he lives, perhaps he won't fight again."

Ronan's mouth dried. "What did Wulfhere do to him?"

"Did he wish to secure him, or to punish?" Selgi whispered, hoarse with some remembered horror,

"Both." Bryn's face was a bleak mask. "Eadhun tried to speak sense to Malla, and at that time was not aware that Wulfhere had fetched in the Saxons. None of us knew. But Wulfhere would think himself shamed before his hirelings, and he must be seen by them to punish Eadhun." He took a breath. "What was done?"

The young man was colourless. "Steel hooks were threaded through the muscles of your friend's back. So sharp, they can barely be felt to slide in, but they won't come out, for they are barbed like fish hooks. Soon enough, your friend would feel them, and would try to move. And then he would not dare move, or speak. There is no dread like it, my lord. I have seen warriors go cowed on their knees." He rocked Dafydd. "I have seen men crippled, and die, for being bound that way."

"Sweet merciful gods," Ronan whispered. "Is it an Angle thing?"

"Or merely cruel?" Bryn rubbed his face, knuckled his eyes. "The best physicians I have ever seen ride for Gareth. If Eadhun is in their hands, he may live."

"And we," Ronan added, "must return to the field. Gareth will need every sword he can get."

Bryn was surveying the four surviving slaves. "Who are they? Were they trained with the warband?"

"No. They're more like me," Ronan guessed. "Lads plucked from the hamlets and thrust into harm's way. . .become warriors to survive. Not trained, Bryn, but they can kill. It was the Angles who put the hammer and the axe into their hands, and flogged them until they learned those skills

"And now the Angles will die by those same skills." Bryn looped Cora's baldric about his shoulder and fixed Selgi and his fellows with a speculative look. "Are you game?"

"To fight?" Selgi hugged Dafydd closer. "Aye, we'll fight. Let me get this little one to your ranks first. Let me take him on one of the horses, and then show me the field! Show me Malla's Angles, or the Halfhand's men, give me the hammer they taught me to use, and tell me what to smash." His teeth were bare, like fangs. "I'm no warrior, but I'll take the field for Gareth."

"You could be a warrior," Bryn said softly, looking then at Ronan. "I'll speak to Gareth for you, after this fight is over." He almost laughed, a bitter, choked sound of something that was not humour. "You're already blooded! I saw you take that one. No warrior could have made a cleaner kill."

"Then, help me with Dafydd," Selgi demanded, "and I'll take the field for you. We all will. It's our honour we win back today, my lord. And Derventio's honour!"

"Don't call me that," Bryn said darkly as Ronan fetched one of the pack horse and cut away its burden. "I'm no one's lord, no one's master. I'm just a cavalry hand in Eboracum's service. And proud of it," he added has he opened his arms to take Dafydd's small weight while Selgi put boot to stirrup and mounted.

Ronan held the horse's bridle till Selgi was up and safe, and helped Bryn lift Dafydd up, across the saddle. The boy was so shocked, he had not the will to make a sound, but he caught Ronan's hand and kissed it, and his eyes were full of tears. Grief was healthy, and Ronan was glad to see those tears, for he remembered how long it had taken himself to find the ability to weep for all that had been lost.

"You're safe now," he promised Dafydd. "And this one seems to care for you." He looked up into Selgi's dirty face, noticing just how handsome he was, under the grime and bruises he wore.

"Care for him? Selgi's mouth quirked. "I love him, Ronan. I would hold him in the night, when Wulfhere did not desire him, and when we were thrust together in the pens. He came to me first, to tend me after a whipping, and I loved him for his gentleness and his beauty." He cradled the boy against his chest. "He is mine now . . .not that I've the right to challenge a warrior for him, but I will. And if I must become a warrior before I can make that challenge, then I'll do what I must."

But Ronan shook his head and slung an arm around Bryn's waist. "Dafydd is safe in your arms, and at peace there. You think I can't see? And I found my own love, the night Derventio burned. Now, go, Selgi. You know the way?"

"By the woods and the bridge," Bryn added.

The youth gave a snort of derision. "I was born here!" He

gathered the reins and summoned his three surviving fellows with a low whistle. "If you'll fight, take the field with me. If you won't, join the Ironhand's back ranks, lend your hands to the old women who tend the men who fought for your freedom!"

Every one of them had been born in Derventio, and they knew the riverside woods as well as Bryn and Ronan. Selgi lagged behind, since the horse had to pick its way around boulders and the gnarled masses of trees, but soon enough they joined the trail which opened onto the bridge, and beyond the river they saw the woods Ronan had always thought of as being in Derventio's back pocket. Just north along the bank was the water meadow below the paddock where Cuddy had trained the warband, and the flats where he himself had trained Red, in another lifetime. He would have said, a happier time, but then Bryn was beside him, looking searchingly into his face, and Ronan would have changed nothing.

"You *are* all right?" Bryn said, for Ronan's ears alone. "Those were not lies, for the benefit of these boys?"

"My skull is throbbing and my neck is sore," Ronan admitted, "but what of it? I've had worse, Bryn, falling off a horse. Save your care for these boys. For Dafydd."

They were lucky, and they knew it. If the Saxon camp had been beyond Wulfhere's reach, or if the Halfhand's son had put a sword in Wulfhere's belly and pulled out, back to the coast where a ship must surely lie, they would have been lost, beyond even hope. Ronan saw the battle light in their eyes as they crossed the bridge, and it brightened as they came up through the woods, retracing the path Wulfhere had cut when he fled the battlefield.

They heard the fracas before they saw it, a terrible sound, once heard, never forgotten. A confusion of cries, chiming steel, screaming horses, and the blood roaring in a man's ears as he knew his life was once again in the balance. Ronan's sword was in his hand and his senses cleared as they stepped from the trees. Bryn was at his left hand, and they stopped in the shadows to get their bearings before showing themselves.

The field was strewn with dead, Britons, Angles and Saxons alike. Malla's hostages were loose and gone, and for that Ronan gave thanks. But Eboracum's cavalry was scattered wide across the common land, separated by a dozen Saxon mercenaries and twice than many Angles. Loose horses strayed around the fringes of the field, and Ronan whistled to them. A dappled grey mare answered him, came to him and thrust her nose into his hand, perhaps for reassurance.

Where was Gareth? Bryn was muttering lividly as he grabbed

for the trailing reins of another horse, and the animal tossed its head, trying to evade him. Selgi was going around the very fringe of the battlefield, and as Ronan hauled himself up into the saddle he saw several archers come up to cover him, as if there was still some danger of arrows from the Angle ranks. Selgi brought the horse to a slithering halt by the wagons, and Ronan watched with narrowed eyes as Dafydd slid from his arms into the hands of the old men and women who worked with the injured.

"In the gods' names, where is Gareth?" Bryn demanded as he got boot to stirrup at last and hauled himself up. Selgi spun the horse about and came back around the field to join his companions, but as he reined back and kicked his feet free of stirrup iron, Bryn gave them a hard look. "You stay well back," he barked. "This isn't the same. If you get the chance to strike like snakes — do it, but don't get out there among them, don't try to fight. You'll die for your trouble. Understand?"

They were filled with resentment, but they understood. Selgi thrust his hand up at Ronan, and when Ronan gave him a warrior's clasp the younger man found a smile. "We'll hold back unless the warband fails. If it does, we'll be in behind you. Watch out for hammers, Ronan, for they'll take a man's head clean off his shoulders as surely as a sword will."

"I don't doubt it." Ronan let go Selgi's hand and gathered the reins, for he had seen Gareth while Selgi was speaking. "Bryn, see? There."

"I see him." Bryn shortened his own reins, and Ronan urged his horse with heels and curses to keep up with him.

Gareth was down, off his horse and bloody from shoulder to thigh, along his left side. His face was a grey mask of pain but he was still on his feet, still swinging a sword that, a little time ago, Ronan could not even have lifted. He was fighting alone, and Ronan could not begin to guess where Kyn and Taran and Cora were. Never more than a pace apart, he and Bryn dived through the stinking shambles of the battlefield, and Ronan heard the rasping cry from Bryn's throat as he tore a javelin out of the ground and hurled it with all the strength of his right arm.

The filthy blade buried itself between a Saxon's shoulders and the force of the impact sent the man plunging forward. Gareth was still fast enough to step back and aside, and the mercenary went down at his feet, dead and twitching. Ronan dragged a hand across his eyes. His horse side-stepped, coming up hard against Bryn's as they joined Gareth, and for the moment they were safe. The Saxons were occupied elsewhere.

"Gareth, you're injured, you should be off the field!" Bryn barked, and it was the voice of a chieftain. Bryn ap Gruffydd was blooded within sight and sound of the place where he should have been chief, and Ronan was filled with pride.

"It's just a nick, and just a moment ago," Gareth told him, shifting his sword into his left hand and using the right to explore his side. "Ah, gods! It will be winter before it's mended. I'm getting too old for this."

"Rubbish," Ronan retorted. "But let me catch you a horse, for Bryn is right. You should be off the field. The wound needs care. Where are the others?"

"Taran was wounded a while ago. He went to the wagons," Gareth said breathlessly as the gash in his side began to pain him badly. "Cora, I don't know. I have not seen her since she fetched the news that the second band of Saxons would fall on us from behind. Thank gods she is like a deer, or we would have been on our funeral pyres! And Kyn — there he is, trying to round up the archers. They've been gathering arrows, trying to find enough to bring these last stragglers down. We have them, Ronan! The day is ours."

"Is Eadhun alive?" Bryn asked, as Ronan called to a loose horse.

"I don't know." Gareth's face was waxen and sweated. "The last I heard of him, they were trying to cut something out of his back."

"Wait, Ironhand, before you order the archers," Ronan panted, putting the reins of a big piebald warhorse into Gareth's blood-slick fingers. He cupped his hands about his mouth and shouted, cutting over the din of battle, "Selgi! Selgi!"

The youth was poised, intent on Gareth's group, and at the sound of his name he dived forward. Too eager to get onto the battlefield, Ronan thought, though he could only admire Selgi's suppleness, the sleek roundness of young muscles that had been force-built at the forge. In his right hand he carried a hammer, the only weapon he possessed, and likely, the one with which he was most adept.

"Who is this?" Gareth wanted to know as he hauled himself into the saddle with a blistering oath.

"Another slave from Derventio," Bryn said darkly. "Wulfhere sold off five, part of the hire-price of his mercenaries. Four survive, and one of them has made himself half a warrior, Gareth, without the training. Keep your eye on Selgi. This one would die for you, but better that you should made an Ironhand of him." He looked at Ronan as he spoke, and Ronan saw the wraith of a smile on his lips. "There is more, Gareth," Bryn went on as Selgi fell panting to his knees at the shoulder of the Ironhand's horse. "This lad knows the face of the Saxon chieftain who commands Wulfhere's mercenaries." He lifted a brow at Gareth. "Would having Cerdic Halfhand's youngest son for your hostage interest you?"

"The price of peace here, for as long as he lives," Ronan added.

For a moment the news banished Gareth's pain, and his eyes widened. "He is on the field this moment, Ronan? This is why you advised me to stay the archers?"

"Aye." Ronan beckoned Selgi to his feet, and as the boy scrambled up, gestured at the fracas. "Does the Halfhand's son still live? Which is he?"

Sharp young eyes, keen as the raven's, searched the knot of Saxons and Angles who still fought, holding off the body of Kynddelig's mercenaries. Had the chieftain already fallen? For a moment Ronan feared that the prize had been snatched away, but Selgi pointed, breathless with excitement.

"There, the bronze helmet with the scarlet hackles, the big man with the chain mail about his right arm, and his left arm bare, save for the black leather band. He is Aella, Cerdic's youngest and proudest."

"I see him." Gareth was holding his wounded side. "Bryn, fetch Kynddelig to me. This must be with care, or we may still win the battle and lose the war."

Kyn was with the men who had ridden with him from Lindum, and Ronan watched as Bryn swung wide about the melee, coming up on Kynddelig's blind side. Swords and javelins thrust toward him for a dangerous moment, before Kyn shouted for his men to let Bryn through, and listened to words that were too distant for Ronan's ears.

They came back together, covering the churned ground fast, but Gareth was too near spent to tell Kynddelig what must be done. Ronan came to his side, lifted aside the centurion's cloak and swore as he saw the wound. A nick, Gareth had said. A *new* nick, then — and the old wound, recently re-cauterised, had broken open again. His whole side was blood, and his face was like ashes. Ronan gave him a reproachful look, and raised his voice over the continuing clash of steel.

"Have the archers stand to, Kyn. Have them pick off every Saxon save one, until the whole company surrenders. Leave unharmed the chieftain, with the scarlet hackle and the bare left arm. He is blood of Cerdic Halfhand's blood, and worth all the rest put together."

"I want him alive," Gareth growled through clenched teeth. "And I want Wulfhere Mallasson alive. Bring him to me, on his knees, when this is done!"

Astonishment diminished Kyn's obvious weariness, and he whistled his surprise. "It will be done, Gareth. Now, get off the field, have that wound tended!"

"In my own good time," Gareth snarled. "Bring me those bastards — alive!"

"Count it done, Ironhand." Kyn sketched a salute with the broadsword and spun the horse low on its haunches. He was bellowing at his captains as he spurred back to the Lindum cavalry, and Ronan's heart began to race as he watched the archers stand to.

Those arrows had been salvaged from the dead, he knew. Under cover of the weary, wounded cavalry from Eboracum, the archers had gone out and fetched back every shaft that would still fire true. They dismounted now, knelt in the grass on the slope, with just a little height to set them above the field, and Kyn continued to shout over their heads. Ronan could catch one word in three and knew he was insisting again, they would leave alive the Saxon chieftain, and Malla's malignant son, for the Ironhand wanted them as war prizes.

Cerdic Halfhand's frontier scouts were neither deaf nor blind. They saw the archers drop into position to fire, and Aella's voice cut like a whip as he drew his men together. They fell back into a knot, protected on every side by their shields, with Aella and Wulfhere in their midst. But the shields did not interlock as Roman shields might have. They were round rather than elongated, each armoured with a javelin-blade boss, superb for protecting a man's blind side in the chaos of battle, but poor cover under a deliberate hail of arrows.

Limbs were unprotected on the edge of the ravel of men, and Ronan caught his breath as he saw the best archers from Lindum deliberately target those men. The screams were terrible, many wounds so dire that those limbs would be lost. The Saxons toppled, the knot of men and bloody steel unravelling until Wulfhere was exposed on one side, Aella Cerdicsson on the other. And Kyn raised his sword over his head.

Thirty warspears, each taller than a man, fell in a ragged circle about the Saxons and hemmed them in like a prison stockade. Wulfhere was wild-eyed, his face contorted with rage or madness, and Ronan heard him screaming what might have been challenges to battle.

But even then Kyn was signalling enough. "They are done!"

he shouted, beckoning the weary men of Ebor's cavalry, most of whom were on foot now, and many injured. "Truss them like pigs, and find me Malla, if he still lives."

Only then did Gareth permit himself to slump in the saddle, lean on the neck of his tired horse. Ronan shadowed him on his left, Bryn on his right, and Selgi took the horse's reins. The fight was not yet over, but the last of it was almost token. Wounded Saxons flung themselves into the jagged teeth of swords and spears, and Ronan looked away. How many had died already, he did not know, but to these men it seemed that death was more welcome than defeat.

The ground was churned with mud and blood, and the field stank, but soon enough the clamour stilled, the final chime of steel was swallowed by a near-silence of moans and begging prayers and the laboured breathing of broken horses.

Ronan's belly turned with such sickness, he might have retched. He wondered fleetingly why in the name of anyone's god he had wanted to be trained for this, to call this his trade, and then he saw the dead faces staring up from the mire at his feet. When the Angles took the field, the farmers from Dubgall and many other hamlets between the frontier and Eboracum had been sent to strengthen the cavalry. They were farmers and shepherds, and they had died by the score. But for Gruffydd and Cuddy, Ronan would have been one of them.

Voices bellowed from the north side of the common ground, and he turned with Bryn, eyes shaded against the afternoon sun. A small band of Angles was still on the loose, still putting up a desperate defence, and in their back ranks Ronan recognised the thick, thunderous face of Malla. "Bryn, do you see?" Was that his voice? Hoarse and rasping, he hardly knew it.

"I see him." Bryn drew the sword that he had only sheathed moments before. The blade was notched, worn, scummy. "You want him, Gareth?"

"Aye, bring him to Eboracum in irons," Gareth panted as every step his horse took lanced through him. "With him in our hands, Derventio is ours." He managed a faint, bruised smile. "The honour of his capture should be yours, ap Gruffydd."

"My thanks," Bryn breathed, as if a prayer had been answered. "Ronan, will you ride with me one last time today?"

"I will." Ronan shifted his grip on his sword, not surprised to find that his arm was wrenched, his shoulder angry, his palm tattered with blisters. "But you," he said sharply to Selgi as the boy seemed about to invite himself along, "you stay beside Gareth!"

He opened his mouth to protest and then closed it again and lifted his chin. "Then let me be Gareth's most personal guard," he said, and hefted the swordsmith's hammer, which in his hands was so fierce a weapon.

A whistle fetched Kynddelig about, and Bryn waved, shouted for a small company to be drawn from the Lindum cavalry. Eight men rallied, and Kyn himself was at their head as they wheeled about and struck north across the common land. The Angles ranks about Malla were swineherds, Ronan thought with a sense of pity. They should have been tilling fields, not carrying weapons. Yet they fought well, as if they believed their enemies would put them to the torture if they were captured alive.

A flurry of steel took Ronan unawares. Desperate men were capable of a terrible ferocity, and at the very end of the battle, when there was no chance of victory for Malla, this was the time when Ronan fought hardest, struggling to keep his head on his shoulders and his limbs intact as two wild-eyed Angles no older than himself came at him from either side at once.

Every instinct Cuddy had trained served him now, and he held them off with an effort that taxed him to his limits. He was through them and almost within reach of Malla himself, when Bryn's voice cried out hoarsely, and Ronan's heart squeezed tight.

He spun his horse, and some instinct brought his sword about in a tight arc as a javelin probed for his heart. He turned aside the cut with nothing to spare and the Angle lunged again, but the weapon was cumbersome in the hands of a farmer, and before he could find his mark Ronan had him.

"Bryn! For the love of Camulus!" He leaned over to catch Bryn by the arm as he sagged, and as Bryn moved he saw the knife wedged fast in his shoulder. Blood streamed the length of his arm, and Ronan's hand was already wet. Somehow Bryn clung to the saddle, but he was dizzy, gasping. Ronan took his bridle and kicked his own horse hard. Kyn was shouting, the Lindum mercenaries had fallen like ravens on the Angles, and as Ronan made his way off the field toward the wagons where the physicians worked he saw Taran coming out to meet him.

Rags padded the side of Taran's neck and were tied about his head. The collar of his tunic was dark with blood, and he was glassy eyed, but he took Bryn's reins from Ronan. "It's a knife," Ronan panted.

"I can see." Taran's words were slurred, and Ronan wondered how he was still on his feet. Necessity was a cruel taskmaster.

"Gareth," Ronan began.

"The boy brought his horse in." Taran gestured along the line of wagons, and Ronan saw him now, sitting up on the high driver's seat, where he could survey the field while his wound was tended. An old man was working on him while a woman brought him water.

Clear across the field, Ronan heard Malla's voice, for the air was hot and still. He did not understand the words, but Selgi had come up behind Taran, and he had picked up a little of the Angle language in the months he had slaved for them. "He is calling to Wotan and Tor," Selgi said in a voice that rasped. "It means he is spent, it is over. I can see only three of the Saxons left standing."

"Then Cerdic Halfhand's frontier scouts are done for this season, by gods." Ronan dragged both hands over his sweated face and turned his back on the field. He slid to the ground and was under Bryn when his mate slithered out of the saddle. "Careful, careful," Ronan cautioned, breathless with dread, and he held Bryn in his arms while Selgi swabbed at the shoulder and muttered, and Taran shouted for help.

"Ronan?" Bryn could not lift his head.

"Shh, don't move." Ronan looked over his lover's bowed shoulders at Taran. "Is it very bad? I've never seen such wounds to know. This. . .this is my first battle. I've seen hunting accidents, but nothing like this."

"It's bad enough," Taran mused. "He had best go to the surgeon at Eboracum. The butchers on this battlefield don't have time or craft enough to treat this. You, boy —"

"My name is Selgi," the youth said, surly and stubborn, as if he was determined to defend the honour he had just won back.

"Selgi," Taran echoed, not quite mocking. "Fetch up a wagon. That one will do. Can you handle horses? Throw the load out, for we've injured men to take back at once — and this is one of them."

Blue eyes fluttered dizzily, and Bryn looked up at Ronan with a rueful expression. "I am. . .well blooded, Ronan. Three, I put down, and maybe four, and injured a fifth before. . .this."

"It was well done," Ronan said, trying to ease him. "Don't try to talk. They'll put you in a wagon and take you to the surgeon at home." Home? For the first time, he thought automatically of Eboracum as their home. Ronan took Bryn's right hand in a warrior's clasp. "It is over, Bryn. The battle is won — and the war, I think."

"Cerdic's son?" Bryn was too dizzy to even look across the field.

But Ronan could see, and he said grimly, "Kyn has him, Malla and Wulfhere too. They are bound like pigs for slaughter, Bryn. Now, rest yourself."

The sight was branded into his memory. If he lived a hundred years, Ronan knew that he would never forget this moment, as he watched the Angle warlord and his son, and the captain of Cerdic's frontier scouts, driven off the field like chattels for market. They were roped about the hands and feet, stumbling at every step, surrounded on every side by the filthy blades of warspears and javelins, and Kyn deliberately drove them by the men and women they had held captive and abused.

The tattered prisoners, Derventio's survivors, were out of their fetters, sitting under the trees by the wagons that had brought out the cargo Malla would never receive. Pale, hollow-eyed, still frightened, they pressed together as if they could not believe that liberation had been granted, and only a few of them had the spirit to jeer and spit as their enemies were driven by. Ronan looked once at them, and then returned to Bryn.

The knife was still in the wound, and Taran's decision was to leave it there, since the bleeding would only worsen if it was removed. The first of the wagons that would carry back the injured had already been unloaded, and Taran beckoned for men to lift the wounded into it. Bryn held tight to Ronan's arm until Taran and Selgi physically tugged him away.

Their hands slipped apart, and Ronan felt very much alone. The common land was strewn with the dead, and he did not care to count them. His belly churned, and yet Ronan could only count himself among the fortunate. He had come through the day without a wound. Most of the dead were farmers, woodsmen, hunters. He took a breath and swung up into the saddle. Away on his left Bryn lay in the wagon with several wounded men, but now Ronan could do nothing for him save pray.

Standing in the bed of a wagon was Gareth, bare to the hips, his left side swathed in ragging and reeking of bitter herbs, a cup still in his right hand, his eyes glassy with the herbs that smothered pain. Still, his face was like a thundercloud as Kyn brought him the three he had asked for, and when they were before the wagon, shoved them to their knees in the dirt. The Eboracum cavalry had rallied into a ragged band, and if Gareth had given the word, Malla, Wulfhere and Aella Cerdicsson would have died where they knelt.

Even now, Malla was defiant, his eyes flaying Gareth to the marrow. For some minutes neither chief spoke, and at last it was the Angle who cleared his throat noisily and said in that thick, guttural accent, "Well met, Ironhand. I have heard of you. Eadhun told me of you." His mouth twisted. "There will be no bargain today."

"No bargain," Gareth rasped. "Not for a betrayer who offered me a fair trade and then brought Saxon mercenaries to meet us!"

"What choice, at the last?" Malla growled bitterly. "Did I know what was to be, when I offered the trade?"

"Did you? I wonder." Gareth cocked his head at the older man.

Malla looked sidelong at his son, and if looks could have killed, Wulfhere would have fallen dead. "I did not hire Cerdic's men. Never trust Saxonkind, Ironhand. You know this for truth?"

"I'm fast coming to suspect it." Gareth made a face as he finished the bitter liquid and threw the cup down. "Yet you yourself hired Saxon mercenaries. Ronan and Bryn saw them, when they brought you Eadhun's message."

"I hire, from need," Malla said sourly. "Many die in the fires when we take this place, and we are close by Eboracum. Too close. Why you not attack before? We think you come for us long ago! So I hire Saxons. But not Cerdic's men. And when Halfhand's dogs come in, my Saxons fight with them, may Wotan rot them in Hel!"

"And it was your loving son, Wulfhere, hired the Halfhand's frontier scouts behind your back," Gareth finished. "You were betrayed."

"Is lucky man who never make mistake." Malla glared up at him, defiant even in defeat. "Saxons all dead. You got Aella Cerdicsson. You got Malla and his crazy mongrel son. Greatest hour for Eboracum, I think."

"Perhaps." Gareth put out a hand for balance as the powerful herbs began to overtake him, and before he could fall Selgi hopped nimbly into the wagon bed and was against his side. Gareth peered down at the boy, surprised and pleased, and Selgi gave him the kind of smile for which a man would make a day's march. But when Gareth touched Selgi's back, perhaps to support himself there, his hand came away red, and he turned the youth, saw the oozing welts through his torn shirt, and his face was black as the sky before a thunderstorm.

Kyn was waiting, never more than a few paces away, ready to catch Gareth if he fell. It was to him Gareth turned now, and Kyn clambered up onto the wagon. "I'll have them in irons," Gareth said windedly. "Take them back to Ebor, and they'll stand before a council of elders there."

"Count it done," Kynddelig promised. "And Derventio?"

Gareth gave the stockade, far off across the common land, a

bitter look. "Derventio has not existed since the night of the fires. That is Mallatun. And it is ours. Garrison it, Kyn. Send to Lindum, send anywhere you must, to get men for the frontier. Round up the Angles, pen them where they are safe, and Eadhun's crew with them. No harm comes to them. . .they are innocents, I think, and they've paid a cruel price already. But I don't want to turn my back on them, for I don't trust them." He was glaring at Wulfhere as he spoke.

"The very stockade they built will make a convenient prison," Kyn said ruefully. "We guard its walls to keep them in, rather than them mounting sentries to keep us out."

"Do it." Gareth was leaning more heavily on Selgi now.

"Get you to the wagons, with the injured," Kyn said quietly. "Ronan? Help him, for this lovesome fool can barely stand, though you'll never hear the confession from him."

Weary, sore, Ronan felt a hundred nicks and scrapes begin to smart as the excitement of battled ebbed and left his limbs like lead. He knelt on the tail of the wagon, and between them he and Selgi manoeuvred Gareth down, and out. Still, he held to his feet though he sagged between them as they took him to the wains, and with a rough, bass groan he let himself go down onto a bed of straw and old linen.

The ancient cavalry quack began to fuss at once, and Ronan swallowed on a dry throat as he watched Gareth's bandages cut away, watched the blood swabbed away from the wound. Twice, the old injury had been cauterised, but it was in a place where Gareth could not twist his upper body without pulling it and opening it. How he had ridden today, how he had fought, Ronan did not know, and he felt a tide of guilt rush through him, filling his face with heat. This should have been a simple exchange of hostages. It was no one's fault, only Wulfhere's terrible ambition, that it had become a killing field.

"Gareth," Ronan began, not knowing what was on his face.

But the Ironhand knew. "The day was well spent," he said, breathless with pain and groggy with the bitter herbs. "After this, we may not fight for ten years. We may not fight until I am so old and grey, it is my son who carries the standard of Eboracum in my place. Don't punish yourself, Ronan, for our scheme was a good one." From somewhere, he found the very wraith of a smile. "But Wulfhere's was better."

"He'll die for it," Ronan said quietly.

"I think he will." And Gareth's eyes closed at last.

As the chief began to drowse, mercifully spared the physician's hands, Ronan moved on to the next wagon, climbed up into its bed. Bryn was there, and beside him, the last man Ronan might have expected to see. Eadhun was awake but his eyes were so dark with the herbs in him, they seemed to be vacant. He was on his belly, and a wad of ragging lay on his back. It was soaked through, yellow with the herbs that warded off maggots and canker, and he breathed as if every moment were an effort. Bryn was propped against the timber-slatted side of the wain, with his left hand holding a bundle of linen around the knife, and his face was waxen. Ronan's heart quickened, and he laid his hand on Bryn's shoulder.

"Try to rest," he said softly as the driver climbed up onto the high seat and shook out the reins. "You sleep at home soon enough. The surgeons will mend you."

Bryn tried to smile, but as the wagon moved off every jolt of its wheels made him gasp. Eadhun cried out once, and then his eyes rolled up and Ronan was grateful to see him slide into oblivion. He looked anxiously into Bryn's face, but Bryn said with a curious lightness, "It is for the gods to decide, love, not you and I. Do you know a friendly god? If you do, speak nicely to him." His face twisted. "But speak soon, Ronan. While you have the time."

"While we both do," Ronan whispered, and clasped his hand tightly.

18

The sound of Bryn's voice, screaming just once before he passed out, was etched into Ronan's memory. The knife wrenched out, and by the time the brand was lifted out of the hearth to seal and cauterise the wound, Bryn was too deeply unconscious to feel it. The air filled with the reek of burning and Ronan's flesh shrank, but Bryn was limp. His face was the colour of old ash, but he was far from pain, and Ronan was grateful.

The surgeon was an old soldier, bald and fat, who knew his job better than any man Ronan had ever watched. He was deft, quick, and before Ronan had stopped quivering, long before Bryn would wake, the knife was placed in Ronan's hand and a pad of rags bound over the wound. It was high in Bryn's right shoulder, not high enough to have nicked the great veins in his neck, but too high to have pierced the lung. The surgeon explained all this as he worked, but Ronan listened to only half of what he said.

Still Bryn did not stir. Ronan turned the knife over and over in his hand, and at last threw it into the timbers by the door. It stuck fast by the point, sharp as a razor, and the surgeon looked up at him with a wary expression.

"I did the best I could, boy. He won't use the arm for a while, but if this is the worst wound he suffers in his life, he should give thanks!"

"Then he'll live?" Ronan clutched like a drowning man at the straw.

"He will sicken if the knife was dirty, or poisoned." The surgeon thrust away his tools and slung his pack over his shoulder. "But he is young and strong. If he grows fevered, send for me. Even if the blade was poisoned, my trade owns a few tricks."

"What tricks?" Ronan whispered as he sat down on the bedside and took Bryn's hand in his.

"I can poultice the wound with onions and hot stones to draw out the poison." The surgeon was at the door, and blue twilight and woodsmoke swept into the house as he made to leave. "As I said, he is young. Often, youth is the best medicine. But if he worsens, send for me." The door banged behind him.

Weariness assaulted Ronan. The ride home had seemed a century long. Bryn had wandered in and out of consciousness, and in the last few miles Ronan had taken him over his lap, held him there and braced him while the wagon jolted, and every rut in the road seemed to bleed him anew.

Eadhun had slept most of the way back, and twice, when the column of wagons paused to rest and change the horses, the surgeons cauterised the wounds on his back. Ronan saw them and was appalled.

The barbed hooks with which Wulfhere had held him would not come out as they had gone in; the only way to remove them was to push them right through, and the gods knew what they had torn. Eadhun would not stand for a week, and it would be next spring before he ran or rode or picked up a sword. Yet he was little worse wounded than Gareth, and of the three of them, Ronan thought Bryn had escaped most lightly.

Kyn had helped him carry Bryn into the house, strip and bathe him, and they had just set him down on the bed when the surgeon arrived. Ronan still wore the same soiled tunic and breeches in which he had ridden to battle. He longed to lie down, just to hold Bryn, perhaps to try to breathe life into him, but he stank, he was filthy, and before he even dared touch Bryn he boiled a cauldron of water to wash. Dirt made wounds poison faster than anything, this Ronan knew. He had seen a woodsman with a clean nick from an axe. The wound was small and neat, and he neglected it. A week later he was raving, and two days after that, a cavalry surgeon came up from Catreath and took off his arm to save his life.

So Ronan stood by the hearth, stripped to the skin and scrubbed himself from head to foot with a scrap of sacking wrung out in near-boiling water. He was bent over, washing his legs, when Bryn's voice said groggily, "I must have died, since this can only be Avalon, and my heart's dream has come to meet me."

"Bryn?" Ronan dropped the rags and spun. "Bryn, are you hurting? The surgeon took out the knife. Don't move, or you'll bleed again."

"I'll be still." Bryn's nose wrinkled as he sniffed the wound. "He roasted me like a pig over the fire."

"It's sealed tight," Ronan assured him.

"I know." Bryn blinked foolishly, trying to gather his wits. "Have you ever been scorched with the iron?" But Ronan shook his head and Bryn have a grunt. "Then you're lucky. I was injured on the practice field three years ago, just a boy at the time. You know the scar?" He flung back the sleeping skins, beneath which he was naked.

The scar was on his left hip. Ronan knew it well, and tonight he knelt at the bedside to kiss it with his tongue until Bryn gave a low groan that was more about pleasure than pain. "The surgeon made a mess of it," he said wryly. "Did more damage with the iron than Brock did when he cut me. My father was so furious, he had them both punished. A surgeon and a lad from the cavalry, hung side by side on the fence, and sweating under the whip! What a sight it was." He was exploring the bandage as he spoke in a hoarse whisper. "Oh, but that hurts. What did the scullion stick me with? Remember, I've not seen it."

"This." Ronan fetched the knife from the timber by the door, and gave it to him. "Lie down, Bryn! You're to rest. You poured out enough blood to float a boat."

"Lie down with me," Bryn whispered. "I shall lie abed, but not alone. Leave me, and I shall be on my feet in a trice, I promise you."

"Foolish, even to think it," Ronan accused, but he stretched out at Bryn's side and tried to take him in his arms. "How can I hold you without hurting you?"

"Open your arms." Bryn threw away the knife, and when Ronan lay waiting he turned very carefully and manoeuvred himself into Ronan's cautious embrace. Exhausted, he put his head down on the sheepskin beside Ronan's and sighed. "I will get up shortly."

"Tomorrow," Ronan whispered.

"Tonight," Bryn argued. "I have to see the girl, Aemilia. I have to know what became of her, Ronan. She was to be mine, once. And now you are mine. Oh, Ronan."

"What?" Ronan stoked his face, found it no warmer than was natural and breathed a prayer of thanks.

"I took men's lives," Bryn said quietly. "Your lover is blooded. A warrior and a man."

"I know. I took men's lives too." Ronan's arms tightened and he rested his head on Bryn's. "Tell me. How did it happen? What did you feel?"

"The first kill? The blooding." Bryn took a deep, careful breath. "He was big and yellow-haired, and he came at me from the right. I looked down into his face, I saw his eyes, so pale blue. His teeth were bare, he was snarling at me. He would have killed me, and almost did. What did I feel? Fear, and. . .I think, fury, that a man should come at me like that, wanting to kill me. But you were on my left side, shielding me there, as I shield your blind side from attack, and I knew that if I fell the Saxon would have you next. So I turned aside his spear thrusts with my sword. Two, three cuts of the spear. One was so close, it tore the sleeve of my shirt, but not the skin beneath. But when he drew the spear back to lunge a fourth time — then, I had his rhythm, and I was too fast. My sword took his life." He shuddered, Ronan felt it clearly. "It felt strange and terrible, but I had no time to sicken. I pulled out the sword and he fell to his side. He lay on his face and I thought, is this the blooding? I had expected glory,"

"Had you?" Ronan's lips feathered about his cheek, and Bryn turned his face in search of kisses. "There is no glory, Bryn. Just survival." They kissed again, deeply, tongues entwined. "You'll not be strong enough to ride with Kyn, when he goes to hire mercenaries, but he's asked me to go with him. Riders went out on fast horses, before dusk tonight, carrying the word of this victory. Within a week, Artos himself, and the great Druid who works sorcery for him, will know that we have pushed back the frontier, that we need men to garrison land that we have won back. The name of Gareth Ironhand will be sung at every chief's hearth, and the warbands will stream in to join us. Kyn will be on the road till winter, recruiting."

"You won't go with him, till winter?" Bryn lifted his head to look into Ronan's face. "Not till winter!"

"No. Would I leave you?" Ronan kissed him. "My place is here, with you."

"I love you," Bryn whispered. "Oh, how I do love you." He nibbled Ronan's full lower lips. "And now, let me get out of this bed."

"You can't!" Ronan's hands on his breast held Bryn down, but Bryn would not be so easily dissuaded. "Bryn, don't," Ronan said sharply.

"There is another, for whom I feel a kind of care," Bryn reminded him. "I don't love her, but. . ." He looked Ronan's beautiful body up and down, from his slender, muscular legs and the quiescent cock resting on his thigh, to the broad, bony shoulders and the curves of his smooth chest. "Everything I want and need is here with me, Ronan. Aemilia belongs to a past that is gone. But she is kindred to us in a way you can't deny. To us, and Dafydd, and Selgi and his fellows. We are the last of the Derventio that was, and I must know what became of her. Now, help me up, or stand out of my way!"

So Ronan gave him both hands to pull him up to his feet, held him whole he swayed with dizziness, dressed him while he gasped, weak as a day-old kitten, and gave Bryn his shoulder to lean on as they left the house. But Bryn walked into the great hall, stood up straight in the firelight, and Ronan was proud.

Gareth was in his great, craved wood chair, but he was in a sleeping robe, and that was a blanket around him, not the scarlet Roman cloak. He looked up out of dark, sleepy eyes as Ronan appeared, and managed a mocking grin as he saw Bryn. Taran was sitting on the floor by the hearth, rocking himself against the pain of his wounds; Kynddelig was rubbing his shoulders and spine to ease him, for Kyn himself had come through without so much as a scratch. The man who might have been looking for a passage to the Otherworld to join the lover he had lost, seemed untouchable. Beyond him was Cora, limping badly on a leg that had been feathered with arrows as she raced back with the news. One of the arrowheads was buried so deeply, it could not be removed. She would carry a piece of Saxon steel in her as long as she lived, and every cold winter's day, she would remember the battle for Derventio. But she had lived, and Ronan thanked his gods for that too.

At the next hearth, reserved for the freemen who were high in Gareth's favour, were Selgi and Dafydd. Still, Dafydd seemed withdrawn and aloof. He sat with his face pressed to Selgi's shoulder, and Selgi had one arm about him. Ronan saw fresh bandages, stuck to Selgi's back with a greasy ointment of yellow herbs, and the young man was smiling. He was alive, he was free, and he was young. How well Ronan knew what Selgi was feeling tonight. He wished he could go to Dafydd, make him speak, share with him everything he had suffered, but Dafydd was mute now, and Ronan realised it might be many years before the boy told of what have befallen him. He might never speak of it at all. Perhaps the last pride left to him was to bear his own wounds in silence.

And there in the firelight, at the same hearth as Selgi and Dafydd, were the six women who had come out of Derventio. Ronan stole a sidelong glance at Bryn, who was intent on the woman who had once been betrothed to him. Bryn was pale, his eyes wide and dark, and his mouth compressed into a grim line.

The girl was hollow-eyed, thin, clad in a shapeless grey wool gown, but she knew him. Aemilia Duratius looked once at him and then dropped her eyes and studied the ground before his feet. She was waiting to be spoken to now, and Ronan wondered how many times she had been punished for speaking up first.

"She has changed," Bryn said softly. "How could she not? She has done the kind of service that dishonours a slave! And for the spoiled brat of a rich, freeman Christian. . ."

Her face was a blank mask now, her eyes looking inward, lacking any lustre, and while Ronan waited Bryn seemed to search vainly for words. He leaned heavily on Ronan's shoulder as if he needed the warmth of another body, not merely Ronan's physical support.

"Bryn, sit," Ronan began, and beckoned for a chair. A bondsman fetched a three-legged stool, and Bryn sank gratefully onto it. "I'm so sorry," he said at last, to Aemilia. She did not reply, nor even look up, and he looked over her head at Kyn and Taran and Cora, who flanked Gareth, as always. "Your father," Bryn prompted. "Was Marcus in Derventio? Did he escape?"

"He is dead," she said, flat and low. "Along with your own father, and all the others."

Bryn took a breath and whispered to Ronan, "Even her voice has changed. I would never have recognised it."

"Bryn?" Ronan's hands were on his shoulders. "What do you feel?"

"Numb," Bryn said slowly. "I don't. . .feel grief any longer." He frowned, and Ronan's arms tightened about him. "It's over," he said softly, and then louder, to the woman: "It is over. I am sure Gareth would make a home for you in Eboracum, as he made a home for Ronan and me. I'll look after you, if you would like that, Aemilia. You've no cause for worry."

"As our fathers arranged?" Abruptly, she looked up at him,

but her eyes were as hollow as two pits. "You would wed me?"

"I can't," Bryn began levelly.

"You would not wed a whore." Bitterness honed the words like razors. "That's what they made of me, and well do you know it."

"That is not what I meant, Aemilia," Bryn continued in the same level tone, painfully aware of the others in the hall. Perhaps these words should have been spoken in private. And then, what secrets had he, or any of them, from the rest of the company? When a company of people had shared the blood, the killing and dying with you, how could there be secrets? "My lady, I have found my own love. Not quite the mate Gruffydd chose for me, but my own love nonetheless. He is here with me now, and fought with me at Derventio."

She looked up at Ronan as if she could not comprehend a word Bryn had said, and then averted her eyes and shook her head. "Our arrangement burned with Derventio, Bryn. You cannot stand by what no longer exists. I have in my heart already taken vows. Long ago, I took them. One night when all seemed blackest."

"Vows?" Bryn and Ronan frowned at each other. "Marriage vows?" Bryn wondered.

"Holy vows," she corrected. "I will make them again, if the Church will accept me."

"A nun?" Bryn blinked in surprise. "Is that what you desire?"

It was Gareth who said, low and gentle, "If it will ease her heart, Bryn, it is for the best. There is a nunnery on the hill above Ebor. Sister Brigid herself ran wild and played with wooden swords with me when we were children. If the shelter of the nunnery would ease her heart, perhaps the lady is wise to go there."

"Let me go there," Aemilia said softly, perhaps even begging, and her eyes were on the floor before Bryn's feet again.

"If that's what you want." Bryn clasped Ronan's hand. "I have a little money put by, and Gareth might trust a loan to me." He glanced at Gareth, who nodded. "I can buy you a position of respect among the vowed women. If this is really what you want."

She seemed to draw herself up, square her thin shoulders, and some glimmer of warmth appeared in her eyes. "I am sure. My blessed saints did not abandon me in all that time. They were there, always comforting me, no matter what befell me. They called to me, Bryn. All I want now is to answer."

With a sigh, Bryn allowed Ronan to put a cup of mulled wine into his hand, and he drank deeply as Aemilia returned to the freed woman and sat with her arms about her knees, gazing into the fire as if she saw through its curtain into a Christian Otherworld that Ronan could not really imagine. Bryn turned haunted eyes to him, and Ronan tangled his hand into the dark mane he loved.

"A nun, Ronan," Bryn murmured. "Vowed and chaste, and shut up in a place like a dungeon."

"A refuge without pain," Ronan corrected gently. "With strong, high walls to keep out the world. Walls to keep out men." He leaned down and kissed Bryn's forehead. "She knows what is best for her, Bryn. Let her go."

"She's not mine to keep." Bryn closed his eyes and leaned on Ronan's shoulder. Their heads rested together and for the first time in so long Ronan let himself feel that old pain, the half-spent sorrow. He was silent, one arm about Bryn, and they listened as the ballad singer began a new song in honour of the occasion.

The song inspired grief for a time, but at the end there were cheers. Kyn and Gareth listened to most of it, and began to talk in whispers under the harp, drum and flute, and as the ballad singer took his bows and retreated for a cup of ale Kyn clapped his hands and called for the hall's guard to stand to. Ronan's skin prickled and his belly flip-flopped. His hand tightened on Bryn's shoulder and he muttered into his lover's ear, "I think we will see justice done. Will you stay to see, or come home to bed with me?"

"Both — by turns," Bryn said stubbornly. "I want love. . .but, just for tonight, I want to see justice first!"

"And I think you're about to." Ronan stood behind Bryn, kneading his shoulders as he watched over Bryn's head.

The assembly of chieftains, warriors and freemen moved back. Even the bondsmen and Eboracum's few slaves crowded into the corners of the hall to see. Gareth leaned forward, elbows on his knees, and very carefully Kynddelig twisted an ancient torc about his neck and placed a fine gold circlet on his brow. They were worn thin with age, and Ronan had heard that they had been buried for centuries. When the warrior queen of the Iceni was defeated her people scattered to every part of the island. Some came to Brigantia; one married an ancestor of Gareth's, and lore had it that Gareth Ironhand wore the torc and circlet that had graced the throat and brow of Prasutagas, the chief of the Iceni, Boudicca's husband.

Yet Gareth's face was gaunt with pain, lined with suffering tonight, and Ronan saw death in his eyes. Bryn ouched as Ronan's hands tightened, and he murmured an apology. Kyn withdrew and stood to Gareth's left. Cora took position at his right and Taran sat at his feet. All three drew their swords, and Ronan's breath caught in his throat. All but Kyn were injured, and Kyn's suffering was of the heart, perhaps the most painful of all. He was grieving for Fergal more than ever tonight, when he had come through the battle without even a scratch. Bryn moaned softly, and Ronan leaned down to kiss the top of his head.

A commotion at the rear door which opened onto the yards by the kitchens announced the arrival of the prisoners. Ronan held his breath as they came in, and Bryn muttered the kind of oaths that blistered the ears. Wulfhere was bare to the waist, and his back was already flogged bloody; he carried such a weight of chains, he could barely stand, and the lower half of his face was muzzled, perhaps to stop him biting or bellowing. A pace behind him, Aella Cerdicsson was limping, and his eyes were black, his lips split, his teeth likely broken.

"What is this?" Gareth demanded in a disinterested tone as the two young men and Malla were fetched before him.

And Kyn leaned down to his shoulder. "They fought. Wulfhere killed his guard. After he was chained, he would bite anyone near him, and if you want to hear yourself think, it's the muzzle or a gag! For the death of the guard, he was flogged on the road before the wagons reached Derventio. Should I have stopped it?"

"No." Gareth sat back. "Who was killed?"

"The third son of Eamon the swordsmith," Kyn said regretfully.

"Then the scourger laid on too lightly for the crime." Gareth's fists clenched, and he glared down into Malla's face as the three prisoners were shoved to their knees and kept there at swords' point. "What would you have me do with your adle-headed son, Malla?"

The Angle was not about to play games. "Do not mock. Make no matter what is said, Wulfhere dies."

"You don't plead for his life?" Gareth cocked his head at the chief, and at the wild-faced young man. "I have heard his story. I know how loss has stolen his mind from him."

"You know this?" Malla was surprised.

"We know." Gareth fingered the torc. "Did you counsel strengthening your warband and waiting a year or three, or five, before you tested the frontier? And did Wulfhere desire only to come at us, and let blood *this* season, unable to wait? Is that why he invited Cerdic Halfhand's men into your camp?"

"Maybe." Malla thrust out his chin. "I know nothing about it, before. . .too late."

"Yes." The Ironhand tucked his right hand against the wound, pressing it to ease it, as pain raised a bloom of colour in his face. "I believe you, Malla."

"You believe?" Malla almost recoiled. "You not murder us all?"

"Enough blood to float a ship as been let in these lands," Gareth said hoarsely, and as Kyn handed him a cup, he drank deeply. Wine was not a cure, but it dulled pain just as it dulled a man's senses. Gareth rested his head back against the carved wood and studied Malla out of slitted eyes. "Do you know the name of Artos? The great chieftain from the south, who has chased the Saxons right back to the sea, when he could. And treated with them, when he could not."

"The Bear," Malla grunted. "I know his name."

"Then you know that Artos offers a treaty," Gareth went on, his words slurring just a little, "to save blood. Many a battle has been avoided, with words and paper."

Malla's whole body was wary. "I hear this. Eadhun trade, whole south coast, every river port where Saxon and Angle and Jute make safe. He trade even with chief who got treaty with Artos."

"All right." Gareth's eyes closed. He took a breath and his face twisted as he pulled it to the bottom of his lungs. "I'm going to execute your son, Malla."

Silence. In the long hall the loudest sound was the crackle of wood in the hearths and the panting of drowsing dogs, the rustle of feathers from the hawks' high perches. Gareth did not move a muscle as he went on,

"Wulfhere dies in the morning. I'll take his head, quick and clean. I can offer you no more than this: *you* will not be dishonoured by his dying. But you accept his dying, Malla, for it is the price of the deal I am going to offer you."

Dark eyes wide in the firelight, Malla looked from Kyn to Cora and back, since Gareth's eyes were closed. "You offer Malla deal? In Wotan's name, for why?"

Now Gareth stirred, lifted his head with an effort and blinked owlishly at Malla. "Because I'm tired of fighting. Because enough innocents have been punished. Because if I don't treaty with you, I'll be killing your people like spearing rats in a trough, and I'm not a murderer, Malla, no matter what you think of me. Artos would treaty with you. So will I. . .if you make me believe that I can trust you."

Surprise brought the Angle chief up short. "You not kill Malla's people?"

"Not if you were my ally," Gareth said, hoarse with pain and wine. "If we are allies, the frontier is open. Trade in our markets.

We trade in yours. This is the magic Artos is working in the south."
He leaned forward, both elbows on his knees. "But there are sins
to be paid for, Malla. There should have been no blood today.
Many died, among your people and mine. And *he* —" stabbing a
blunt finger at Wulfhere "— murdered them. You are betrayed.
The traitor in your camp is blood of your blood."

"I. . .know." Malla looked away, and while Ronan watched he
seemed to age ten years. He chewed over every word the Ironhand
had said for a long moment, and Gareth gave him the time to work
through it. At last, when Ronan had begun to think Malla either
did not have the words to understand what was meant, or was
uncooperative, the old man lifted an ashen face to Gareth and said
in that strange, troubling accent,

"I ask the Ironhand one favour."

"A favour?" Gareth was weary to the marrow of his bones.
"What manner of favour?"

"I ask," Malla said, and it seemed that his teeth were clenched,
"that you give to me the axe. Give to me the axe that takes the life
of my son. It is *Malla* who is betrayed worst. Malla who is duped,
shamed by flesh of his flesh, yes?"

"Yes." Gareth's brow creased deeply. "Are you asking me to
let you take the life of Wulfhere?"

The old man's chin thrust out. "I ask this. Like, beg favour.
Give this to Malla, and my people will treaty." He sighed noisily.
"Wotan! You not know? In my camp this night, if we won battle,
Wulfhere would pay for betrayal. My chieftains make him dog
meat. My chieftains," Malla added sourly, "all dead. Malla is last."

As he spoke, Bryn breathed a soft sound of surprise, and the
Ironhand was equally as astonished. "Then, I grant you the favour,"
he said slowly. "Dawn, Malla. It is done at dawn."

"Dawn." Malla's mouth worked as if he struggled to contain
some private purgatory of grief. "Soon, he stand before Wotan,
father of all, and *then* he answer for sin and crime."

"May your gods be merciful," Gareth said with gruff generosity.

"Would yours show mercy?" Malla demanded.

And Gareth's head shook slowly. "No, Malla, I don't think
they would." Painfully, he leaned forward again, far enough to offer
his hand. "Clasp my wrist. Be my ally on the north frontier.
Guard me there, and I will guard you in the south, yes?"

Malla's hand extended, almost but not quite clasping Gareth's.
"You guard me from Cerdic Halfhand?"

"I will." Gareth looked deliberately at his hand, and then back into Malla's sharp, crow-like eyes.

The old hand clasped the young. "I treaty." The words might have been ripped out of Malla's throat, and Ronan could scarcely breathe. Artos of Caerleon would have done this, he knew, and together, Eboracum and Derventio would buttress each other. Yet for a moment Ronan felt a deep sense of betrayal, as if Malla *must* be his enemy, and he must make war upon Angles. And then the old man dispelled all that and Ronan felt a rush of something very like shame, that he could have thought those things.

"This, our home," Malla warned. "Nothing lie behind. No place go back, understand?" He waved a hand at his son, who was bowed down with a weight of chains, his flogged back still bleeding, his jaw muzzled, lest he bellow like an enraged beast. "Pain make my son mad. Woman, child, sister, blood-brother, even he-mate, all gone. All dead."

"I know," Gareth sighed. "Every man and woman in this hall has suffered that loss. We are all children of war, Malla. But we don't have to kill every day. Treaty with me, make pace here, as Artos makes peace in the south, and we will keep each other safe from enemies we share."

"Aye." Malla gazed sadly at his son. "You have saying? Enemy of my enemy, this man is my friend."

"We have the saying," Gareth agreed. "Then, you are my ally, Malla, for Cerdic Halfhand will murder your people and mine alike, if we allow it."

The old man made dismissive gestures. "Dawn, Malla take life of own son. What more you ask?"

"Nothing more," Gareth assured him. "In fact, I *give* you more." Malla looked hawkishly at him. "His head will not be on a spike over Eboracum's gate," Gareth said quietly. "You may have him to bury or burn, decently. Take him back to Mallatun, your own priests can pray for him."

Ronan took a breath, Bryn murmured his astonishment, and as for Malla, tears welled in his eyes and spilled.

"Wulfhere's death is the end of it," Gareth swore. "No more shame. No more betrayal. You treaty, you stand by me. Your word of honour, Malla, for as long as you live."

The Angle inclined his head. "Malla's word, good as bond. Better."

"Good enough." Gareth seemed to relax, and frowned deeply at the other, the Saxon, who rested back with his buttocks on his heels, listening to the exchange between the two as if he understood. Gareth fixed him with a look that might have flayed him alive. "You are Aella, son of the Saxon warlord, Cerdic Halfhand?"

Not quite to Ronan's surprise, the Saxon's yellow head bobbed and he said, "You know my father?" His voice was deep, his words only slightly slurred as he spoke through split the lips and loosened teeth of a sound beating.

"I fought against him," Gareth said thoughtfully. "He almost killed me. . .I almost killed him. You would have been too young to be on the battlefield. Tell me, Cerdicsson, does your father cherish you?"

"As much as any father loves any youngest son," Aella said slowly, suspiciously. "Will you set a ransom price?"

"Oh, yes." Gareth shifted painfully in the chair and reached out for another cup of wine. Kyn was hovering at his left hand, as if he were concerned that Gareth might simply topple. "I will set a ransom price that your father can pay easily," the Ironhand went on, punctuating his words with sips of the drugged wine.

"Any price," Aella began, eager to brag.

"No price," Gareth barked. "No price at all. Not one coin, not a gem. Nothing." His eyes widened, feverish and red in the firelight. "This is your ransom, Cerdicsson. You live out your days here in comfort. Have a woman, make children. But Eboracum is your home until the day you die. You stay here, and I will chain you to the ground if you or the Halfhand dispute it! Here is Cerdic's price." He glared over Aella's head at the crowd that had steadily crept closer until they were almost at his feet. "Peace is the price," Gareth told them all. "For so long as the Halfhand leaves Eboracum and Derven. . .Mallatun unmollested, so shall Aella Cerdicsson live here with every right and privilege of a freeman, save that he may not leave. And this more do I swear." He looked down into Aella's face now. "The Halfhand raids on my river, and I'll have you flogged till you cannot stand. He comes at my walls, and I'll have your head off your shoulders so fast, yours will be the first death of the battle." He leaned back in the chair, head lolling in weariness now. "Can you write?"

Aella was stunned, speechless.

"I said, can you write?" Gareth shouted, as if the man had been struck deaf.

"I cannot," Aella stammered.

"Then, fetch me a man who can write Saxon words," Gareth said to no one in particular as he began to succumb to the effects of wine, herbs, pain and fatigue.

It was Malla who offered, "I got good slave. Blind all life long. Got nothing to do but talk. He know words, and I got scribe to write. You. . .can share."

Gareth actually smiled. "I'm grateful, Malla. And in return, tell me if your physicians need medicines to treat your wounded. Tell me if your people are hungry. Ebor has enough to trade, and friends should care for one another. You agree?"

"You think, maybe Cerdic ransom his son with this?" Malla mused.

"I don't know," Gareth admitted. "But perhaps, using Aella, we can secure ourselves the next few seasons to grow strong before we have to face him."

"Aye, that we can." Malla huffed a sigh and gave Gareth a hard look. "We. . .strange allies, Angle, Briton."

"Rather strange allies than enemies." Gareth was frowning at Wulfhere. "This is his last night alive. Are there prayers to be said? There are priests in Eboracum who would speak to your gods for you."

But Malla's shaggy head shook. "Soon he stand before the All-Father. My son go before Wotan of the one eye, and he speak for himself. Fool of a boy." And there was such anger in his voice, such burning shame, that for a moment they eclipsed the grief.

Even if his people had won the battle, Ronan thought, still would Wulfhere have faced the council of Angle elders. And perhaps the death they arranged for him would not be so kind as the sharp edge of an axe. Malla seemed accepting of the judgement — would he have been expected to pass this same judgement before the council of Angle chieftains? How much more easy it was for him, then, to have Gareth Ironhand pass sentence. Honour, justice and vengeance were satisfied in one swift stroke.

Beneath Ronan's hands Bryn was stirring, and Ronan looked down to find him pale and drawn. "You should rest now, Bryn," he warned, "You have seen justice done. Go now, and sleep, and you'll see Wulfhere's execution at dawn."

For once Bryn did not argue, but accepted Ronan's hands to help him rise, and his shoulder to help him out of the hall. The air was sharply cold, summer night or no, and Ronan smelt the river. The moon was up, full and white as a lantern, almost overhead, and beyond her face the stars of midsummer told him the station of night.

Dawn lay but two hours away. Malla would likely sit out a vigil tonight, watching over his son and trying to make peace with him in any way he could. Ronan did not envy Malla; he envied Gareth even less, for the decision to take a life was never easily made.

He pressed Bryn onto the bed and covered him with rugs, but for himself Ronan did not lie down. He wanted Bryn to rest, and it was easier to sleep alone. And he wanted to think, and he never thought with much clarity when Bryn's lean, hard body was pressed against him. It seemed a lifetime since he had met Gruffydd on the road to Derventio, since he had been hired to train a horse and finished out the season as a warrior. In reality it was just a few months, and Ronan could not believe the turns his life and Bryn's had taken.

In the shadows cast by the firelight he saw the faces of his mother, his brothers and sisters. Gruffydd and Sian, Cuddy and so many others he had known in Whitestonecliff and Derventio. The old people believed that at Samhaine, when the veil between the worlds was thinnest, the dead could walk in this world, be seen, and talk with the living. People hugged their hearths that night, perhaps fearing that they would accidentally cross over into the Otherworld and be lost. But this Samhaine coming, when autumn fetched mist and cold and hoar frost along the river, and when the forest was like a thousand skeletons clawing at the sky, Ronan thought he would walk abroad and seek out the ghosts of Derventio and Whitestonecliff, for he wanted to be sure that they knew. They were avenged, they could rest easily, and they would never be forgotten by the living.

The sky was thick with clouds when dawn broke, and the sun was no more than a bright place in a deep, grey overcast. Ronan had dozed, crook-backed in a chair, and he woke with an ache in his spine and a mouth like old parchment. Bryn was already awake, lying on his side in their bed and studying his lover with a rueful, almost mocking smile.

His colour was better this morning, Ronan thought, but when Bryn moved, needing to go to the pail in the corner to make water, his wound pulled and he winced sharply. Ronan was boiling water, laying out his shaving knives, and threw open the shutters to admit the pale, pre-dawn light.

It seemed that all of Eboracum was gathering. They streamed by the window, headed for the marketplace, as Ronan shaved and Bryn heated a poker, mulled a deep pitcher of last night's ale. They shared it as Bryn dressed, and Ronan was swinging a cloak about his own shoulders just as Kynddelig's face appeared at the window.

"Good morning," he called in. "Are you coming to the execution?"

"We are," Ronan said grimly. "I have a sense, Kyn, that I would like to see the end of it, as I saw the beginning."

"The night they came over the moor." Kyn's brow creased deeply, and he looked at Bryn, who was leaning against the wall, trying to find his bearings and his balance. "How is he?"

"Hurting." Ronan fastened his cloak with a big silver brooch. "How is Gareth?"

"Hurting," Kyn told him. "Like Taran and Cora. And Eadhun." He left the window, came around to the door, and offered Bryn his shoulder. "You slept?"

"After a fashion," Bryn said tiredly. "There will be plenty of time to sleep when I'm dead! For now. . ." He gave Ronan a wry look and shook his head.

"Rest," Kyn said soberly. "Take the time while you can, and get well. See Gareth, and know what is in store for you if you drive yourself back onto the battlefield before you are mended." A muscle in his jaw betrayed his grinding teeth. "I held him while the surgeons took the iron to his wound again. I have never heard Gareth scream before."

"He'll heal, won't he?" Ronan joined them at the door, closed it behind them.

"If he sits on his backside till winter is out, and then pursues his strength one step at a time," Kyn said darkly. "And I think Aella Cerdicsson is the magic to bring that about. Here, Bryn, slowly. Slowly, I said!"

They were making their way to the marketplace by the alley between the houses, more or less a direct rout to the gate. When the wind was southerly it shrieked through this alley, but this morning it was quiet, and under the overcast, simply dark.

Every soul in Eboracum was there, and Ronan was only a little surprised to see Eadhun, up on his feet, though he walked with an old man's stoop and was clad in a blanket. His skin was pale as lily petals, his yellow hair lank, and Ronan thought he saw blood in the merchant's eyes as Wulfhere was fetched out, bound hand and foot, and tied face-down over a bench in the middle of the marketplace.

At Eadhun's right hand were Selgi and Dafydd, and Ronan watched the two with a peculiar thrill of pain. Dafydd looked once at him, blushed scarlet and lowered his eyes. It was shame that made him colour, but Ronan did not know what to say to ease his mind. It was as if Dafydd believed that Ronan would see him as a whore now, and it mattered very much to him because Ronan was a warrior, one of Gareth's elite. Nothing could be further from the truth, but Dafydd must come to realise this himself.

Only time would heal. Time, and Selgi. The young smith had Dafydd in his arms even then, and *he* looked Ronan in the eye. He knew that Ronan had come out of a mud-hole village on the moor, and if one young man could make that magic out of courage and ambition, determination, then another could do it. Ronan smiled at him, and Selgi returned the smile, albeit grimly.

"Look after him," Ronan said quietly as he and Bryn joined Cora and Eadhun.

"I will," Selgi swore. "Life-long, Ronan. Trust me."

"I trust you, Selgi." Ronan nodded good morning to Cora, but spoke to Eadhun. "Wulfhere's death may be the best medicine for your wounds, Captain."

Pale, haunted eyes blinked at him. Eadhun was shadowed, smudged, and to Ronan looked no better than Gareth. He licked his lips, which were dry as dust, and seemed to struggle to find words in a foreign language. Too much wine would do that to a man. "My people say, 'Be sure, thy sins will hunt thee down.' I think Wulfhere will discover the truth of this. Wotan will be waiting for him, and I am sure he will freeze in Hel."

"The Christians would say, burn," Bryn mused.

"You're thinking of the woman," Ronan guessed.

"Yes." Bryn gave him an apologetic look.

Before Ronan could speak footsteps in the market square announced Gareth and Malla, and in the Angle's hands was a great, shining steel axe, so heavy that Ronan knew how it would punish his shoulders to lift it. Malla's arms were like the limbs of young trees, even at that age. He hefted it as if he spent all his life logging timber, and as he came to the bench where his son was tied down, he turned his face to the sky and called Wotan to bear witness to the scene. Ronan did not understand the words; he did not need to.

The axe swung just once, swift and clean. Ronan watched it rise but looked away as it came down, and he only knew from the rushed sigh of the onlookers that Wulfhere's life was over. His pain was over, too, with that stroke, and Ronan wondered if any man but himself felt a twist of compassion for one whose loss had driven him past the edge of madness.

Where would Ronan stand, he wondered, if Bryn also were taken from him? If Eadhun had told the story truthfully, Wulfhere had once been a husband and father. Not a gentle man, but not the crazed animal he became. *And I?* Ronan wondered, watching Bryn as they went on around the fringe of the crowd to join Gareth's group. Kyn looked well satisfied, but Gareth was too weary, too drugged this morning, to display much reaction. Malla was stoic, his face like granite. Only his eyes displayed the emotion he kept masked, for they were red after a night's grief. But, Ronan was sure, he grieved for the son he had lost months or years before, when Wulfhere became someone he barely knew.

He dropped the axe by the bench where Wulfhere's body was twitching slightly, and turned his back almost contemptuously on the remains of his son. Wulfhere was the All-Father's responsibility now, and Malla was done. He glared defiantly at Gareth, challenging Gareth to belittle the act, but the Ironhand only nodded and gave Malla his hand in a warrior's clasp.

"It was well done," Gareth said to Malla, for the crowd to hear. "And you will take him back to Mallatun for his burial. Ride back today, with a cavalry escort. Come and trade in the market here. Send your young men to train as warriors alongside our own."

The words were brave, but for the moment, Ronan saw bleak, sour faces among the crowd. Every one of them had lost kin, friends, lovers. Were these people ready to make peace? Ronan was unsure, but Gareth's was a powerful voice in Eboracum. If any man could persuade them that enough blood had been let, the Ironhand was the one.

Even Eadhun was impressed. He was leaning on Cora — who was herself limping, but she could stand straight while Eadhun was bent-backed, like a man thrice his age. His right arm was useless by his side, and every step brought him a wince of pain. Yet he looked up at Ronan and Bryn and gave them a grim little nod. "Malla will honour his word. Justice was swift, and even merciful. No man in our camp would claim that Wulfhere had not brought this price upon his own head. It had to be to be paid, or Malla would be shamed forever."

"And now?" Bryn was watching the bondsmen gather Wulfhere's remains in thick sacking.

"And now, we will defend each other's borders against Cerdic Halfhand," Eadhun said windedly, blinking across the market square at the tall young son of the Saxon warlord. "Cerdic will bellow like a bull, flog his slaves and butcher his prisoners in fury when he has this news from Malla's scribe. But we will have what we want." He closed his eyes. "Peace. Please, Wotan, peace for our children to grow up and grow old."

Moved, Ronan held Bryn against him while Cora helped Eadhun back to his lodgings. Bryn also was spent already, and Kynddelig was shaking his head over him in some exasperation. It seemed Bryn had lost track of time, and Ronan whispered into his ear, "Come home, let me bathe you and lie down with you. You're ill."

"Only aching," Bryn corrected, stirring with a great effort, but he allowed himself to be manhandled around and urged back to the house.

The priests and acolytes of the island's old religion, and the new church, were working with Derventio's survivors. Aemilia Duratius had come to the marketplace to see Wulfhere's execution, but she was already in the company of an elderly monk, and if she saw Bryn this morning, she did not acknowledge him. Dafydd and Selgi were eating with the cavalry, where Taran seemed to be showing Selgi an assortment of swords. Ronan shivered with a sense of coming full circle, returning to source. It was Selgi's turn now. And Selgi would do it. Ronan hugged Bryn against him as he watched the youth. By autumn he would be a man.

"What was that for?" Bryn wondered. "Not that I mind being hugged, but I did nothing to earn it."

"I love you," Ronan told him. "You don't have to earn my affections."

And Bryn lifted his mouth for kisses in the first morning sun.

Much later, when the fire had burned down to glowing embers, Ronan held a cup to Bryn's lips and said, "Aemilia will be well with the vowed women. You've no cause for concern."

"I know." Bryn sipped deeply and made a face as he tasted the herbs there, hiding in the sweet wine. Herbs to make him rest, and to heal from within. "I never loved her, but I suppose I might have learned how. As a boy, I fell in and out of love so often, in the end it was the same as if I had never loved at all." He touched Ronan's mouth with one fingertip. Ronan kissed it. "And then you came to Derventio —"

"And you wanted to beat me bloody, to prove you could!" Ronan took Bryn's finger between his teeth and bit, not quite hard. "Don't look back, Bryn. You can't. The past exists only in your memory. The birds still sing, children still laugh, no matter how miserable a man makes himself, weeping for what is lost."

"Spoken," Bryn accused, "like a bard, which is what you should have been. Save that you can't remember a verse or string two notes together."

"There are other kinds of magic, just as sweet." Ronan moved against him, and Bryn was hard and warm, comfortable and familiar.

The freedmen would soon disperse, he knew. Some of them would remain in Eboracum, but some had kin elsewhere, and as soon as they were reaccustomed to their freedom, and healed of their wounds, they would take the old road that Rome had carved out of the landscape with the slave labour of the tribes that were, now, only names. Boudicca's Iceni; the Trinovante and the Silure, the proud Brigante, Ronan thought, remembering the nights he had spent with the bonded people, listening as Dafydd's fey mother wove the timeless stories for enraptured listeners.

Now the horse boy from Whitestonecliff sat at the hearth of a chief, and warrior pride stirred in him. The pride of the Brigante, who had fathered him? Sian would have said so. Ronan hoped she was right. The same blood was rich in Bryn's veins, making them somehow kindred.

Stiff, sore, Bryn moved cautiously and slowly even in bed. But he was mending, Ronan could tell. They slept the day through in each other's arms and stood on the rampart at sunset to watch a group of monks and priests leave by Eboracum's gates. A woman was with them, hooded and cloaked, her eyes downcast. Bryn cradled his aching shoulder and sighed.

The wind was warm out of the southeast, and along the coast the old Roman signal towers were manned. Ronan clasped the hilt of the sword Gruffydd had put into his hand. It was so short a time ago, and yet it might have been another world. Bryn was tiring again, growing pinched about the mouth with fatigue, and as the churchmen took the woman out of Ebor, Ronan put a hand on his lover's brow. Bryn was cool, he found no suggestion of fever.

"I am merely weary," Bryn remonstrated. "I shan't be a lover to you just yet! Be patient with me."

"So long as you rest and grow well, I shall be the very soul of patience," Ronan promised. "Come and sleep now." He slid his arm about Bryn's waist and urged him away from the wall, down into the noise and music, and the safe embrace of Eboracum.

Send for our free catalogue to GMP Publishers Ltd,
BCM 6159, London WC1X 3NN, England

Gay Men's Press books can be ordered from any bookshop in the
UK, North America and Australia, and from
specialised bookshops elsewhere.

Our distributors whose addresses are given in the front pages of
this book can also supply individual customers by mail order.
Send retail price as given plus 10% for
postage and packing.

*For payment by Mastercard/American Express/Visa, please give
number, expiry date and signature.*

———————————————————————————————

———————————————————————————————

Name and address in block letters please:

Name
———————————————————————————————

Address
———————————————————————————————

———————————————————————————————

———————————————————————————————